THE ART OF WRITING
Made Simple

Geoffrey Ashe

Made Simple Books
W. H. ALLEN   London

© Geoffrey Ashe, 1972

Made and printed in Great Britain
by Richard Clay & Co. Ltd, (The Chaucer Press),
Bungay, Suffolk
for the publishers W. H. Allen & Company, Ltd.,
Essex Street, London WC2R 3JG

ISBN 0 491 00359 5 Casebound
ISBN 0 491 00369 2 Paperbound

This new instructive series
has been created
primarily for self-education
but can equally well
be used as
an aid to group study.
However complex the subject,
the reader is taken
step by step,
clearly and methodically,
through the course. Each volume
has been prepared by experts,
using throughout the
Made Simple technique of teaching.
Consequently the gaining
of knowledge now becomes
an experience to be enjoyed.

Accounting
Advanced Algebra
  & Calculus
Anthropology
Applied Economics
Applied Mathematics
Applied Mechanics
Art Appreciation
Art of Speaking
Art of Writing
Biology
Book-keeping
Chemistry
Commerce
Cookery
Economics
Electricity
Electronic Computers
Electronics
English
French
Geology

German
Human Anatomy
Intermediate Algebra
  & Analytic Geometry
Italian
Journalism
Latin
Law
Management
Marketing
Mathematics
New Mathematics
Organic Chemistry
Philosophy
Physics
Psychology
Russian
Salesmanship
Spanish
Statistics
Typing

OTHER BOOKS BY GEOFFREY ASHE

The Tale of the Tub
King Arthur's Avalon
From Caesar to Arthur
Land to the West
The Land and the Book
Gandhi: a Study in Revolution
The Quest for Arthur's Britain
All About King Arthur
Camelot and the Vision of Albion
The Quest for America

Acknowledgments

For permission to quote, the Publishers and author gratefully thank the following:
The Publishers of *Nature* for extracts from two issues of that journal; Times Newspapers Ltd. for extracts from two articles in *The Times*; The Reader's Digest Association for an excerpt from *British Reader's Digest*; Professor N. Cohn for an extract from *The Pursuit of the Millenium* published by Martin Secker & Warburg Ltd.; The *Daily Express* for two quotations of Arthur Christiansen and for an extract from an article in that paper; The Publishers of *IT* for an extract from an article in that magazine; David Higham Associates Ltd. for an excerpt from *Great Short Stories of Detection, Mystery and Horror* published by Victor Gollancz Ltd.; *The Economist* for an excerpt by Sir Ernest Gowers; The London *Daily Mail* for an extract from that paper; Gildrose Productions and Jonathan Cape Ltd. for an extract from *Dr. No*; George Allen & Unwin Ltd. for an extract from *History of Western Philosophy* by Bertrand Russell; Michael Joseph Ltd. for an extract from *Friends at Court* by Henry Cecil; Cambridge University Press for an extract from *On the Art of Writing* by Sir Arthur Quiller-Couch; Robert Graves and Alan Hodge and Jonathan Cape Ltd. for an extract from *The Reader over your Shoulder*; Miss Sonia Brownell and Martin Secker & Warburg Ltd. for an extract from *Politics and the English Language* in *Shooting an Elephant and Other Essays* by George Orwell; Mr. Oliver Jensen and *The New Republic* for an extract from that magazine; The Estate of Aleister Crowley and Jonathan Cape Ltd. for an extract from *The Confessions of Aleister Crowley* edited by John Symonds and Kenneth Grant; Mrs. Laura Huxley for an extract from *Point Counter Point* published by Chatto and Windus Ltd.; The Estate of Sinclair Lewis and Jonathan Cape Ltd. for an extract from *Main Street*; A. D. Peters & Co. for an extract from *Helena* by Evelyn Waugh published by Chapman & Hall Ltd.; Murray Pollinger for three extracts from *Kiss Kiss* by Roald Dahl published by Michael Joseph Ltd. and Penguin Books; The Executors of the Ernest Hemingway Estate and Jonathan Cape Ltd. for an extract from *Fifty Grand* in *The First Forty-Nine Stories*; A. D. Peters & Co. for *Tarantella* in *Sonnets and Verse*; The Trustees for the copyrights of the late Dylan Thomas and J. M. Dent & Sons Ltd. for lines from *Fern Hill* in *Collected Poems* by Dylan Thomas; Diane Conlan, Rosemarie Dale and Intiaz Malek for three poems from *Stepney Words* published by Reality Press; The *Daily Mirror* for an extract from an article in that paper; Rapp and Whiting Ltd. for Brigid Brophy's Anti-list in *Fifty Works of English Literature We Could Do Without* by Brigid Brophy, Michael Levey and Charles Osborne. The Publishers apologise for any unintentional omissions.

Preface

'The Art of Writing' is a topic which can be treated in many ways. Indeed, it already has been. There are classic discussions by famous critics and scholars, with a frankly literary approach. There are hand-books on technique: 'writing for magazines', 'writing for radio', and so on. There are established manuals of correct English usage.

As a writer myself, I have gained from the reading of books of all these types. Yet I have also had to learn lessons which no book taught me, and they were apt to be the most important. For instance, in a career that has involved writing for several widely different media, I have often run into problems adapting my ideas on writing-in-general to the needs of a particular market, such as a Sunday paper. Again, much of the advice offered in existing works, however sound when they first came out, rests on assumptions about society and its media of communication which have become obsolete. The modern writer has to think in new ways, sometimes altering or re-interpreting the rules that guided his predecessors.

This book, therefore, combines several modes of treatment. It considers the writer as a human being in the contemporary context, and what he does, and what he should do. It describes various literary forms—fiction, drama, poetry—and their special features, always with practical applications. It surveys the media and markets as they exist today, and explains how a writer should proceed so as to have the best hope of success in his chosen field. And it puts forward some unifying ideas to hold all these themes together.

The Art of Writing Made Simple is designed to be useful to as broad a spectrum of writers (and intending writers) as possible. School-leavers should find that it helps them to develop their gifts and avoid wasting time in blind alleys. The more experienced freelance, dissatis-fied with his progress, should be able to pick up the hints needed to get him moving again. Students of English, both 'Literature' and 'Com-position', can use the book to approach their subjects from original angles. The hopeful contributor to magazines, the hopeful script-writer for television, the staff man in industry who has to compose a report—these and others can all find something here to assist them. The more ambitious writer with a promising notion for a book can learn how to present it to a publisher, and carry the project through to completion.

I have included many quotations and examples to illustrate the points

viii   *Preface*

made in the text. However, it is impossible to give adequate extracts from novels and plays. Some of the exercises at the ends of the chapters supply recommended reading to fill such needs.

A further word on these exercises. In the whole book, there are seventy altogether. Many are substantial. To work through them all would be a large undertaking. Many readers will doubtless prefer to make a selection. Hence, the choice is wide.

Obviously I have taken hints and advice from more people than I can recollect or thank individually. But special thanks are due to Jane With of the National Book League, for her aid in unearthing statistics; to David Wainwright, for his excellent practical advice on journalism, and constructive comments; to Correlli Barnett and Michael Bakewell, for their immense help with the chapter on television; to Anthony Jones, for his expert information on the writer's market in broadcasting. None of them, of course, should be held responsible for anything that is said in the text.

I must especially thank Irene Slade, who launched the idea of this book, and supplied constructive help and valuable criticism in every part of it, on a generous scale. She also made available to me, for the chapters where they were applicable, all the lecture notes and other material from her own courses on the art of writing, given at the City Literary Institute, London.

GEOFFREY ASHE

Table of Contents

Table of Contents

PART ONE: *THE WRITER IN HIS WORLD*

CHAPTER ONE

YOURSELF

The First Question

Here at the start we must face a question, and face it honestly. Can I teach you to write at all? Can anybody?

Once upon a time Sinclair Lewis, the American novelist and Nobel prizewinner, was invited to launch a university course on creative authorship. When the class assembled, he rose and said: 'Well, now, to begin with, how many of you actually want to write? Please put up your hands.'

Every student raised a hand. The great man looked his audience over, then snapped: 'In that case, why the hell aren't you at home writing?'

Of course there are answers to Sinclair Lewis's challenge. But there is no single answer. Much depends on the sort of writing you are going to do. If any of those would-be authors did think of a rejoinder, it was certainly different from some that might be given today at a class in television script-writing. Again, there are contexts where the challenge itself would be out of place. It would be stupid to put it to a report-writing class at a school of management studies: the trainees in such a class aren't there because they want to write, but because their jobs will require them to.

Still, when every qualification has been made, the issue remains a serious one. Anybody who has written with the slightest success knows that you learn by doing. We may well ask how much you can learn about writing by any other method.

Stop now and question yourself frankly, in Sinclair Lewis's manner. Why are you reading this book? What do you hope to get out of it, and what do you hope to do with what you get? Why aren't you doing something else; not even writing, necessarily; but something more active, more amusing, probably more gratifying?

I can't answer those questions for you. I can only suggest some possibilities.

What Can a Book on Writing Do for You?

First, obviously, a book can enlarge your ideas about technique in a broad sense. That includes not only the technique of the written language—vocabulary, phrasing, and all the rest—but also the sheer mechanics of the job: how to lay out your work on the page, where to dig up information, how to correct printers' proofs and deal with editors. All of which we shall be surveying in due course. Much of it can

3

be helpful to a non-author such as a management trainee, as well as to an intending journalist or novelist. If you are a non-author but need to write as part of your job, these basic things may be all you require, and a large part of this book will not concern you much.

But if you are one of those who seriously 'want to write', then hints on technique and mechanics, alone, may not be worth your trouble or even give what you are looking for. The chances are that you're not a complete beginner. You have tried it already. Your retort to Sinclair Lewis's question 'Why aren't you at home writing?' might well be, 'Yesterday (or last week or last month) I was.' It is indeed to be hoped so. An alleged literary aspirant who has never tried to get off the ground unaided will not be made airborne by a textbook.

A young musician asked an old one: 'How should I set about composing a symphony?'

'Perhaps you haven't the experience yet,' said the veteran.

'Mozart was composing symphonies when he was eight.'

'I know. But he never asked how to do it.'

A manual on the Art of Writing can have a number of functions. But the most important, I believe, is to assist the person who wants to write, and has tried to (without asking advice), and is now self-critical enough to be dissatisfied and to want to consider how to do better.

This dissatisfaction with your own efforts, if you feel it, may be no more precise than a feeling—one which is apt to hit poets harder than prose writers. Confrontation with a few lines of the Real Thing can be a recipe for despair. But the cause may be far more solid and mundane: a box of unpublished manuscripts, a pile of rejection slips. Sooner or later the self-tormented victim asks, 'Where am I falling short?' Or more ruthlessly, 'What am I doing wrong?' Then, if ever, teaching and textbooks can help. At the very least they can show *what not to do*.

That sounds like a negative approach. There is a famous precedent for it: the Ten Commandments. But we need not get engulfed in debate about the relative value of *Thou Shalt Not* and *Thou Shalt*, because the positive aspects will become apparent as well.

The shortcoming may be purely in technique, and if so, the hints on technique which you will eventually get to may put it right. More often the truth goes deeper. Technique is unlikely to be the whole trouble. It is axiomatic in journalism and publishing that a script can be re-written, to some extent anyhow; slipshod grammar or phrasing may be off-putting, but if an author has anything to say, the prospects are fair that some alert editor will accept his work and polish it afterwards. The truth, I repeat, usually goes deeper.

It may go so deep as to be fatal. In other words you may just not have the ability. If you haven't, the only service a book can do is to make you face the fact, as quickly and painlessly as possible. But we are assuming that you do have the ability. A credible hope exists. And if it does, then a method of fulfilment also exists, and my task is simply to help you find it.

The Plan of This Book

I have followed a course which may strike you as odd, but the reasons should emerge as we go along. In most of Part One, where we now are, there is no direct advice on writing at all. I suspect that the weakness of most manuals, in this field as in some others, is that they don't start far enough back. We need to do some hard thinking about *you*, your environment, how you regard it, and how you come to terms with it, before any detailed hints on writing can be worth giving. This first part will vary in importance for you according to the kind of writing you expect to do, but you will find it relevant, even if your sole concern is with engineering reports.

Part Two is on 'The Practice of Writing', and offers advice that seems to me to apply universally. Part Three is on 'Writing as a Vocation'. It deals (so far as one can) with the creative work of the novelist, biographer, or other type of author who makes it his chief pursuit in life. The poet, though an intractable character, is not ignored. Part Four is on 'Writing in Prescribed Patterns'. It explains the special methods and styles required in such fields as journalism, where an organization lays down the rules, and it also looks at the problems of the non-author who works to order on a report or thesis. Part Five closes the survey with a practical scrutiny of 'how you do it'—preparation of manuscript, finding a publisher, and so forth.

The 'vocation' and the laid-down 'job', while distinct, are not in watertight compartments. They overlap. To look no farther, even the most dedicated creative author will usually try to make money out of his work, and must attend to at least some of the dictates of writing to suit publishers and editors.

There is also a firmer bond of union between the creative author and the one who works to meet requirements. It explains the omission of what you may feel should have been given a section to itself: writing as a hobby or pastime. The bond I have in mind is *compulsion*, whether by financial pressure, or by the bias of your talents, or by the needs of your personality, or by a profession which entails writing as a by-product. The hobbyist is not compelled. In nearly all respects, he may do what the serious author does—but he is not compelled. To say this is to say all that can be said about the hobbyist as a distinct person. He is not doing a separate kind of writing, he is doing what the others do, but under less pressurized conditions.

To excel in any kind of writing, however, is not easy. It is a sad fact of human nature that few readers of a manual like this will effectually practise even the little it can teach, *unless they have to*. But if you, being a hobbyist-writer, can pick up hints from what is necessarily addressed more to the writer by compulsion, the best of luck to you; and if you apply them, I salute you as a rare being.

The Vital Factor: Attitude

Since we are not going to start by discussing writing directly, how are we going to start? By looking at something which is prior to it, and crucial; something which can make the difference between failure and success; which can be analysed; which can even be taught. I mean the writer's *attitude*.

If you are to write successfully by any standard (sales aren't the only test, though they are not to be despised), then you must bear in mind, unwaveringly and always, that *you work in a context*. A context of other people who are as real as yourself. Most of what you will have to grasp can be shown to follow, in one way or another, from that. You must carry a built-in radar, sensitive to human signals of many kinds. It is not enough to observe fellow-mortals from outside. You must be alive to their interests, their habits, their emotions; to what they know and care about; to all that will enable you, as a writer, to take hold of them and make them read you.

You may think this is a prescription for journalism rather than true authorship. 'A true author,' you may say, 'should express his personality without fussing about his prospective readers. Those who are worthy of him will come anyhow.' To which I reply that one of the chief ingredients of the right attitude is *respect*. Respect for people in general, for the media through which they are reached, for the craft of communication in all its aspects. Unless you are very special indeed, contempt for 'journalism' and the outlook that goes with it is a snobbery you can't afford. Nor (while we are on that subject) should you reserve the right to pick and choose even within journalism itself. Respect for the *Daily Mirror* with all it implies is at least as important as respect for *The Times*. *The Times* may be unrivalled for its content, but the *Mirror*, on the whole, is more skilfully written.[1] Nor should you stop at respect for journalism. Total contempt—contempt that sneers and dismisses— is always wrong, even towards comic-book dialogue and the public that devours it. People *do* exist and the art of communicating with them is always an art; it can be done well or badly, and the qualities that make for goodness or badness always concern you.

'But,' you may object, 'plenty of great and successful authors have written for a small circle, and not cared a bit about communicating with anybody outside it. Some have written for only a handful of readers: Gerard Manley Hopkins, for instance, who invented modern poetry decades before the world was ready for it. Another one wrote for

---

[1] A clergyman is said to have started a prayer: 'O Lord, as thou didst doubtless see in this morning's *Times* . . . ' The assumption that God reads only that paper is, I believe, unwarranted.

himself alone—Samuel Pepys. Would you deny a place in literature to Pepys's *Diary?*'

A fair enough comment. But the point I am making is not that an author should be constantly and obsessively thinking of readers (though in practice he often must), it is that he should have the outlook that *goes with* the power to attract them, whether he is trying to do it or not. Later we will see how far this outlook can be analysed into a set of rules.

To answer the immediate query, 'what about Gerard Manley Hopkins?'—well, here was a poet with intense human sympathies, intense awareness, a passion for experience, a command of language that was staggering and precise and vivid. As a trail-blazer in poetic communication he was willing to wait for readers, even if they never caught up during his lifetime. Nor did they. Yet today he has them in thousands. Hopkins's poetry was communication with people and not solitary vapouring. The attitude was the same; what looks like an exception is due merely to a time-lag.

As for Samuel Pepys, his *Diary* supplies its own answer, if you read it from the beginning. It opens as a dull chronicle of public events, noted down in a difficult shorthand. But although Pepys kept to his shorthand and his secrecy, he was not the man to go on in the same spirit. His wide interests, his gusto for description, his strange inspired ordinariness, his fascination with people and their doings, rapidly took over. He had the outlook to gain a readership, as he since has, even though he didn't want one. Almost everything worth while in the *Diary* is due to Pepys's attitude to people. He is not an exception.

This, then, is the first principle of all. Be conscious of the society round you, and cultivate the right attitude towards it. Maintain awareness, even when you think there's nothing exciting to be aware of. Maintain respect, even when you think there's nothing much to respect. I can assure you that in both cases you are wrong if you do think so. Just an honest effort to see why you are wrong can take you far in the proper direction. As an aid in that effort, read some of the great story-tellers who are mentioned farther on in this book in Chapters Eleven and Twelve. Notice how they can take up experiences which many people would find trivial or dull, and bring them to life by sheer ardour of interest and observation, and often humour. If a little of their attitude rubs off on you, it will give your progress as a writer a flying start.

Exercises

1. Look again at the questions at the end of the first section: 'Why are you reading this book?' and so on. Give your own answers to them.

2. Write a character sketch of yourself (about 200 words) as a candid friend might describe you.

CHAPTER TWO

ENGLISH AND WHAT HAS HAPPENED TO IT

The Art of Writing As It Was

At Cambridge, shortly before the First World War, Arthur Quiller-Couch gave a classic series of lectures on literary composition. In book form, Quiller-Couch's *Art of Writing* remains a gracious, civilized, and sensible work. Towards the close of his course he brought out several of the points I have been urging. Literature, he said, is part of life. It happens in human society. It must respect that context and keep in touch with it, lovingly, ardently. Style is personal, yes; personality will always express itself, as is right and proper; yet it should never obtrude, or domineer, or produce a result too eccentric for others to follow. Good writing, Quiller-Couch argued, has much in common with good manners, which (if genuine) will mould our relationships with everybody, not just a select few.

Having quoted that last remark, and put my praise of its author on record, I must now add that it sounds old-fashioned: significantly old-fashioned. Further, the entire book—with all its many virtues—reveals how deep this matter of social sensitivity goes. The book is an object-lesson itself, in a way its author can scarcely have intended. Addressed to that university audience, in that imperial England, it lived up nobly to its title. Today we can still accept that many of the things Quiller-Couch said in it are wise and true and worth saying. Yet to say them effectively now, we would have to recast almost every page of his book, because society has altered, and English has altered with it. The lecture course itself took place in a context. The context is no longer there. The art of writing in the 1970s is not the art of writing in 1914. Our business is to inquire what it has become.

How English has Changed in the Twentieth Century

To say that a writer should be attuned to the human beings around is our first principle. But we must go farther. A writer should have a feeling for the shape of human society. He needs to grasp that it has changed and is changing now and will go on changing, in ways that concern him. His situation is not static. Often it is the non-author who, within his own sphere, sees this truth most plainly. In management studies, for example, the emphasis shifts and the jargon alters; texts become semi-obsolete every ten years or less. But never suppose that there is anything Olympian and eternal about 'higher' forms of writing.

Everybody knows that society is different today from what it was fifty or a hundred years back. Not everybody sees all the implications of the changes for the writer who wants to understand society and address himself to it. He has a more exacting task than his forerunners. It is also more interesting and challenging.

I am not speaking of such doubtful requirements as keeping up-to-date and with-it. An author may be conspicuously without-it yet still good. He may write on topics lying far outside the blaze of publicity and the trends of fashion. He may do it in a style that seldom employs a word less than fifty years old, or a contemporary cliché. Yet he may write successfully, crisply, and (if you care) saleably, whereas another with the same surface conservatism actually is a has-been or a never-was. Why? Because the first writer has a feeling for our present society and the ways in which it communicates, and the second hasn't.

Several features of that society demand scrutiny. I am not trying to load you down at the outset with new ideas and rules. My object is to point out, and to point up, various facts which you may well find you know already, if you think about them.

When Quiller-Couch gave his lectures in 1913–14, the printed word had no competition from radio or television, and virtually none from films. The writer's status was more secure. The nature of his work was clearer, to himself and to the public. Also, if he was a 'serious' writer, he could make certain assumptions which he can't today.

Quiller-Couch's Cambridge Audience

Those young people whom Quiller-Couch instructed in writing were Cambridge undergraduates. If you go through his lectures carefully, you will realize how much he could take for granted. Nearly all his listeners were male. Nearly all came from families which were better-off than the national average. Nearly all spoke with a certain accent, and, so to speak, thought with it. Hardly an image or idea in the lectures has a working-class reference. Conversely, many things are said which imply that the listeners are gentlemen with some leisure, and safe professional careers lying before them, in Britain or her Empire. Church membership is assumed, and the lecturer goes into raptures over the King James Bible. More crucial still, a classical education is assumed. *The Art of Writing* begins with a long reminiscence of one of Plato's dialogues. Greek quotations are tossed in untranslated. England's Graeco-Roman cultural heritage is extolled, at the expense of the Anglo-Saxon (which is derided) and the Celtic (which is ignored).

Of course the audience was drawn from a privileged minority. But—here is the decisive fact—that minority still set the tone in England. More-or-less educated writers for more-or-less educated readers nearly all accepted the same norms, however widely their styles diverged. A writer of that period might have come from a humbler social origin, as Bernard Shaw had. He might not have gone to a university, as G. K.

Chesterton had not. He might display the rebelliousness of H. G. Wells, or the half-outsiderish quality of Kipling. But he knew that the articulate world belonged to men such as Quiller-Couch addressed, with their background, their values, their responses, their modes of thinking. The art of writing meant the art of writing for a society stamped by such men.

Ever since the imposition of the public-school system on the upper and upper-middle classes, the English language had been in essence a *single* language, shared by most educated people. The literate Victorian and Edwardian public had been a *single* public. Most of its members went to church, where sermons by Oxbridge clergymen helped to fix their ideas of style. Most of them read papers dominated by the same tone. Most of them (the men at least) had had some Latin and Greek drilled into them at school, with allied results. Little by little this public was exerting unconscious pressure on the authors themselves: pressure to standardize.

'Edwardian Pudding-stone Style'

By Quiller-Couch's time, authors, in general, were sounding more and more alike—a fact which his own prose illustrates by being such a perfect norm for the period. Written English with any pretensions seemed to be turning into a featureless compound, a blend of imitations of the established authors—Ruskin, Pater, Stevenson, Henry James, and others. The result (Robert Graves has called it the 'Edwardian pudding-stone style') could still be very agreeable, but it was getting stereotyped.

Also, there was less specialization than there is today. Even a scientist could still write on his subject in much the same English as anybody else. In April 1910 the scientific magazine *Nature* could still carry a paragraph like this:

> The apparatus of the nutrition laboratory proves highly effective, and the experiments already made, on pathological as well as normal subjects, fully justify the confidence hitherto entertained with respect to this line of research. Many additions have been made during the year to the equipment of the laboratory. Among these are a bed-calorimeter into which a recumbent patient may enter with ease and safety; a portable respiration apparatus . . .

And so on. Not distinguished prose, but prose that a layman can follow most of the way. But in April 1970 a fairly typical paragraph in the same magazine could read like this:

> Moving from amorphous to polycrystalline films, Professor C. J. Anderson (Imperial College, London) showed how the Fuchs–Sondheim theory of surface scattering could be applied to semi-conductors and extended to include the effect of surface band

bending. He also showed how scattering at grain boundaries can have a large influence on the transport properties of polycrystalline films.

Scientific language has clearly diverged from literary language, and not merely because science itself has grown more complex. We are getting familiar words—'scattering', 'band', 'grain', 'transport'—with unfamiliar meanings. This is only one instance of a broader phenomenon. The decades since Quiller-Couch have brought a tendency—not unopposed, not finally disruptive, but a tendency—for English to split apart into sub-languages with special functions. The last representative of the old order, the last person who wrote on every sort of topic in the same style, was Bertrand Russell (1872–1970), the mathematician and philosopher.

A writer today can no longer assume the single, homogeneous literate public that Quiller-Couch could. He may have to make up his mind which of several varieties of English he should cultivate for his own use; and his decision must come, or rather grow, through his sensitivity to that section of the public which he most cares about reaching.

Universal Education and its Effects

Special kinds of language are not new. Children and lovers, husbands and wives, have always had special ways of talking to each other. Special crafts and modes of life (seamanship, for instance) have always produced special vocabularies. But the gradual undermining of standard, literate Victorian English—the language learnt and expounded by Quiller-Couch—began with the Education Act of 1870. Today we confront the results of more than a century of its operation.

The 1870 Education Act followed a previous Act which gave the vote to millions of workers. Politicians proclaimed the need to 'educate our masters'. The new voters had to be absorbed into the system. As soon as the 1870 Act became law, all British children were required to go to school till they were fourteen. Most parents could not afford the fees paid by the upper-middle and upper classes. Usually, therefore, they sent their children to the new State schools set up under the Act, where elementary education was given at public expense.

Because of this trend, the main social object of the Act was never fully achieved. Most of the lower-middle and working-class children did not integrate. The State schools gave them a different kind of education. When they left, they retained their parents' interests and outlook, but often with a new liveliness and ambition.

First to realize that a new factor had come into British life was the publisher George Newnes. After the Education Act had been in force for about ten years, it was plain that a reading public was being formed which was not part of the established scene. Millions of children had been taught the Three R's, and acquired various fresh perspectives, without becoming like their 'betters'. An astute business man, Newnes saw a big potential market which could only grow bigger. In 1881 he founded the first popular magazine, *Tit-Bits*. Then Alfred Harmsworth launched a weekly called *Answers;* he also bought the *Evening News*, which he turned into a popular paper; and, in 1896, started the *Daily Mail*.

The New Media

With the birth of these mass-media, run hard-headedly for profit, the English of non-Oxbridge citizens began to achieve importance in print. The process was slow. But, little by little, the ex-pupils of the State schools began to get jobs in Fleet Street and make themselves heard. More new journals sprang up and encroached on their more polite competitors.

The early history of the *Daily Mirror* marks one of the notable transitions. Harmsworth started it in 1903 as an attempt to break into the quality female market. It was to be a paper 'for gentlewomen' written 'by gentlewomen'. Unfortunately the gentlewomen on the staff —the aunts and cousins, probably, of those Cambridge students— proved unequal to journalism at the tempo which it had now acquired. One lady reporter was sent to cover the wedding of an actor and actress from the same show, who appeared on the stage together a few hours later. Having described the ceremony she suddenly realized what the 'news' angle was, and ended: 'The usual performance took place in the evening'. Her story and others like it got by, and the *Mirror* became a laughing-stock. Losing interest, Harmsworth handed it over to his brother Harold. The gentlewomen were swept out, and the paper was turned into a daily with a wider appeal. It adopted the latest techniques in picture printing and became popular through its lavish illustrations.

Quiller-Couch himself was past fifty when he gave his lectures on writing, and he could still virtually ignore what was going on. But writers such as Chesterton, who were journalists of the old school themselves, could not and did not. Some of them denounced the new popular papers, not only as being poorly written (which they often were), but as being unscrupulously exploited by the few magnates who ran them, to mould public opinion and achieve power. Harmsworth, who became Lord Northcliffe, never tried very hard to conceal his belief that he was doing just that. Nor did Max Aitken, afterwards Lord Beaverbrook, who bought the *Daily Express* from predominantly political motives.

In fact the press lords miscalculated, and so did their critics. They never wielded the personal influence they aimed at. Harold Harmsworth (Lord Rothermere) persisted during the 1930s in using the *Daily Mail* for propaganda, and succeeded only in pushing it downhill. What did happen, however, was that in the course of struggling to make their papers influential, one or two outstanding owners like Beaverbrook learned how to give them character, style, and virtues and qualities of their own.

Much could depend on editorship. Whereas Rothermere had a bad habit of changing editors for ideological reasons, the more acute Beaverbrook acquired one of the great editors of all time, Arthur Christiansen, and kept him at the *Express* for many years without ever pushing him too far. Christiansen was one of the geniuses who helped popular English to come of age. The *Mirror*, the other supremely successful daily, owed much of its impact to learning from American tabloids, which its editors began to do in the late 1930s. It outdistanced all competitors in meeting the new demand for papers during the Second World War. In this way it built up a frankly working-class readership on a scale which had eluded even Northcliffe and Beaverbrook.

Sound and Vision

While these developments were in progress, with the book trade plodding behind at a more leisurely pace, technology was creating rival mass-media. Films, radio, and television were not, and are not, substitutes for the printed word. In spite of dark forebodings, there is no sign that they are likely to oust it. But all of them increased the importance of the mass public and the language it would accept. Film-makers, for economic reasons, could only survive by attending to its tastes for most of the time; until the 1940s, only a few of them—and consequently, only a few screen writers—even tried to do anything else. Here again a popular medium did finally come of age, and establish a language that could be good in its own way. Much the same might be said of radio and television, though, in those fields, the BBC always sought to combine different styles, and give what was popular a quality of its own.

Films added a further element to English: Americanization. It led, in the upshot, not so much to an outright takeover as to 'Mid-Atlantic' accents and styles. In the US, because of a more democratic educational system, English had not undergone the same shifts and cleavages as in England. Something like the Victorian class structure, with a pattern of cultured literacy, had flourished for a while in a few cities like Boston, but this was never the norm. American English was closer to the popular idiom. The effect of American speech and writing in England has been chiefly on the mass-media and on the language as employed in them.

The Language of Today

To sum up. After more than a half-century of mass journalism, fiction, films, radio, and television, the cultured Victorian–Edwardian English of Quiller-Couch is out of key. It can no longer subsist as a universal standard in its own right. Yet it preserves valuable qualities which no author should lose sight of. The English of the *Express* or *Mirror* is by no means out of key; however, exactly the same statements apply to it.

Unless you actually work for one of these papers, you shouldn't make either your universal standard. Yet you will be well advised to learn all they can teach you, just as you will be well advised to learn all Quiller-Couch can teach you.

What conclusion does this all lead to? That today there is no single, absolute standard of written English. But neither are there two or more totally distinct standards. The process we have traced has not, after all, split up the written language into 'good English' and 'journalese', or into 'educated English' and 'popular English'. Parlour games such as 'U and Non-U', which are supposed to classify people by their vocabulary, don't really work. The modern writer employs a language which is still single after all, but no longer with the Victorian singleness. It is a language that can *lean in different directions* according to what he is writing about, and for whom. It can lean towards academic English, or *Times* English, or *Express* English, or Mid-Atlantic English . . . and so on. It can change its bearings to suit changing requirements. There are many guide-posts. All are useful, and valid for an apt purpose. You, as a writer, must decide which way to lean. If your attitude is right, your decision will be right.

Here are four extracts: from a work of academic history, from *The Times*, from the *Daily Express*, and from the *Reader's Digest*—not in that order. First, match each extract to its source. That should not be too difficult, though the answers are at the end of the chapter if you need them. Then think a little about the distinctive flavour of each: the tone, the kind of reader who seems to be implied, the phrases and expressions which would be unlikely to appear in the other three contexts.

1.   Onward Christian singers? A new form of marathon takes place in London this weekend at St. Stephen's Church, Hampstead. It is described as a Hymn-In, a complete and continuous performance of the 600 or so hymns in the *English Hymnal*. Par is 33 hours.

   The organ (and sundry other instruments including a harmonium) will be played by a team of enthusiasts led by Nigel Wicken, the St. Stephen's organist. The marathon begins after the morning service on Sunday, and should end on Monday evening.

   I like this final touch: the two neighbouring public houses have been informed.

2.   I raised the revolver and in a voice tight with panic called out to my husband on the other side of the locked door: 'Get away or I'll shoot you!'

   I was delusional again. My husband had been urging me to take the pills prescribed by the doctor. Tranquillizers, he said they were, but I was suddenly convinced that he was trying to poison me. I had locked myself in the bedroom armed with the loaded revolver because of the isolated location of our home.

3. The raw materials out of which a revolutionary eschatology was gradually built up during the later Middle Ages consisted of a miscellaneous collection of prophecies inherited from the ancient world. Originally all these prophecies were devices by which religious groups, at first Jewish and later Christian, consoled, fortified and asserted themselves when confronted by the threat or the reality of oppression.

4. In Ulster the security statistics are depressing. Since August 1969 there is a record of 303 explosions involving the use of nearly a ton of gelignite. In this period of 21 months only nine people have been convicted of explosives offences.

    For several months a team of Scotland Yard detectives have been working day and night investigating, among other crimes, the brutal murder of three British soldiers. They are extremely secretive about their operation. So far there is no record of them having made a single arrest.

Special Language for Special Purposes

Some of the other guide-posts are further off-centre. The past few decades have given birth to a number of special brands of English. There are the technical sub-languages of science, as we have seen, growing ever more alien. There are experimental varieties invented by individuals, such as James Joyce. Long passages of his novel *Ulysses*, and the whole of his later *Finnegans Wake*, are written not so much in English as (to quote T. S. Eliot) in a language based on English, evolved for literary ends and often difficult to follow. Between the wars, critics drew attention to the persistence of what was dubbed Mandarin English—a laboured, derivative, would-be-'cultured' prose that assumed a reader with literary knowledge and sensibilities which most people do not possess.

More recently, the 'generation gap' and the rise of an under-30s culture have inspired 'beat' language, and 'hippie' and 'underground' language, with a swarm of vogue-words and vogue-phrases, often coming and going too fast to be kept up with. The following (which I have deliberately picked as being a few years old but not many) is from a letter in *International Times*, October 1969.

BUSINESSHEADS THRIVE ON YOUR APATHY—AND THE GOOD SCENES DIE FOR LACK OF ENERGY. What it gets down to is just my experience with E.C. and Implosion in the past year— U/g organisers tend to be, first and last, ORGANISERS—people who dig politicking and power games. If they are not like this in the beginning, they are forced into it—MAINLY BECAUSE YOU OPT OUT. Believe it or not, it is a continuous hassle with the powersthatbe to hold these scenes together—and some of us don't want to do it solo for the glory. Help!

Once again, if you are writing for a paper with a special dialect, you can properly use that dialect. But if you are writing for a less tribal public, and trying to do it in a style of your own, should you ever allow yourself to be led by borderline guide-posts such as these? You must never simply imitate, unless to parody, or convey a deliberate echo. In any case an attempt to imitate an author with a highly personal manner, James Joyce for instance, will almost certainly end in confusion. The resulting style will be neither yours nor your model's. It is also unwise to copy specialist jargon, even if you are writing on the topic concerned. Some of the English evolved for restricted purposes tends to get stereotyped, machine-made, low on meaning. We often find this with the jargon of sociology, economics, and certain political schools. Again, it is silly to ape the junior fashion of the moment just to be with-it, if only because fashions change. In the words of Paul Valéry, 'nothing ages more quickly than novelty'.

It is worth familiarizing yourself with at least some of these special sub-languages, so long as you don't use them where they don't belong. They are still within the broader domain of modern English; they are not islands cut off from it altogether. Read great individualists like Joyce; sample the scientific and political jargon; catch the accent of the junior vogue-language of the moment. In your own writing you probably won't feel a need to lean far towards any of them. But you will find that they all help you to open up new vistas, to enter into the minds of others, to hit on words and phrases which are correct in the correct setting, and look fresh and striking when put there.

To draw together all this problem of hitting on the right tone and vocabulary: you shouldn't say to yourself 'For my present purpose I will write like *The Times*' (or like the *Mirror*, or Ian Fleming, or Auberon Waugh, or Norman Mailer). With the attitude which a writer should cultivate, you will get the feel of different ways of communicating. You will be able to sense what is right for such-and-such a theme, such-and-such a readership. Your own language, as it comes to grips with the topic, will incline without undue labouring in the right direction.

If that sounds idealistic and abstract, have patience.

Exercises

1. Re-read the four extracts on pages 14–15, Then choose at least three more specimens of the same kind, from other papers and magazines. Try in every case to find material which has a style of its own, as each of the four extracts has. Pick out words and phrases that make each of your own specimens distinctive, and different from the rest, so that a reader might be able to tell which

of your sources it came from. (*Hint*: Sample the women's magazines, the hobbies magazines, the weeklies, the juvenile press.)

2. Do you think mass-circulation papers influence public opinion? Can you learn anything from them about the technique of using English persuasively?

3. Repeat Exercise 2, substituting 'television programmes' for 'mass-circulation papers'.

4. The King James Bible (or 'Authorized Version') was published in 1611, and had little competition for many years in the churches of the English-speaking world. Recently, there have been several new translations into more or less modern language, e.g. the New English Bible, the Jerusalem Bible. Compare a few passages in at least one of these with the same passages in the King James Bible. Would you say modernization is a good thing?

The extracts on pages 14–15 are from *The Times*, the *Reader's Digest*, the academic work and the *Daily Express*, in that order.

CHAPTER THREE

COMMUNICATION AND FEEDBACK

You and Your Audience

Two large practical questions arise.

First, how do you adapt to your presumed audience, and do it without sacrificing your own personality?

Second, how do you train your mind so that this act of adapting will conjure up a suitably shaped English? How do you get the raw materials there to begin with?

The first question brings us back, as so many will, to that central matter of *attitude*. Readiness to adapt does not imply weakness or compromise or herd-following. I am not advising you to 'give the public what it wants'—*any* public, however distinguished. If you have something to say, your first job is to say it. Never yield to people's opinions (or what you think are their opinions) so much that you warp your statement. You will be wrong if you add things you don't mean, merely in the hope of pleasing. You will be even more wrong if you leave out essentials, or distort them, for fear of not pleasing. As a writer you need to be arrogant in some respects, or at any rate, self-confident. You should yield on a vital point only when faced with incontrovertible proof that you are mistaken. In that case, don't ignore the obstacle or search for an ingenious way round it; pause and reconsider. Otherwise, be firm.

Yet with this arrogance or confidence on the main issues, you should practise humility on all others, including your method of presenting the main ones. *While saying what you have to say, you should be adaptable in choosing the way you say it and the framework you give it.* Hence our consideration of language, which we shall try, in this chapter, to bring down to earth a little; and hence also some subtler points.

The Value of Criticism

Before we pass on to these, let us note one of the most down-to-earth requirements of all—a willingness to accept fair criticism and learn from your errors. Here journalism can be an excellent training. It can go far in itself to adjust the balance between arrogance and humility. Writers usually suffer from too much arrogance. Having poured forth their text, they cherish it as a sacrosanct creation, and wince at any proposal to cut or revise. This is the sort of nonsense a good editor can knock out of you, if you will let him. Most people unfamiliar with the production of papers, magazines, and books, would be shocked at

18

the frequent difference between the script that comes from the author and the text that finally reaches the reader. Business communication is not the only species of writing that bears the stamp of teamwork. Most published writing depends on teamwork to some extent. Whatever contemporary matter you read, more of it than you probably think is due to the editorial hand: changes in detail, suggestions which the author has followed, even the re-writing of text by the editor.

In most cases this mauling is for the good—not least because the editor is, precisely, helping the author to adapt to his prospective audience. Even if you write books you will encounter it, and must learn to acquiesce and co-operate in some degree. But an ability which is vastly more precious (and will gladden editors' hearts if you acquire it) is the ability to forestall the process: to write a text that will do its job substantially as written—will run to the right length, strike the right note, use the right kind of English, and be suited to the readers you hope for.

The Influences at Work

Before all rules and mechanics of prose comes that necessity of getting attuned so that the script can indeed come out right. We have seen how the modern development of English corresponds, in part, to changes in society. I repeat that if a writer is to use the language to best advantage, his sensitivity to his human milieu must go beyond an awareness of individuals. It should give him a feeling for what divides them and what unites them, and for the sort of reverberations that pass among them, today, not a half-century ago.

People's habits of thought and response are different from what they were when Quiller-Couch gave his lectures. For instance, while they still see themselves as 'middle class' or 'working class', the distinctions are not so simple. The generation gap (so far as it exists) cuts across classes altogether. Bonds that used to link nearly everyone, such as religion, have weakened. On the other hand, new links have been forged by the shared mass-media, above all by television. And a TV-conditioned society doesn't think or respond like the society that was conditioned by speech and print.

A Victorian or Edwardian writer not only had a better-defined language and audience, he had a more rigid, logical-seeming frame of reference. There were fixed standards, cut-and-dried forms, predictable reactions. If he tossed out a slab of language, he could more or less trust anyone who read it at all to work through it in due order, and end up understanding it as intended, whether with approval or not. That was how the printed word worked—rationally, sequentially—and it still had no serious competition from media that worked otherwise.

Television

Today, television is the most obvious factor in a vast change of mental habits. The TV-conditioned person absorbs a diet of ever-shifting audio-visual items from all over the world. These are jumbled one after another with almost no inherent logic; they come through into the living-room mixed with the everyday life of the household, and governed in their form by the producers' knowledge that they will be; they are presented through the camera, by teams of technicians and commentators and script-writers and personalities. The citizen of the television age does not function like his grandparents. Even if he never watches television himself, the attitudes it creates spill over on to him. That doesn't mean that all writers are now outmoded except television script-writers. Far from it. But it does mean that all writers have new problems in communicating—problems reinforced, moreover, by other things that have come into the world besides television.

Today more of the comprehension comes from the reader and from what he does with what he receives, in his mobile mosaic world. Despite all that has been said against television and other mass-media, he is less passive and predictable than his immediate forebears.

Advertising

A notorious example of changed communication in practice is the shift that has taken place in advertising. Until about the 1950s, whatever tricks advertisers might use to attract attention, they always relied on the 'proposition'—that is, on what at least purported to be a reasoned argument showing why the product was good. But over the past decade or two (largely through the inspiration of a Madison Avenue Scotsman named Ogilvy) the proposition has lost ground to the 'image'. Advertising copy no longer hammers away solely at the product's tangible virtues. It also surrounds it with an aura, placing it in a contrived setting, with certain associations. By projecting the carefully planned image, it tries to get the consumer—or more precisely, the class of consumer aimed at—to feel about it in the desired way. Depth psychology and the Hidden Persuaders, the techniques appropriate to the TV age, have encroached deeply on the semi-rational persuasion that was appropriate to the age when print reigned supreme.

Drama

Or look at the drama. Compare Bernard Shaw's plays with many that have been staged since John Osborne appeared on the scene in 1956. Shaw does spell everything out, brilliantly. He draws morals. The Osborne of the 1950s still did, but he gave a voice to social elements hitherto silent, and his main moral was that there weren't any more morals, because the rules were obsolete. Since then we have had plays that don't tell a clear story, don't make sense in the traditional way, bring in dance and mime and other kinds of non-realism, and don't necessarily carry an explicit message.[1] The point is *not* that you have a duty to imitate the Pinters and Ardens, and their counterparts in other fields, or even to like them. You may like them, you may have no use for them whatever. It even appears probable that the conscious taste of the television public itself may incline more towards having no use for them whatever. The fact remains that you do have a duty to realize that communication is changing, even in the face of conscious resistance, and the drama is an art form where the changes stand out starkly.

You may protest: 'This applies to dramatists, poets, maybe novelists. But all I am proposing to write myself is a textbook. Surely a textbook is just a presentation of plain facts and consecutive logic? It does spell out, it does lecture to the reader, it does draw conclusions. You can't tell me that *all* communication has changed, that *all* writing demands a new stance on the writer's part.'

I would reply that while such an objection has some weight, the distinction is a matter of degree rather than kind. Consider the subject which some people might imagine to be the most rigid, factual, spelt-out of the lot, the subject which is all proposition and no image: mathematics. If you suppose it to be immutable, take another look. It has no more escaped the flow of change than anything else.

In 1910–13 Bertrand Russell and A. N. Whitehead published *Principia Mathematica*, and in the late 1960s their New Mathematics invaded primary schools. Children today are still taught some traditional mathematics as in the past, but they also do logical puzzles which bewilder their parents. Communication, even from teacher to pupil, even in such an objective field as this, is no longer a one-dimensional one-way traffic. It is no longer a mere handing out of information with closely foreseeable results. Much of the time is spent encouraging children to organize their own mental behaviour so that when information actually is handed out, they will respond to it correctly and make it their own. The same approach—by way of puzzles with words, pictures, and logic—has affected textbooks of English also.

To revert to you as a writer in this contemporary setting, what must you do? You must recognize that success will depend, not so much on being correct or clear by any impersonal standard, as on being correct and clear for the audience you hope to reach; on using the English language so that the reader you are aiming at will respond and think as you want him to. When society has become so multiple, and con-

[1] It has been said of William Blake (1757–1827) that the meaning of his more obscure poetry is not so much 'what it says' as 'what you arrive at for yourself by a sustained effort to understand it'. In that respect, as in some others, Blake was a precursor of much modern writing.

ditioning by print has yielded so much to conditioning by TV and other mass-media, this is plainly a subtle process calling for a fine touch.

Writing and Speaking

Self-attunement, as described, may sound mysterious and daunting. However, you will find it within your powers if you remember always what the right attitude is, and work out its implications. You must think of yourself as a human being *in a human context*.

The basic mode of human intercommunication is speech. In general, therefore, the point of departure defines itself: *write as you speak . . . well, more or less.*

The path to literary attunement is by way of that qualification, 'more or less'. To write *exactly* as you speak could mean producing something unreadable for anyone who doesn't know you. You may be in the habit of pouring yourself out, with endless corrections and repetitions, and in no very distinguished language. Transferred to paper, that sort of speech will look like an over-long, careless letter to a friend who doesn't mind. On the other hand you may not talk much at all, in which case the written version will be even less adequate. But the central point is always the same. You should build up your everyday English into a written instrument that is stronger and more precise and more versatile, yet never loses touch with its roots. This will come to be the language you want, in any given circumstance. You don't have to learn a new 'literary' English. Any attempt to write differently from the way you talk—really, fundamentally differently, so that the result isn't like your voice at all—would sound strained and contrived.

And the *primary* method of developing speech is through speech itself. When you talk, *you are conscious of the person or persons you are talking to*. The all-important attitude should almost force itself on you, if you give it a chance. When writing, you can shut yourself in and lose it. When conversing, you can't. Besides practising oral communication you can observe the effects, the feedback of response from others. Their replies will show you how well or badly you are employing words. Their gestures and interruptions, their signs of approval or boredom, may be more telling than anything they say. Observe, always observe.

The Value of Involvement

Don't neglect small-talk. No talk is so small as to be negligible. But try also to meet people who are interested in more than that: not so much the intellectuals, scholars, and so forth, even if your own themes belong to their realm, but people of marked character who have done things and are doing them, not just talking about doing them. With these, dialogue cuts deeper. While it isn't for me to advise anyone on his private life, there is no harm in urging the value of *involvement*, and the stirrings of personality that go with it. Nobody learns much, even about self-expression, through dilettantism and polite chat alone. Vance Packard, author of books on business, tells how a number of successful executives were asked how they rose. What was it that drew them out and made them promotable? The usual answer was not 'Attending such-and-such a course,' or 'Taking part in such-and-such a project,' but 'Working with So-and-So.'

To press this even nearer, it is surprising what unguessed resources of character, including verbal ones, can be unleashed by involvements with the opposite sex. The eloquence may not be very memorable in its raw state, yet the victim is seldom quite the same again. Richard Steele, the eighteenth-century essayist, wrote gallantly of a certain lady that 'to love her was a liberal education', Anton Chekhov, an author much closer to ourselves, said of a literary rival: 'The trouble with Korolenko is that he'll never write better unless he deceives his wife. He's too noble.' I am not recommending Chekhov's recipe to all aspiring authors, or even to those who may resemble Korolenko. But human relationships that excite and disturb can take one much further, even at this level of getting a truer command of language, than those that stay pleasantly superficial. Another quotation, this time from Nietzsche: 'You say that if you did thus, your life would be intolerable. But why should not your life be intolerable?'

Admittedly hardly anybody has complete freedom to choose his company. For all but a leisured few, the foregoing advice cannot perhaps be much more than advice to seize opportunities of acquaintance rather than let them pass. But it can be that. What is prescribed is simply one more aspect of the recurrent attitude: a positive human awareness, a willingness (in the words of a cliché) to say 'yes' to life.

Talking in Public

There are other steps you can take, where your control over your own course is greater. You can join debating societies and take part in discussion groups. You may be in a position to talk in public on subjects you have a reputation for knowing. Always accept invitations to do so if you can.

On this matter of public speaking, a distinction is called for. I am not thinking of academic lecturing to a class, as a regular job. It may well be doubted whether this does, as a rule, improve the lecturer's talent for writing; at any rate for writing about the subject he lectures on. The relationship to the class is apt to be too much of a one-way traffic. The lecturing is apt to be too much a process of handing out slabs of pre-fabricated information and argument—conduct (as we have seen) which is rarely the best policy for a writer in present society. The academic lecturer can often get tired of his own courses and sink into a rut. After, say, the sixth repeat, he is rather exceptional if he is not sometimes cutting corners, and skimping parts of his subject which he is too weary of to discuss properly. Also he may sometimes neglect to keep his knowledge up to date, and (worse) maintain positions which he ought to be reconsidering; even to the point of defending his favourite orthodoxies by sheer dishonesty. If he does produce a book on his subject, it is quite likely that he will only do so after the bloom has gone and he has become, God help him, an 'authority'. He will be all too liable to write it in a spiritless jargon, long since insulated against dangerous new energies.

No; the lecturing that may help to bring you to life as a writer is other than this. It is the kind that can keep its freshness: talking on topics you understand, not too often, to audiences that have no obligation to take notes or even listen, except in the way of politeness. Preferably, your hearers should ask questions. You should encourage them to do so. But with or without direct questions, the lecture throughout should be a dialogue, not a monologue—a dialogue with speech on one side, and expressions and gestures on the other. You should be able to judge when and how you are getting a point across, and when you are causing incomprehension, hostility, or worse, boredom. You should notice what an audience laughs at, what it applauds. You should try things out, hold fast to whatever modes of speech work best, and then find how to translate them into written terms.

Sources of Feedback

Whether with audiences or individuals, watch for the feedback, and learn to shape your language accordingly. Be flexible, be sympathetic. Always respect the listener, but never let him control you. Remember, also, that respect should extend to everybody you address and converse with, not just to those whom you regard as discriminating or well-informed. Whatever you are learning to do, an expert's reaction *by itself* is a most dubious guide. It may inhibit you from blossoming out as you should.[1] Or it may mislead you. If you have any acquaintance with Public Relations, you may have noticed how many experts in that profession contrive press releases that go straight to the waste-paper basket, and television presentations that make the pub echo with scornful merriment.

Do not put your trust in the well-informed, or in the umpires of debating contests. Your least technically-qualified hearers may be the ones who are most worth attention when they talk back, the sources of your best hints on the use of language. That is a truth which genius has applied long before now, if in ways that are no longer ours. Molière used to read his plays aloud to his cook. Some of the unsurpassed miracles of English were worked by a poet-dramatist who depended on a popular audience for his living; who noted when it clapped, laughed, or

---

[1] Henry Ford said, 'When I want to test a new idea I never consult an expert. An expert is a guy who'll give me six reasons why it won't work.'

stayed away; who responded to its tastes and its fashions; who was utterly careless of preconceived perfections; and who even entitled a comedy *As You Like It*.

At the beginning of Chapter One I said that a writer learns by doing. You may be wondering when the doing begins. The answer is that it should have begun already. If writing is a compulsion for you, you probably made your pioneer attempts long ago, and are still at it today without needing to be driven. At all events, you should be. None of these activities that can help you to write should be treated as preliminaries or warming-up exercises. They don't precede the writing, they go with it and nourish it.

You must not say to yourself: 'I will give talks on sea-shells to the Church Youth Group; I will have an affair with Lorna; I will frequent the studio where Blifil McPeters is producing *The Four Zoas*; and when I've sucked them dry, I'll lock myself in and start on my novel.' If you were to say that, my guess would be that you'd never start at all. Certainly you would be showing an unforgivable lack of respect for the persons concerned. If Lorna and Blifil come your way, cultivate them for their own sakes, while learning from them if you can. Your writing should be going ahead whether they are around or not.

What to Read and How to Read It

Given a true perspective on these social activities, you can see how to fit in a more solitary one—an important one, though it tends to be overstressed. Manifestly, you ought to read. But to say this and stop is to impel you back towards that pre-1914 Oxbridge milieu, where (in principle) the budding gentleman-of-letters *first* picked up all the literacy a gentleman required, and *then* went off to write. The advice 'read' generates reading lists. These in turn imply a standard curriculum, an accepted package-culture prior to any serious writing, which you must digest before you can get moving.

Such an outlook has only a very limited validity. In the later Victorian age, it prevailed, and with more excuse. So versatile a man as Sir John Lubbock—anthropologist, entomologist, politician, inventor of bank holidays—could compile, and be praised for, a list of the *Hundred Best Books* which every educated person ought to have read. To urge that such lists are now of dubious value is not to question the stature of the books, or the desirability of reading them. If forced to choose, I prefer Lubbock to Brigid Brophy, whose anti-list *Fifty Works of English Literature We Could Do Without* inverts his position.[1] What is misleading and a deterrent is the notion of prerequisites. Our world has grown so complex, the impact of non-European cultures and non-Christian

[1] Both lists are given in Appendix Two, page 256.

philosophies has grown so powerful, that there is no longer a single compulsory way of being literate.

Few passages in Quiller-Couch's *Art of Writing* are more dated than a long quotation from Newman—in itself, a superb piece of prose—contending that the civilization of Europe, rooted in Jerusalem, Athens, and Rome, is the only civilization that counts. We may still love that marvellous heritage as warmly as Newman and Quiller-Couch. Yet the heritage has altered under our eyes. Before 1914, for instance, the truly literate man was expected not only to have read Greek and Latin books, but to have read them in the original. Reliance on translations made him a second-rater. Today the classical education has withered, while the translations have improved. The classical corpus has become, for us, a different thing; and thanks to the anthropologists and the archaeologists, we look at it differently in other respects also. As for its being at the basis of the only civilization that counts . . . try telling that to a Chinese, an Indian, a Ghanaian.

Read—yes, of course; but as you go along, not as a prior training in prescribed literacy which you have to endure. Lean a shade towards conservatism in spite of what I have just said, because the current temptation is to reject. Recognize that the classics, ancient and modern, remain classics. Try to absorb as many of them as possible. Don't be scared away from translations by snobs who know the originals; simply make sure that the translations you read are good. (Sometimes, as with Flaubert's *Madame Bovary*, the most recent is the best almost automatically, because the earlier ones are expurgated.) Read the Bible, with an open mind if you can, like an intelligent pagan not brought up on it.

But never be held back by the delusion that you have to read such-and-such books to acquire culture, before you can write a book of your own. Coleridge made a wise remark, wiser now than when he made it, about 'having the courage to be ignorant about many things'. There are no absolutes. If you can't manage Henry James, don't force yourself; you and he can get along happily without each other; only, don't let your personal dislike beguile you into damning him as overrated.

All this has a converse. Leave a classic alone without shame, if it repels you; likewise, read a non-classic without shame, if it attracts you. Snobbery (that word again) will get you nowhere. Good and bad taste are relative terms. A book which is 'in bad taste' may well not deserve your trouble, but usually for a better reason than that. The conclusive objection to many works of pornography is not that they are in bad taste but that they are empty and dull. *Fanny Hill*, in equally bad taste, survives after two centuries.

Once you are outside the acknowledged classics, your own interests must guide you. I will merely end this chapter with three overlapping suggestions to bear in mind.

(1) Read freely, expansively, variously: fiction, non-fiction, magazines,

newspapers. Leave the paths laid down for you. If a man, look at the women's magazines, and if a woman, look at the men's magazines. If you are writing (say) ecclesiastical history, make a habit of buying lurid paperback novels to read on the train.

(2) Use libraries, and don't go there for particular books only, coming away empty-handed if they are not in. Browse.

(3) Read functionally—that is, read what fits into your pursuits as a writer; but do some non-functional reading as well. Always have a library book out which is not on your subject.

Exercises

1. Did you ever have a teacher who was outstandingly good or stimulating? If so, give an account of this teacher's methods, showing what was special about them.

2. Look at a few newspapers, and pick out a controversial current topic that interests you. Imagine you are going to give a talk on it. How would you present it to each of the following audiences?

(a) A Women's Institute in a country town.

(b) A roomful of restless school-leavers aged 15 to 17.

(c) A conference of ministers of religion—any church or denomination you please.

There is no need to draft any of the actual talk. Just explain, in a paragraph or two, what your approach would be.

3. Turn to Appendix Two.

(a) Choose one of Lubbock's 'hundred best books'—one which you don't already know. Read at least enough of it to form a fair impression. Write two pages saying why you think it either *is* or *is not* a work of interest and value for present-day readers.

(b) Give the same treatment to one of Brigid Brophy's 'works we could do without'.

CHAPTER FOUR

THE WAY YOU SHOULD BE GOING

Two Abilities that Matter

So, what practical results emerge from all this?

First should come an ever-increasing command of language. Talking and reading should give you a wider, truer, readier vocabulary; a sense of phrasing; a feeling for what is effective and what isn't, whether in the most erudite study or in the lightest journalism. If you keep a dictionary handy, and look up unknown words whenever you strike them, you will expand your range that much faster.

Besides mastering literal meanings, you should be grasping nuances. While English is rich in words that may pass for synonyms, it has very few complete synonyms: several words may refer to the same thing, but they seldom have exactly the same connotation, and a feeling for connotations is an important part of good usage. 'Horse', 'mount', 'nag', 'steed' and 'gee-gee' all denote the same four-footed beast. But one would not speak of Lester Piggott winning a race on a gee-gee, or Sir Lancelot bestriding a nag. A fine instance of misfiring connotation was supplied by an ode on the death of Queen Victoria. Its author, one of her loyal Indian subjects, wanted to convey the suddenness of her passing after so long a reign. Unfortunately he wrote:

> *Dust to dust, ashes to ashes,*
> *Into her tomb the Great Queen dashes.*

For this reason and others, it is not so important to have a big vocabulary as to have an accurate one, with the knack of aligning it for the task in hand. Here your personal contacts should come in strongly, the conversation and debating and so on. As a rule I doubt if there is any complete substitute. Vance Packard, in his study of successful executives, noted that nearly all of them had a spoken vocabulary that was larger than most, and far more to the point. These bosses might be wrapped up in their jobs, but, within that field, they had an impressive command of the language needed to talk to the people whom they dealt with, about the topics that concerned them. As a writer you should possess the same quality, both orally and on paper. We have seen how you can acquire it through the attitude you should cultivate in life.

The second practical ability you will acquire as a result of cultivating the right attitude and increasing your command of language is this: *you will become able to appreciate the advice of experienced authors.* There really are rules of writing which have been stated by competent people, and are well worth remembering. Yet in practice they seem hard for a would-be writer to take in if they are simply dictated to him. He may note them down as copybook maxims, but he then goes off and does something else. That is one reason why I have not put them at the beginning. When you have talked and read and reflected, and tried out your writing as well as communication by word of mouth, you should attain a frame of mind in which you can digest them and act accordingly.

Six Basic Principles

Here are some rules of the sort I mean. I have seen all of them gaining force in a writer's mind as his appraisal of the human context improved.

(1) Write about what you know and care for

This is a platitude which an odd quirk in human nature tends to reject. If a teacher gives his students a choice of essay topics, most of them will probably pick a remote or abstract theme, rather than a familiar one which they could handle a great deal better. I once heard of an amateur art class in a prairie town, where the instructor had the utmost difficulty in inducing the members to draw cows, which they all met frequently, rather than castles on the Rhine, which none had ever seen. This quirk may be due to escapism, or pretentiousness, or familiarity breeding contempt; whatever the cause, exhortation seems useless.

But when you have had a taste of talking on a subject without special knowledge or conviction, to those who possess both, you must be very thick-skinned and uncritical if the soundness of the rule doesn't begin to dawn on you. Such behaviour is at best futile and at worst offensive. Conversely, the effect you can produce by talking well and feelingly of what you do know, to sympathetic hearers who don't, ought to convince you that this is always the path to follow if you are free to choose.

Meanwhile your reading should clarify what, in fact, you do and don't know, and should help you to define your profounder enthusiasms.

(2) Approach people through their interests rather than your own

Neglect of this rule is a besetting sin of writers and speakers who have a Cause. The protester, the pacifist, the revolutionary, insists on saying his own piece in his own style; he asserts his burning issues in seeming unawareness that ordinary households and pub-gatherings are scarcely conscious of them at all; his terms may be almost unintelligible to an outsider. If you tell him so, and cite the rule given above, his reaction is either to deny the fact or to say: '*Their* interests? Sport and booze and sex and the pay packet. If I'm to pander to that, I might as well shut up. My whole object is to rouse them, force them to care about something else.'

Quite so. Yet the plain truth is that he usually fails, unless some catastrophe like a war does his work for him. What is the formula that eludes his ardour? I am not arguing that if you have a message you should give up trying to reach the public at large, or alter the message to make it more palatable. Not at all. Speak it out aloud. But relate it to the interests which people have already. Make it relevant to them. Everyday life supplies endless handles and levers. As Lenin put it, 'A true revolutionary can use a dish-rag to further the revolution.'

For anyone with a message, the early history of the Jesuit missions ought to be required reading. When the Jesuits got to China, they found that the Chinese were fascinated by mechanical gadgetry; so they wooed them with gadgets, and followed up with sermons. One of the Fathers sent the Emperor a clock with no key. When it ran down the Jesuit had to be fetched to wind it, and thus obtained an audience. In Paraguay the Jesuits learned that the Indians loved music; so, when they paddled up the river to parley with them, they had an instrumental group playing in the foremost canoe.

If you have lectured to an audience without engaging its interest, you will have seen how it fidgets and becomes glassy-eyed. And if you have been more successful, you will have found how interest can be engaged by the timely anecdote, the instance that brings your topic home. The American correspondent Eddie Gilmore, speaking on Russia to Mid-Western housewives, used to catch hold of them by giving the price, in US currency, of an orange in Moscow.

(3) Don't let the reader hover uncertainly. Make it plain fairly quickly what you are talking about, and leave him with an ending as strong and expressive as the beginning

A rule observed by several of the great epic poets. European literature begins with the opening line of Homer's *Iliad*:

> *Sing, O Muse, the wrath of Achilles . . .*

from which the entire action of the story follows. Or Milton:

> *Of Man's first disobedience, and the fruit*
> *Of that forbidden tree . . .*

As a backwoods preacher put it, less exaltedly, but with the same insight: 'First I tells 'em what I'm going to tell 'em.' Then I tells 'em. Then I tells 'em what I've told 'em.' Sometimes a firm rubbing-in of the main theme (not of course throughout, but at suitable intervals) is actually best. It is a practice of Communist writers, including some, such as Brecht, who are by no means to be despised. In other cases you will prefer not to rub the theme in repetitively, but to remind the reader of it from different aspects. The need for coherence, for definition, for making the reader see what it's all about—and that it's all about the same thing—is a constant.

A classic instance of prose that does 'tell 'em', unswervingly, is President Lincoln's Gettysburg Address. He gave it at the consecration of a national cemetery for the Northern dead in a crucial battle of the American Civil War. A previous speaker poured out rhetoric for over an hour extolling the fallen heroes of the Republic. Lincoln did not try to compete. He wanted to make a single point only—that the war was *about* the American ideal of democratic equality, challenged by the slave-owning, aristocratic South. This is the entire text of his speech:

> Fourscore and seven years ago our fathers brought forth upon this continent a new nation, conceived in liberty, and dedicated to the proposition that all men are created equal.
>
> Now we are engaged in a great civil war, testing whether that nation, or any nation so conceived and so dedicated, can long endure. We are met on a great battlefield of that war. We have come to dedicate a portion of that field as a final resting-place for those who here gave their lives that their nation might live. It is altogether fitting and proper that we should do this.
>
> But in a larger sense we cannot dedicate, we cannot consecrate, we cannot hallow this ground. The brave men, living and dead, who struggled here, have consecrated it far above our power to add or detract. The world will little note nor long remember what we say here, but it can never forget what they did here. It is for us, the living, rather, to be dedicated here to the unfinished work which they who fought here have thus far so nobly advanced. It is rather for us to be here dedicated to the great task remaining before us: that from these honoured dead we take increased devotion to that cause for which they gave the last full measure of devotion; that we here highly resolve that these dead shall not have died in vain; that this nation, under God, shall have a new birth of freedom; and that government of the people, by the people, and for the people, shall not perish from the earth.

Lincoln begins with the democratic ideal; he ends with the democratic ideal; and between, he speaks not only of the dead but of the living in relation to his single theme. Owing to the boredom caused by the long preceding speech, the Gettysburg Address fell flat. Some papers did not even quote it in their reports of the ceremony. Yet it has won recognition since as a compact masterpiece of language, whereas the other speaker's oration is forgotten.[1]

(4) Start from what is familiar and easily grasped, and proceed from that to the unfamiliar and difficult

This is a rule to bear in mind always, but especially when presenting a specialized subject to a non-specialist audience. Thus, a skilful

[1] See further what is said about journalistic writing on pages 195–204.

popular-science writer will begin with an everyday experience like lighting a match, or seeing how a flower grows, and work from that into the mysteries of chemistry or botany. An account of past happenings on some historic site might well open with a description of the place as it looks to an uninstructed tourist today. Once the scene is set, the historic events can be fed in with far more vividness.

Let me illustrate with a topic I have often had to speak on myself: the reality behind the legends of King Arthur, as partly disclosed by historical and archaeological research. If I were to follow an abstractly logical order, I would have to start from the truth, so far as this can be ascertained—from a still-obscure train of events in Britain somewhere about AD 500—and go on to show how stories were told about these events, and grew steadily more romantic and remote from the facts. This procedure would be all right for a learned society, well briefed on Arthur already. But with any other audience, the abstract logic of the theme must yield to a human logic which is the precise opposite.

Many listeners will have at least a vague picture of the legendary King, of Camelot and Guinevere and the Round Table and the Quest of the Grail. Far fewer will respond to such names as Gildas, Nennius and Badon, or know what is meant by Tintagel-B pottery. Human logic requires a speaker to begin by evoking the Arthurian Legend, which plants the audience on fairly familiar ground, and then to say: 'Now what were the facts behind it all? Did Arthur exist? Where was Camelot?' and lead from such questions into the dark-age labyrinth which, displayed at the outset, would have been merely baffling. This method is right for a lecture and it is just as right for a book. The only substantial difference will be in fullness of treatment.

(5) Tell things, so far as you can, through concrete examples and anecdotes, and through people rather than abstractions

As Christiansen, the great *Daily Express* editor, used to impress on his team, 'There is nothing that can't be told in terms of people.' To some extent this rule repeats (2), and much the same distinction holds. You aren't being asked to confine your writing to gossip and trivia. What you can do is to use the raw material of gossip and trivia to make statements carrying infinitely more weight. One of the masters of this art (indeed, one of the supreme practitioners of the whole rule) is Jesus Christ, especially as portrayed in the first and third Gospels. The word 'parable' should be reminder enough. A parable is, precisely, an application of Christiansen's point. It is a story that teaches general truths through people—in this case, imagined ones. In *Luke* xv: 11–32, when Jesus wants to make his audience think about repentance and forgiveness, he is not content with edifying remarks like 'It's never too late to mend'. He tells them a short, clear, beautiful story—the story usually called *The Prodigal Son*—which, once heard, is not easily forgotten.

(6) Treat your readers with respect

Once again that perennial theme 'respect'. But in addition to everything said already, realize that it is double-edged.

On the one hand you must put yourself in the reader's place, appreciate his difficulties, and try to meet them. Never talk needlessly above his head, or drive him into endless mulling-over and looking-up, with the implication that you don't care how much trouble you cause him. If you try things out as I have suggested, and run into patches of incomprehension, don't react either by dismissing your audience as stupid and pressing on (over-arrogance), or by withdrawing (over-humility). Recast your material. This is all part of the courtesy you should observe, not only as a virtue in itself, but in your own interests.

Granted, it is not always possible to be easily understandable. Writing a book on a technical subject will always involve you in complications. So may the problem of producing a purely literary effect, if the effect desired is extremely rich and subtle. James Joyce made outrageous demands on his readers, and was perfectly candid about it. Difficulty of comprehension can be excused if there is no alternative. However, it is as well to recall the notice said to be pinned on Frank Sinatra's door: 'If you haven't been invited you'd better have a damn good reason for ringing this bell.' If you do make heavy demands on your readers, be damn sure it's the sole and proper means to the end. First exhaust every possibility of simplicity.

Now for the converse. In your readiness to sympathize with the reader's position, and meet him courteously half-way, don't topple into a contrary disrespect and talk down to him. Inexpert writers for children are apt to do this. Many teachers and parents imagine that although they have no special talent for authorship, they can write for children. The trouble is that they can so easily try out their attempts on a captive audience and get misleading results. The would-be author says in all truth, 'I read this story to my class' (or 'my own children') 'and they liked it.' That in itself proves nothing; the children probably responded to the person rather than the story.

Good writing for children presupposes what these well-meaning people so often lack: the ability to write. If you possess that ability, you may be able to adapt it to juvenile readers. Of course you can't write for them exactly as you would for adults. But without talking down to them, you can adjust the subject-matter to their knowledge and tastes, keep your vocabulary on the right level, and address them sensibly as sensible beings, very likely your equals in native intelligence.

Children are not the only readers who inspire the literary misconduct of talking down. For many years advertising, journalism, and popular fiction suffered miserably from a well-known belief that the public's mental age is twelve. Even if that belief is correct, the practical consequences deduced from it were often dismal. Frank Harris, whose editorship in the 1880s profoundly affected the *Evening News*, conceded that his public might be mentally as old as fourteen; but the result was much the same. Harris asked himself, 'What was I interested in at fourteen?' and filled his paper with suitably chosen items. His recipe was 'kissing and fighting', or as we might put it now, sex and violence. Following his example, other papers worked to the formula of giving the public what it wanted, in a spirit which was, at heart, contemptuous or condescending, and unduly restrictive.

Again Christiansen was one of those who gave journalism a wiser lead. He rejected the Harris approach, and he also rejected the would-be-'quality' approach that merely ignores popular concerns. In a memo to his staff at the *Express*, he once wrote:

I journeyed from Rhyl to Prestatyn on Sunday past lines of boarding houses, caravans, wooden huts, shacks, tents and heaven knows what else. In every one of them there were newspaper readers. Happy citizens, worthy, fine people but not in the least like the reader Fleet Street seems to be writing for. These people are not interested in Glyndebourne or vintage claret or opera or the Sitwells or dry-as-dust economics or tough politics. *It is our job to interest them in everything.* [Italics mine.] It requires the highest degree of skill and ingenuity.

Respect them genuinely, don't just cater to what you assume to be their taste. Write what they can grasp and enjoy, but use it to take them somewhere. They will come with you if you do it well enough.

Christiansen's case has been strengthened by the BBC. The changes in English thought and behaviour induced by broadcasting, and especially television, have been so vast that they are largely unconscious. One major watershed was the satirical programme *That Was The Week, That Was* (1962–3). It was denounced as irreverent. In fact, at its best, it was one of the most reverent of all TV programmes. It acted on a faith in the mass viewer's potential maturity, his willingness to think about anything and everything in an uninhibited style. That faith was wildly daring and, in the outcome, justified. Having unleashed all that it did unleash, TV satire died of its own success, and nothing has looked the same since.

Doubtless the idea of talking down to a supposedly dim public is not extinct. George Orwell thought it worth warning against, and in *Nineteen Eighty-Four* he imagined machines churning out trashy reading matter for the masses, under the name of 'prolefeed'. But if that ever happens it will be a reversion. The 1984 world, with its cut-down English and its planned stultification, is not (linguistically at any rate) a nightmare which we are headed for at present.

While your respect for the reader should be invariable, it remains true that you must adapt your style to suit readers on various levels of age and education. You can learn to do it; you can even learn to do it by numbers. Here, however, we are at last leaving 'attitude' behind and entering the realm of technique.

Exercises

1. On page 28, five words meaning 'horse' are given, each with a different connotation. Can you bring out the differences by making up five sentences, using *one* of these words in each, in such a way that you couldn't substitute any of the others? If you can't manage all five, how many can you manage?

(Suppose, as an illustration, that you wanted to distinguish the words 'violinist' and 'fiddler'. You might say 'He was first violinist in the symphony orchestra' and 'As the peasants danced, the fiddler played faster and faster'. You couldn't substitute 'fiddler' in the first sentence or 'violinist' in the second.)

2. You are going to address an audience of small-town businessmen on (*a*) hill farming or (*b*) amateur photography or (*c*) your recent visit to Ethiopia. Write out the first 150 words of your talk.

3. Write a page giving the main facts on one of the following topics, for readers twelve years old.

(*a*) Napoleon.
(*b*) The Gulf Stream.
(*c*) The Olympic Games.

4. See page 34. Christiansen mentions 'Glyndebourne, vintage claret, opera, the Sitwells' as topics that don't normally interest the mass public. How would you go about interesting the mass public in one of them?

PART TWO: THE PRACTICE OF WRITING

CHAPTER FIVE

ACHIEVING THE BASIC OBJECTS

Writing and Thinking

Prose should be *clear*. It should be *right*, both in meaning and in tone. It should also be *persuasive*. If these qualities are to come through on paper, they must reflect corresponding qualities in the writer's mind. Always be cautious about beginning to write while you are still inwardly hazy or unsure of yourself. If you do go ahead, try to eliminate these shortcomings as soon as you can, and revise carefully afterwards.

You want to communicate with the reader. In some sense or other, you want to convey information. That purpose places you in a varied company, both human and non-human. With the advent of computers and related equipment, the modern science of communication has grown vastly. It ranges far outside everyday speech into realms of mathematical symbolism and logic. You are not a computer yourself, and shouldn't try to behave as if you were. Yet at least one lesson of computer technique is worth bearing in mind.

Behind all the jargon about 'bits of information' and binary code, a basic principle pervades everything—the principle of exact analysis, exact definition, exact solution. A computer's programming and input cannot be vague or non-committal. Nor can the processes that go on inside it. On a magnetic tape, every spot must be either charged or not charged. It has no method of saying, 'Well, I don't quite know how to put this into words, but surely you can see what I mean.' Computers can't invoke feelings as a substitute for thought—their own type of thought.

Indeed, even the simplest mathematical problem—whether computerized or jotted down on a scratch pad—has a single answer which is *the right answer*. It is like the bull's-eye of a target. We cannot recognize any such thing as 'the wrong answer', only an infinite number of wrong possibilities, an infinite number of ways of missing. To handle the problem we must know what it is, state it accurately, work it out correctly, and thus arrive at *the right answer*. If we start with a muddle or get into one, we shall not arrive at the right answer unless by a fluke.

While writing could never be reduced to a branch of mathematics, it is more like it than unlike. Already computers can reason their way through arguments, draw up astrological horoscopes, translate from foreign languages (after a fashion) and compose verses (of a sort). Of course these machines are only applying skills which their designers have built into them. Still, it is a challenging fact that the building-in can be done at all, that the writer's craft can be computerized even to the extent it has been.

Precision in Prose

For the moment we are leaving the verse aspect aside and concentrating on prose. When you read a competent passage by a human author, what are you getting? A series of well-defined ideas ('ideas' in a very broad sense), each lucidly expressed in words which are right for it. Further, the series is linked so as to give the right effect over all, and evoke the responses from a reader which the author intends. If a thought is clear, there is probably one form of words for it which is best: not 'best' by some absolute rule, or all good authors would have the same style; but *best for that author, in that context, with that audience*. Besides this best way of putting it, there are endless others which would be weaker. A surrounding blur of conceivable out-of-focus phrases stretches off into obscurity. Whenever a thought is not well-defined to begin with, the blur closes in and takes over. There is then no best way, nothing verbal corresponding to 'the right answer' or hitting the bull's-eye. Communication becomes uncertain or worse.

This ideal of precision was well understood by many of the great writers of the nineteenth century, from Gustave Flaubert onward. Unfortunately some of them pressed it so far that they provoked a reaction. The agonized search for the *mot juste* by such novelists as Henry James became a joke. It is said that Oscar Wilde, on a week-end visit, did not appear till lunch. He told his host that he had spent the entire morning working on his new play; and he had put in a comma.

'Is that all you did?'

'Oh, no. After prolonged thought I took it out again.'

All the same, Wilde erred on the right side. George Orwell was one of the last English authors who took comparable pains. His attacks on slipshod language, and his 'Newspeak' nightmare in *Nineteen Eighty-Four*, show how deeply he felt and how profoundly he reflected. The ideal does need to be re-asserted, so long as it is kept within bounds, and perhaps computer technology will help.

'Foolproofification'

You may feel that you should have no trouble in finding words which are at least adequate, because your own mind is clear and you always know what you are trying to express. But do you—always? And even if you have this feeling, is it the whole story? Think of your writing once again in relation to your use of the spoken word. Isn't it a sadly familiar fact that even when you do feel clear in your own mind, people whom you talk to may misunderstand? In speech, you can blame the normal hurry and carelessness of conversation. But as a writer, with time to ponder and revise, you must certainly learn not to rest content with your own feeling of clarity. It will cheat you. The truly well-defined idea demands more. Mentally and on paper, you must learn to take a step beyond.

No single word for that step exists. Ronald Knox, a brilliant satirist, detective-story writer, and theologian, once coined a word which we might adopt if it were not so clumsy: 'foolproofification'. Ideas should be so sharply defined that their written form is not only satisfying to you, the author, but also proof against the propensity of other people to trip and go wrong. You may find this annoying, but as I stressed in Part One, you must treat your readers with respect and see through their eyes.

Your text may look right to you because, for you, it has a background. You can read it in the light of additional thoughts and knowledge in your mind. But you cannot always assume the same of readers. They have only the text by itself. When read in the light of their own thoughts and knowledge, which may be very different from yours, it may look very different. The word 'foolproof' should not be taken to imply that anybody who misconstrues your text, or hesitates over it, is a fool. He may be brighter than you, and see flaws which escape you.

A well-worn but classic example of unclarity is the order which unleashed the Charge of the Light Brigade, at the Battle of Balaclava in 1854. The British Commander-in-Chief, Lord Raglan, looked down from a high vantage-point and saw a Russian force capture some British guns on a ridge. He scribbled an order to the Light Brigade, below in a valley, to advance rapidly and prevent the Russians from carrying off 'the guns'. From where he sat, the meaning was obvious. Unhappily Lord Cardigan, the Light Brigade's commander, was too far down to see the crest of the ridge. The only guns he was aware of were those which covered the main Russian army at the end of the valley. Getting insufficient guidance from Raglan's courier, the officers made what sense they could of the order, and their cavalry rode to disaster against the wrong enemy force with the wrong guns.

Raglan had been quite clear about the guns, but not about the landscape which, for a reader below, would alter the meaning of his message. Hence he failed to take that step beyond clarity in his own mind which was vital for foolproof communication. He failed to amplify. When the order was read in the light of other knowledge, it was misunderstood.

Downright misunderstanding is not the only hazard. Sentences can be written which will in practice be taken correctly, but which remain faulty as communication, because they pull the reader up, or start him momentarily on a false trail, or put wrong notions in his head. To 'foolproofify' is not only to rule out mistaken meanings, but to rule out extra ones—overtones, as it were—which you don't want, and which spoil the effect.

Countless jokes have been based on this peril. A newspaper is said to have carried an advertisement saying:

For sale, bulldog. Will eat anything. Very fond of children.

An early manual on child-rearing gave the immortal instruction:

If the baby does not thrive on raw milk, boil it.

In both cases the reader would, actually, get the message. The dog's purchaser would not offer him children's legs to gnaw. The young mother would not boil her complaining infant. But neither message is stated in the best or most cogent form. Both reflect the confusion of writers who have not fully grasped their own implications.

The same mental failure that causes unintended meanings can also cause unintended images; and the same comments apply. To quote a student:

Dante stands with one foot in the Middle Ages, while with the other he salutes the rising star of the Renaissance.

Or this, a fine juxtaposition of a third-rate metaphor with a slipshod misuse of the word 'literally':

Throughout the long debate Mr. Gladstone sat literally glued to the Treasury Bench.

Yes, one does know what the writer was driving at . . . but oh dear . . .

Sorting it Out as you Go Along

So, think before you pour yourself out on paper. Yet not too much, not too laboriously. As with your practice of spoken communication, and as with your reading, so with this. It is not a hard-and-fast question of *first* thinking out all you want to say, to the minutest detail, and *then* switching over from brain to hand and setting down a flawless fair copy. You may be able to do this with one sentence, even with several. Edward Gibbon, author of *The Decline and Fall of the Roman Empire*, could compose an elaborate paragraph in his head and then transfer it to paper intact. But you are under no obligation to do likewise. Your basic thinking must precede writing—of course. However, once you have the main message clear, you can at least contemplate starting work. Further clarification will be needed. So will further improvement of the logic, and tightening-up and refinement in detail. But you may find that they come in the course of writing; as you make your rough drafts, read them over, consider, and re-shape. The point is simply that this revision does have to come at some stage, and the faster the better. It must never be shirked.

To revert to your non-human colleagues, the age of the computer is also the age of the servomechanism. Complex control systems, such as those that direct moon shots, are programmed to watch what they are controlling and keep the process adjusted as it unfolds. Besides the instructions flowing out, there is a feedback of data flowing in, and the feedback affects the further instructions. These machines are imitating what human nerves and muscles have been doing expertly for thousands of years. To shoot a series of arrows at a target, to ride a bicycle, to perform any one of countless other actions, is to pass repeatedly through a rapid, barely-conscious rhythm of doing, observation of the result, feedback, and adjustment.

Writing is apt to be like that. An author must have his main drift clear from the outset. He is riding his bicycle to point *A*, not to point *B* or *C*. But everything else, from the choice of single words to the logical structure of entire chapters (occasionally even entire books), may develop in the course of writing. The author's acts of self-expression and would-be communication may make him clearer to himself as he goes along.

To a certain extent this always happens. No author composes a whole book or even an article in his head before writing any of it down. But no firm rule can be given for the proper proportion between advance planning and playing-by-ear. Authors vary. An extreme case was John Galsworthy, author of *The Forsyte Saga*. Once he had got a novel under way, he carried it on by a method which he described as follows:

> I sink into my morning chair, a blotter on my knee, the last words or deed of some character in ink before my eyes, a pen in my hand, a pipe in my mouth, and nothing in my head. I sit. I don't intend; I don't expect, I don't even hope . . . Suddenly, my pen jots down a movement or remark . . . When the result is read through it surprises me by seeming to come out of what went before, and by ministering to some sort of possible future.

Galsworthy's technique is hardly a model for less experienced writers. It depends, not on eliminating thought, but on doing an unusual amount of it subconsciously, and as you go along. On the whole, the nearer you are to being a novice, the more you should plan in advance, the more you should crystallize your ideas first in outlines and notes (see Chapter Twenty). But once again, don't labour it. Never allow planning to paralyse you or hold you back. Never be afraid of making rough copies, trying things out on old envelopes, reflecting on what you have put down, crossing out and re-phrasing and re-phrasing again. This is a valid approach to clarity and rightness and persuasiveness, quite apart from any question of literary polish or elegance, which we have not yet come to at all.

You may prefer to dictate, rather than physically write or type. As usual, to carry authorship back to the spoken word is to see its nature more fully. If you compose aloud—if, even, you write quickly and spontaneously as you might to a friend, to whom you are, in effect, talking—you place that advice about 'writing as you speak *more or less*' in bolder relief. We are now coming to closer grips with the all-important 'more or less'. With only a few very experienced authors, a dictated text, typed back by someone else, can be satisfactory as it stands. With most writers it will only be the preliminary sketch for the finished thing. The difference between speech and its ideal written counterpart consists largely in the process of enriching and amplifying on the one hand, cutting and shaping on the other, which we are now considering. If we think along that line, we shall see in more detail how to go about it.

The Crucial Differences between Writing and Speech

We said on page 22 'write as you speak . . . well, more or less,' and discussed the practical development of speech as an essential instrument of writing. Now we will see how this has to be adapted to the actual process of writing.

Why the 'more or less'? In everyday life, the spoken word does (with a little makeshift 'foolproofification') convey your meaning. Why, then, does written communication have to be so different? Why take so much extra trouble over clarity, precision, and so forth?

Chiefly, because the relationships are not the same as in everyday life.

When you talk to somebody face to face, the two of you are together. When you talk on the telephone, there is still a dialogue of voices. When you write to a friend, there is at least mutual knowledge. You can picture him as a person, with foreseeable responses; you are present to him yourself in imagination. But when you write a story or article or book, and it reaches its reader, you are not there yourself. He doesn't know you, nor do you know him. Therefore there is a blunt basic necessity prior to all others—the necessity for *making up for lack of direct contact*.

Even apart from the effects of acquaintance, talking allows you to do things which are impracticable on paper, or misleading, or off-putting. It supplies instant feedback, and therefore, on-the-spot 'foolproofification': the other partner in the dialogue will soon reveal to you when you are being obscure, illogical, unconvincing, or silly. You can then repeat yourself and improve on yourself till your point is made, whether or not it is accepted. If Raglan had come down to the valley at Balaclava, and Cardigan had asked what guns he meant, he could have replied, 'The guns over that ridge'. Absence of direct contact was the cause of the blunder. The wording of the written message should have supplied the lack, and didn't.

Again, there are loose modes of speaking which are quite proper as such, but less so if transposed into a more formal medium. To take one very minor instance, you can convey ideas in conversation by exaggerating and over-emphasizing. 'X ought to be shot' is acceptable as a spoken phrase between friends, but not as a verdict in sober print. 'In Scotland it rains all the time' would pass as a warning to a tourist, but not in a textbook of meteorology. These and similar turns of speech depend on an informal, face-to-face situation, and can misfire badly without it.

When talking, you can think aloud. You can digress, hesitate, amend as you go along, till your real meaning works its way through. This behaviour is natural, and expected. Indeed, anyone who talks in neat sentences with no second thoughts is in danger of failing to persuade, because he sounds too slick—like a salesman who has learnt the patter. On paper the opposite is true. Prose that lurches around and back-tracks is apt to be merely irritating. It is obvious that the author could have done more thinking and correction before letting the script go as a final copy. Hence, his conversational air is either slovenly or bogus.

Deliberate Conversational Groping

A few authors, who knew what they were doing and kept it under control, have made good use of a wandering, off-target effect, often for the sake of humour. Laurence Sterne did it in *Tristram Shandy* and *A Sentimental Journey*. Jerome K. Jerome, of *Three Men in a Boat* fame, could contrive engaging chat. Here is a sentence from his description of a furnished bed-sitter in the 1880s:

> There are the two—what do you call them? they stand at each end of the mantelpiece, where they are never safe; and they are hung round with long triangular slips of glass that clank against one another and make you nervous.

He probably knew what these ornaments were called, and he could certainly have found out; but the pretence of conversational groping is part of his style. More serious effects of the same kind are produced by James Joyce and various American novelists who have experimented with the 'stream of consciousness'.

Outside fiction, however, sham conversational hesitation or self-amendment is seldom right. W. S. Gilbert satirized it in *The Yeomen of the Guard*. Two men give their account of a faked prison escape:

Wilfred	After mighty tug and tussle—
Point	It resembled more a struggle—
W	He, by dint of stronger muscle—
P	Or by some infernal juggle—
W	From my clutches quickly sliding—
P	I should rather call it slipping—
W	With the view, no doubt, of hiding—
P	Or escaping to the shipping—
W	With a gasp, and with a quiver—
P	I'd describe it as a shiver—
W	Down he dived into the river,
	And, alas, I cannot swim.

By putting the second thoughts into verse, where they are so blatantly contrived, Gilbert rubs in the falsity and artificiality of the whole tale. But this was intentional and wittily successful in its context. For purposeful writing where the object is not a special brand of humour, it is best to end up with a text that reads straightforwardly—and is therefore an improvement on speech.

Shades of Meaning in Speech

Yet another thing. In speech you can convey shades of meaning by the tone of your voice and the expression of your face. You can make it clear, for example, when you are being funny or sarcastic. On the printed page you cannot. Since a reader neither hears nor sees you, the text alone may cause him to wonder. Just how do you intend him to take it?

Authors have got into trouble by publishing satires and parodies that were misconstrued. One historic instance is that of Daniel Defoe. He brought out a pamphlet presenting a tongue-in-cheek 'case' for religious persecution—and then found that the persecuting bigots were hailing him as an ally. We can still see today how such doubt is exploited by a certain type of controversialist. First he attacks somebody with gross unfairness, and then, when his victim protests, he replies that he was just being funny, and scores a second time by insinuating that his victim can't take a joke.

Don't do it. You may think it very handy that by coming through in print only, and not in person, you can create ambiguities and keep a line of retreat open. But don't do it. Honesty (trite as it may sound) is the best policy. Where, in speaking, you would define your intent by tone or expression, you should clarify your words on paper till the lack is made up, and the reader will know which way to take you as surely as if you were there yourself.

Words Written to be Spoken

What about drama? Is writing for the theatre an exception? If your words are meant to be spoken as well as read—if, in fact, your end-product is simulated speech—may you not be justified in a certain relaxation, in a degree of blurring for realism's sake? The same principle remains. Relaxation and blurring must be introduced with skill, and they must be under control. All major dramatists—Shakespeare and Bernard Shaw, for a start—give us dialogue which, in various ways, is far more highly-wrought than real conversation, even where it is meant to sound conversational. It has more bite, more direction, a heavier charge. A television script-writer, portraying ordinary men and women in a popular serial, will still work at the dialogue so as to make it more pointed and economical than the real thing, while preserving the illusion of ordinariness. He is still writing like speech *more or less*—not simply writing like speech.

A dramatist has the same problem as other writers: in his own person, he is no more present to the audience than a novelist. But the actors are. When they deliver his lines they *can* add effects of tone, expression, and gesture. He may take advantage of that asset, as a writer for the printed page cannot. Or he may leave interpreting to the producer and cast. Unless he is extremely strong-willed, he is likely to succumb to the second alternative in the end; and it will prevail anyhow if the play is revived in his absence or after his death.

Shakespeare's fascination is due in part to the number of meanings that can be found in his many-faceted language. No single production can exhaust the potentialities of any of his major plays. When Macbeth is discussing the proposed murder of Duncan, he says:

If we should fail?

To which Lady Macbeth replies:

We fail!

Is that a stoical 'What will be, will be'? or a scornful dismissal of her husband's lack of confidence? or an incredulous protest at a foolish anxiety? Different intonations give it different senses, suggesting different views of Lady Macbeth. And this in a speech of two words only.

Our study of play-writing as a special form must be deferred (Chapter Twelve, page 153). But for the moment the main argument stands. Your primary axiom in addressing your unseen reader—and your primary reason for hammering your spoken language into a sharper instrument —is that you have no direct contact with him. Before all else you are coping with a gap; you are piercing the barrier of an absence.

Exercises

1. A job which you often do yourself is going to be done by somebody else, who is unfamiliar with it. You don't know who, and you can't be there to explain in person. Write an adequate and 'foolproof' set of instructions. (Don't get involved in anything complicated. If your instructions look like covering more than three pages, try a simpler job.)

2. While away from home, you hear that a neighbour—whom you know only by sight and name—has let his children play in your garden, pick flowers, and cause damage. Write a letter asking him to see that it stops. (If you are merely rude to him it probably won't stop, and there may be further unpleasantness after you return.)

CHAPTER SIX

THE INVISIBLE READER

Shaw's Intelligent Woman

The key to the process outlined in Chapter Five—making your text clear and right and persuasive—should now be manifest. It was grasped by Bernard Shaw when composing some of his popular handbooks of politics and economics. You must mentally bridge the gap, you must suitably supply the absence. *The first step towards mastering the fact that your intended reader isn't in front of you is to imagine that he is.* Not as an individual, but as a type; and not as a guest whom you can chat with, but as a figure sitting across the room, picking up your script page by page, reading it to himself, and quietly commenting.

Shaw was a pioneer. There were no exact precedents for his kind of popularization. He judged that he would get it right if he did it so that an intelligent woman would understand it. Therefore he imagined such a woman actually trying to follow what he said; and that is why his *Intelligent Woman's Guide to Socialism* was so called.

What Sort of Reader?

Is this practical advice for anyone with a less vivid imagination than Shaw's? Could you picture, say, an intelligent woman as a type—or would she only be some particular intelligent woman, someone you've met, who may not be typical?

We must break the exercise down into manageable components.

Ask yourself, for instance, whether you are writing for a *general* audience or a *specialist* audience. 'General' does not necessarily mean that you are aiming at the entire public which consumes television and mass-circulation papers. What it means is that you are thinking of your reader as pretty well anybody at a certain level of intelligence and general knowledge, with nothing further assumed. Writing for a 'specialist' audience means addressing yourself to readers who start with more knowledge of the subject than most people at that mental level. Specialist writing is not confined to scholarly and technical fields. An article for a magazine concerned with football, pop music or cat-breeding makes the same kind of assumption about the reader as an article for a journal of chemistry or philology. It is aimed at a specialist audience rather than a general one.

In other words, to get your reader in mental focus, one of the first questions you should consider is this: what do you expect him to know? Once you can picture somebody reading your text with a certain mental equipment, you can begin trying to picture his reactions. Thus, if you are writing for specialists, have you put in too much elementary discussion of topics which the reader is likely to be familiar with? Do you ever see him, in your mind's eye, looking impatient and skipping paragraphs? Or, if you think of him as a 'general' reader (on whatever intellectual plane), are you running a risk of upsetting him with allusions he can't understand and terms he hasn't heard? Are you treating him like a specialist when he isn't, and thereby failing to be clear?

The hazards that relate to the general reader are the more important and far-reaching of the two categories. As we said in Chapter Two, an author writing sixty years ago knew that the literate public shared an established culture, and that he could make assumptions which he can't make today. He could cite Greek and Latin classics with little explanation or none, being sure that an educated reader would take his point. And while at that time the classical net spread wide, the scriptural net spread wider. For over two hundred years the English Bible was the daily reading of millions on both sides of the Atlantic—not only the expensively educated, but many in the middle and working classes as well. Those who lacked book-learning often possessed a Bible as their only book; and when they did own a second volume, it might well be Bunyan's *The Pilgrim's Progress*, the work of an author steeped in the Bible.[1] Scriptural phrases, and allusions to scriptural characters and stories, would then evoke a reliable response. Today they do not. More survives of the biblical heritage than the classical: such names as Judas, Solomon, Cain, still have notions attached to them. But as a writer, you can no longer take it for granted that biblical references will make sense to the general reader, or elucidate your meaning.

For bridging the gap between yourself and your absent audience, Greeks, Romans, and Hebrews have become untrustworthy allies. That is not a reason to consign them all to the scrap-heap (God forbid), but it is a reason to be careful what use you make of them. Someone has claimed that in the present state of English-speaking civilization, there are just three literary allusions which are safe anywhere: to Romeo, Robinson Crusoe, and Sherlock Holmes. It hardly seems an illuminating list.

The 'general reader' of today, even when highly educated, is difficult to pin down. As a culturally-defined figure you cannot assume so very much about him. A first experiment towards picturing him, as a test for your prose, is to make him a composite of several people you know, on the mental level you envisage. Think of your friends X, Y, and Z looking over what you have written; imagine their faces; imagine their

[1] Jerome K. Jerome, in 1887, credits his charwoman Mrs. Cutting with a more original second choice. 'She never reads anything but the Bible and *Lloyd's Weekly News*. All other literature she considers unnecessary and sinful.'

pauses, their re-readings, if any; imagine their comments (preferably after a few drinks); and see what guidance emerges. We shall try to do better . . . but, just for a moment, pause here.

The Translation Guide

By way of illustration, take a problem which would seem almost to compel this act of imagining the reader or readers: what to do with quotations in foreign languages. Do you give the original without a translation, or a translation alone, or both together?

Suppose you are writing for a fairly literate general readership. You want to introduce a passage in a language most readers are unlikely to know, such as Chinese. In that case a translation by itself will be best. Picture, say, your dentist turning the page and confronting a sudden array of Chinese characters. It would be a jolt, a hindrance. Where the language is known to many, as German is, the decision is more exacting. It may be wise to give the original as well as a translation, especially if the precise meaning is important. Readers able to follow the original will want to see it for themselves. You can hear some of them muttering suspiciously, 'I wonder what the actual German word was?'

More delicate decisions still can arise from French. It is so widely taught in schools that most readers can be trusted to know a little—but how much? Normally you should quote a French original, unless it is inconveniently long. Do you also translate or not? Further reflection on the kind of reader you aim at, and the exact nature of your quotation, must supply the answer. If your text were intended for students of French literature—that is, specialists—anything in French would stand alone; a translation would be downright discourteous. You must carefully picture your 'general reader' and decide how much French he is likely to have picked up.

A choice demanding exquisite judgment confronted a writer of modern French history who mentioned the nickname of a politician's mistress. The politician's first name was Georges. His career depended largely on the lady's wealth and social connections. She was therefore called the *soutien-Georges* (Georges-sustainer)—the joke being that a *soutien-gorge* (breast-sustainer) is the garment now known in English as a bra. An attentive reader of French women's magazines would know this. But do readers of modern French history also read French women's magazines? To explain or not to explain?

What Educational Level?

In trying to picture your 'general reader' we looked at the problem of foreign words because it compels you to begin defining him. It also leads naturally to a larger issue. In the linguistic context we are driven to press the question 'What sort of general reader?' And in answering, there is one thing we can scarcely avoid taking into account—his educational standard. French quotations, if brief and simple, will get through for at least a high proportion of readers above such-and-such an academic level, but not below it. This is a principle of far wider uses.

Broadly speaking, education is related to age. In most English-speaking countries, every child goes to school. There is a fixed system of public examinations. Most universities have a family likeness to each other. So do colleges of further education. Hence, in theory, we can say that a piece of prose is right for a reader who is at least a certain age, and we may be able to link this with a certain number of years of education.[1] The converse is also true. If the writer knows that many of his readers are likely to be younger than that, or to have had less than the corresponding amount of education, then he should re-think and re-write till he has got his prose on to the proper level. *The 'general reader' in any given case begins to acquire substance when you picture him as having had such-and-such an amount of formal education.* Education simply; we are not talking about intelligence, or even achievement—just academic survival up to a given point.

The issue of age stands out plainly in journalism. *The Times* assumes a readership with more formal schooling than that of the *Daily Mirror*: a readership, therefore, of at least the age corresponding to that amount of schooling. Faced with both papers, children usually pick up the *Mirror* rather than *The Times*, and not solely because of the pictures. They can understand more of it. The same distinction also affects the style of books.

But far more is involved than the crude question of whether you are writing for children or adults. Your presumed reader may be an adult of any age. It still matters how old he probably was when a certain turning-point occurred in his life. It matters whether he is likely to have left school at fifteen, to have stayed on longer and then gone to work, or to have taken a degree at a university.

If you think hard about your reader's educational level, the next important guideline is to ask yourself what is the *minimum* age, the *minimum* educational level that you seriously hope to contact. Are you writing lucidly and simply enough to reach it? If you can feel assured that a reader on that level will follow you, then you will also be followed by readers who are older than that, better educated (whether through school and college or through courses taken later in life), and, one hopes, wiser. When in doubt it is always better to err on the side of clarity, both of explanation and of expression.

---

[1] Clearly there are wide differences between schools, and such factors as race, class, and parental income affect the quality of the education which children get. But in Britain, Ireland, Australia, New Zealand, and most parts of the United States, certain broad generalizations remain viable.

Three Tests of Prose

What about the marginal reader, the touchstone? What happens when you picture him reading your script? Three kinds of test emerge here.

(1) Test of academic knowledge assumed

The question of education brings this up most obviously. You must judge how much academic knowledge you can assume in your reader, and the main basis for this judgment can only be your experience of people and what they know. Recall the 'attitude' discussed in Part One. Some help may also come from a little study of school and college curricula.

You can work out your own points of reference, and will form certain basic ideas. For instance, if you write for the broadest readership—a readership including many without formal education past the age of fifteen or so—you can assume that anyone in this group who reads you at all will know the names of Columbus, Shakespeare, and Napoleon. He would also be able to tell you which of the three discovered America, which wrote plays, and which led armies. If, however, you wanted to mention Dante at any length, you would be well advised to explain briefly who he was. The Florentine poet will not be known reliably, except, perhaps, as a meaningless constituent of the phrase 'Dante's Inferno'. (When a film was made entitled 'Dante's Inferno', a popular reviewer described it as 'a vivid version of Milton's classic'.) Newton is fairly safe, so long as you are talking about gravity and nothing else. George Washington will pass, in England or America; Calvin Coolidge won't. You cannot, I have found, take Gandhi for granted.

Authors tend to be vague on such matters, and to estrange readers by not bothering to meet them half-way—an inexcusable failure of respect. Macaulay, the great nineteenth-century historian, never lived down a sentence which he once tossed off in passing: 'Every schoolboy knows who imprisoned Montezuma, and who strangled Atahualpa.' Every schoolboy doesn't. It is a pity, because Macaulay's style is far easier than this monstrous assumption might lead us to expect. If you are writing for schoolboys, or for readers whose last contact with formal education occurred at school, you may well take hints from Macaulay's literary practice, but not from his implied precept. A sounder assessment was made in more recent times by W. C. Sellar and R. J. Yeatman, whose parody-textbook *1066 and All That* professes to contain 'all the history you can remember'. It lives up to that claim, and remains a masterpiece of humour.

To give this warning is not to dismiss millions of citizens as ignorant blockheads, or excuse the insulting error of writing down to them. But over a wide range of academic knowledge, they have been told only so much, and have rarely been given any convincing reasons to keep it in mind longer than necessary, or to learn more for themselves. Hence, where that sort of knowledge is concerned, a writer should recognize the limits at various levels, and the need to explain and awaken interest. This recognition has nothing to do with other sorts of knowledge. Take the most scholastically-blank person, and you will often find that there is some subject on which he has a special knowledge as well as a native appreciation of things he never learned at school. But where we are seeking to define a 'general reader', we must stick to knowledge that can be generalized about.[1]

The other two tests we can apply are of a more objective kind, also based on schooling. As a child passes through the educational mill, his reading accustoms him to longer words, and to longer sentences. In both respects a gradual progress takes place, and this, also, can be generalized about to some extent. *Word-length* and *sentence-length* are qualities of prose that can give some idea of the sort of reader it demands. Again the converse is true. If your intended reader seems likely to have trouble on either count, you should reduce the number of long words in your text, and shorten the sentences.

(2) Test of word-length

A profusion of long words will always make for heavy going. The higher the proportion of such words in your prose, the more education you are requiring in your reader, and the more mature—by that standard—you are assuming him to be. Will he measure up or not?

It is true that small children like and accept long words in stories and rhymes read to them, but this is more a matter of sound and imagery than of meaning. A skilful author can employ big words with potent effect, for children as well as adults. He will be right to do so if there is no other way of creating the effect. A teacher, reading Kipling's *Just So Stories* to her class, came to the passage about the Parsee's hat from which 'the rays of the sun were reflected in more-than-oriental splendour.' A few days later the teacher met a little girl from the class, and remarked on the large white hat she was wearing. 'Yes,' the child replied, 'it reflects the rays of the sun in more-than-oriental splendour.' Kipling's grandiloquence has caught the imagination of many thousands of children in exactly the same way since the publication of the *Just So Stories* in 1902.

As a child gets older, however, and he is expected to apply himself to

---

[1] And with no prejudice as to comparative value. During the heyday of the British Empire, a chieftain from a Pacific island colony visited England and was taken on a tour of schools. Afterwards he looked puzzled, and said to his guide: 'You did tell me that all children come to these places from the age of five to fourteen?' 'Yes,' replied the official proudly, 'and at public expense if necessary.' 'Well,' said the chief, 'I don't understand. That's just the time of life when they ought to be learning things.'

school work, long words tend to defeat him. Even after he knows how to spell them out, he will not feel at ease with any passage that has a large number. At senior school levels, and at university if he goes there, he must eventually learn to live with such words if he is to read the books and pass the exams. But a writer should always be careful with them.

No rigid rule can be prescribed. In the adult world, champions of plain language often point to the politicians, and contrast the woolly verbosity of most with the superb pile-driving of Churchill's war speeches:

> I have nothing to offer but blood, toil, tears and sweat.

> We shall defend our island, whatever the cost may be. We shall fight on the beaches, we shall fight on the landing grounds, we shall fight in the fields and in the streets, we shall fight in the hills; we shall never surrender.

Both these memorable passages depend on the use of short words. Yet it was also Churchill who coined the often-quoted phrase 'terminological inexactitude'. The most inspiring and enduring of all political slogans was made up of three fairly long words: 'Liberty, Equality, Fraternity'.

Long words, in fact, can be functional and correct for a literary or rhetorical purpose. They are also functional in a scientific text, where the technical term, however forbidding, is the right one. It is when they are not functional, or not clearly so, that they impede most gravely. If you find yourself putting many in, you should picture your reader once again, ask yourself how accustomed he is to handling such words, and, perhaps, try to break them down or find shorter synonyms.

Sir Ernest Gowers, who wrote manuals on 'plain words' for the guidance of British civil servants, asked why people are so easily lured into polysyllables. Recalling H. G. Wells's engaging hero Mr. Polly, who revelled in 'sesquippledan verboojuice', he suggested that we are all apt to be seduced by the air of grandeur, distinction, and out-of-the-ordinariness which the long word carries. This, however, is a personal and rather infantile feeling which does not rub off on the reader, and is no excuse for putting obstacles in his path.

Gowers collected some dreadful examples of pointless overloading. From *The Economist*:

> NATO has expressed its fundamental change of policy as 'evolving in place of the overriding medium-term defence hypothesis to which all economic planning was functionally subordinate, an antithesis of balancing *desiderata*, such as the politico-strategical necessity against the economico-social possibility and further these two components against the need for a maximum of flexibility.'

The Economist attempted a translation of this, which Gowers quotes (*The Complete Plain Words*.) He also gives the following, from an unnamed source, without any translation:

> Diffusibility of knowledge throughout the environment in which the families are to move is essential if the full expression of their potentiality is to become explicit in action. Facts pertaining to experience of every sort that the family is in course of digesting give the context and the full flavour of consciousness to their experience.

Even here, where the piling up of long words is not quite so appalling, notice how they deaden the impact and leave the meaning uncertain. They are actively anti-functional.

Such passages underline that second quality which is a gauge of what a piece of prose demands in the reader: sentence-length.

(3) Test of sentence-length

Some authors can run sentences on for line after line without losing the thread, or the reader. Others are less capable. There is no objection to the occasional long sentence, any more than there is to the occasional long word. But if too many are needlessly long, the reader is apt to flag. He is compelled too often to retain thirty or forty words, to marshal them in his head, and to recall the first link of a winding chain as he nears the last. It is not the length of the odd sentence that counts, but the average length of all the sentences. If this is high, indicating a large number of long ones, then the demand which is being made on the reader is correspondingly high and perhaps excessive.

English sentences have tended to shrink during the past century or two. At least, the intervals between full-stops have tended to shorten. However, if we study some of the masters of prose before 1800, we shall sometimes find that the journey from full-stop to full-stop is by way (grammatically speaking) of several sentences, not one. Divided by colons or semi-colons, they form a logical sequence, and the length we shall assign to the sentence may depend on our notion of what a sentence is.

Here is Gibbon on the decline of the Roman Empire:

> Prosperity ripened the principle of decay; the causes of destruction multiplied with the extent of conquest; and as soon as time or accident had removed the artificial supports, the stupendous fabric yielded to the pressure of its own weight.

Here he is describing the camel:

> Alive or dead, almost every part of the camel is serviceable to man: her milk is plentiful and nutritious: the young and tender flesh has the taste of veal: a valuable salt is extracted from the urine:

the dung supplies the deficiency of fuel; and the long hair, which falls each year and is renewed, is coarsely manufactured into the garments, the furniture, and the tents of the Bedouins.

Each of the single units is fairly compact. But something larger, a kind of musical structure, connects them. Gibbon does not expect the reader to retain many words together; he does expect him to retain a series of ideas, and let them build up.

This leisurely, receptive, reflective manner of reading is what our age of mass-media has partially banished. Conditioning has gone too far to reverse: conditioning by such factors as the highly compressed news item, and by the necessary brevity of the spoken sentence on radio and TV—necessary, because the listener or viewer can't go back for a repeat, and the broadcaster must govern himself accordingly. To point out that modern prose has (and needs to have) shorter intervals between the full-stops than Gibbon's is not so much to lay down a statistical law as to say that most modern readers are adjusted to prose which is less artistically patterned; which is more broken up, more 'one-thing-at-a-time' in its rhythm and impact; which provides more frequent pauses in the voice and the mind.

When children compose essays, their sentences are usually brief and disjointed. They toss out packets of simple words without much logical interweaving. Gowers quotes the following, by a child of ten asked to write on a bird and a beast:

> The bird that I am going to write about is the owl. The owl cannot see at all by day and at night is as blind as a bat.
>
> I do not know much about the owl, so I will go on to the beast which I am going to choose. It is the cow. The cow is a mammal. It has six sides—right, left, and upper and below . . .

We do outgrow this. However charming it may be, it is not what we would desire, as adults, to read or write all the time. The percentage of adults who outgrow it as completely as Gibbon did is lower now than it was in the eighteenth century. But throughout the years of school and college, the sheer stern necessity of coping with books and passing exams gradually forces the process on, even if nothing else does.

The Fog Index

We said at the end of Chapter Four (page 35) that you could learn to adapt your style to suit readers on various levels of age and education, and that you could even do it by numbers. Robert Gunning, an American business teacher, has distilled both the word-length test and the sentence-length test into an interesting technique for measuring readability, and it will be very much worth your while learning how it works.

Gunning's 'Fog Index' combines the two objective tests, word-length and sentence-length, so as to assess the minimum age and educational level for which a text is suitable. To speak in terms of our present approach: if you work out this index for your own prose, and judge that the reader you have in mind won't measure up to it, you will have a clear directive to re-write.

Any such measuring technique must, of course, be hedged round with qualifications. It assumes that the sense is not obscured by a highly unfamiliar or specialized content, which no brevity of words or sentences could ever make easy. It assumes that the prose is contemporary, in manner and punctuation; Gibbon, for instance, might create hazards. Also it assumes a sensible, practised user. Gunning does not pretend to have reduced his test to a mere clerical routine. Still, after all these warnings, the Fog Index remains a helpful tool of criticism and self-criticism.

This is how you work it out for a given text.

1. Take a sample of about 100 words from a typical-looking passage. Start the sample at the beginning of a sentence, finish at the end of a sentence. Count the exact number of words (the closer to the round hundred the better).

2. Divide the number of words by the number of sentences, to get the *average sentence-length*. Punctuation may cause doubt as to what is a 'sentence'. Thus you may find two grammatical sentences with a semi-colon between instead of a full-stop. Use judgment, but you should generally count them as two. 'He chose the northerly road; this turned out to be a mistake.' Two rather than one. The semi-colon here could be a full-stop.

3. Also count the *number of long words* in the sample. A long word means a word of three or more syllables. But don't count (*a*) capitalized words; (*b*) words which are combinations of short easy ones, e.g. 'book-keeper', 'butterfly'; or (*c*) words made up to three syllables by adding-ed or -es to shorter ones, e.g. 'invaded'.

4. Add the *average sentence-length* and the *number of long words* together.

5. Multiply the result by 0·4 to get the Fog Index.

Gunning added the final step in order to make his Index fit the grades in the US school system. An Index of 10 means that a reader must have reached at least grade 10 if he is to follow prose of this texture easily for any length of time. However, the Index can be applied in most English-speaking countries. Roughly, it shows the *minimum number of years of formal education* required for sustained understanding and attention.

The Fog Index of 10 corresponds to readers who are somewhere about fifteen years old, or who left school at that age—plus or minus a year or so. The range 11–13 implies a senior school level, up to sixth form in the English system. The range 14–16 goes with a university-educated reader, or, at any rate, a reader who has equivalent practice with fairly difficult books. Beyond 16 the ground is shaky. 17 and 18 are marginal cases. A Fog Index over 18, persisting through more than the odd passage, is too hard. It wanders away from any meaning in educational terms. Prose of that sort will be heavy going for almost all readers. If you find that you are guilty of it yourself, you should try to simplify. One good feature of the Fog Index is that it keeps the spotlight on the two instant methods of lightening your prose: to break up long sentences, and to replace long words by shorter ones, where you can do so without serious loss.

Let us look at some examples. Newspapers first. The Fog Index is not quite so significant here, because papers are usually read in small doses, and the question of sustained attention arises less often than in books. However, the results of the test can still be interesting.

Here is a sample from the *Daily Mail* (August 8th, 1970):

> Thousands of homes, shops and offices were flooded, theatres were evacuated and traffic was thrown into chaos when a thunderstorm swamped London last night.
> Firemen were inundated with calls for help from a 30-mile radius.
> Many roads were flooded to a depth of two feet. Some drivers abandoned their waterlogged cars.
> Several Tube stations were closed as torrents poured on to the tracks.
> Near Isleworth station, in West London, a policeman on point duty took off his boots and socks, rolled up his trousers and carried on.
> Shows at three West End theatres—the Duchess, Garrick and Victoria Palace—were abandoned and the audiences left.

There are 106 words, in 7 sentences—average sentence-length (to one decimal place), 15·1. There are 7 long words—'evacuated', 'indundated', 'radius', 'abandoned' (twice), 'theatres', 'audience'. Adding 15·1 to 7, and multiplying by 0·4, we end up with an index of 8·8. In practice, of course, 'about 9' is all the accuracy we should pretend to. Hence the item is quite well suited to a mass-circulation paper. It is adult, but it assumes no reading habits more advanced than those acquired by all ordinary adults in the last year or so before the minimum school leaving age.

Now, from *The Times*, an example of prose creeping out of hand, in a long news story about a proposal to ease the internal problems of Jordan (July 10th, 1970):

> It [the proposal] calls for guarantees that the sovereignty of King Hussein will be honoured and that the guerrillas will be allowed

freedom of action from Jordanian territory. This in itself is a major contradiction.

According to most versions, the King would withdraw Jordanian forces from around Amman in return for a similar guerrilla withdrawal.

However, the King has shown himself to be dissatisfied with the guerrillas' promises that their 'regular' forces would be withdrawn from inside the capital and has called for a total withdrawal of the guerrilla militia, the irregular force composed of part-time soldiers drawn from the refugee camps and the Palestinian population generally.

Average sentence-length, 26·5 words; number of long words, 20; Fog Index, 18·6. Prose that went on like this would become most fatiguing. The last sentence could be broken up into three with no trouble at all. That change alone would lower the Index to about 15, still high, but more manageable.

And now to books, where, because of the need for sustained attention, the Fog Index matters more.

From Ian Fleming's *Dr. No:*

Bond took the opportunity to glance at his watch. Ten o'clock. His eyes slid to the gun and holster on the desk. He thought of his fifteen years' marriage to the ugly bit of metal. He remembered the times its single word had saved his life—and the times when its threat alone had been enough. He thought of the days when he had literally dressed to kill—when he had dismantled the gun and oiled it and packed the bullets carefully into the springloaded magazine and tried the action once or twice, pumping the cartridges out on to the bedspread in some hotel bedroom somewhere around the world.

Average sentence-length, 18·2 words; number of long words, 6; Fog Index, 9·7. Say 10.

From Bertrand Russell's *History of Western Philosophy:*

Subjectively, every philosopher appears to himself to be engaged in the pursuit of something which may be called 'truth'. Philosophers may differ as to the definition of 'truth', but at any rate it is something objective, something which, in some sense, everybody ought to accept. No man would engage in the pursuit of philosophy if he thought that *all* philosophy is *merely* an expression of irrational bias. But every philosopher will agree that many other philosophers have been actuated by bias, and have had extra-rational reasons, of which they were usually unconscious, for many of their opinions.

Average sentence-length, 24·5 words; number of long words, 16; Fog Index, 16·2. Say 16.

From Anthony West's *All About the Crusades*, a book for children:

Conrad had his way. He went through Constantinople and presently set out from Nicea with his army of ten thousand men. He was back in less than a month. All his baggage was lost, and nine out of every ten of his men were dead or taken prisoner. His army had been attacked one evening after a hard day's marching through waterless desert. It was almost dark. The knights were resting; their squires were watering the horses along the banks of a river some distance from the camp; the men-at-arms were pitching tents and unloading the pack horses.

Average sentence-length, 15·1 or 18·3 words, according to whether you count the last portion as three sentences or one; number of long words, 4; Fog Index, 6·4 or 7·3. Say 6 or 7.

The Fog Index of a book may vary considerably from one passage to another, because of changes in subject-matter (a wholly proper reason) or in the author's mood at the time of writing (a less proper one). It is wise to take several samples, a long distance apart. Random spot-checks in *The Art of Writing Made Simple* suggest a range from about 8 to 12—up to secondary education, but never, I hope, beyond that. The densest Fog Index in my experience was 22. It occurred in an article by an educational expert, published in a teachers' journal as a choice specimen of that expert's wisdom.

Exercises

1. Do you agree with Shaw that the best imaginary reader, for an author popularizing an abstruse subject, may be female rather than male? Might the answer be different today from what it was in an earlier generation?

2. See page 49. Why do you think it is that 'everybody' has heard of Romeo, Robinson Crusoe, and Sherlock Holmes? This is *not* a question about the works these characters appear in, because only a minority has read them. What would you say is special about the characters themselves, and how have they become known to non-readers?

3. See page 55. Try re-stating the 'Diffusibility of knowledge' extract in plain language. Has it a comprehensible meaning at all?

4. Look at your answers to the longer exercises after Chapters One to Five (or anything else you may have written) and calculate your own Fog Index.

CHAPTER SEVEN

LOGIC BEFORE RULES

Three Kinds of Criticism to Apply

We must now close in from advice in general to advice in detail. With a creative art, such advice is always liable to be stronger on the negative side. Warning (here as elsewhere, but especially here) is easier than precept. But we must try to make negation a springboard for positive action.

There are books that offer rules which are meant to give a writer every warning he needs—at least in matters that can be pinned down exactly enough. One of the best lists is in *The Reader Over Your Shoulder*, by Robert Graves and Alan Hodge. Such lists, however, can grow alarmingly long. Graves and Hodge give forty-one rules altogether. The implication that you are picking your way over ground strewn with forty-one traps may be a shade forbidding. Also, to apply rules is to risk classifying and compartmentalizing too much. A passage that requires alteration does not always require it for a single, precise reason.

Learn rules of writing if you like. In Chapter Four we already encountered a few of the more general sort, and, of course, you can't dispense with them entirely as you narrow down to particulars. I shall soon be offering some rules, or at least guidelines, of my own. But don't be too rigid about them; don't treat them as if they were the laws of some complicated game, which you must know and obey exactly in order to play it. Put them in a context which keeps them in due proportion, and get the context right first.

Press on a little farther, in fact, along the line proposed in the last chapter. Thus far, 'thinking of your reader' has meant chiefly thinking of one typical person from a single point of view: will he be broadly able to follow you? Suppose you have cleared the hurdles in that respect. You feel satisfied that your writing is correctly attuned. Now take another step and test it more carefully. Knowing what range of readership you have in mind, picture several different readers within that range. More particularly, three.

Reader No. 1

Imagine a reader who is quicker-witted than most—a lively, questioning type whose mind works on what he reads. He isn't hostile, he's simply critical in a fair way, and not disposed to slide over anything that strikes him as obscure, muddled, or false.

Reader No. 2

This reader is quite different from the first. He is slow and uncertain in the uptake. While equipped to read you, and interested enough to try, he won't try very hard. If he finds a lack anywhere he won't make a mental effort to supply it, he will just get confused or irritated.

Reader No. 3

This one is neither very lively nor very lazy, but has an eye for the comic, the incongruous, the unfortunate—a person who laughs, and starts others laughing, when he isn't meant to.

Imagine these readers singly to begin with, mentally submitting your work (or samples of it) first to No. 1, then to No. 2, then to No. 3, and picturing their reactions as honestly as you can. With practice the trio should merge into a single presence, an advisory panel in the background, whenever you review your drafts.

Having your ghost-readers as sharply outlined as this, you may know real people who fit the descriptions. If so, then possibly you can humanize the process by showing them your script. But unless they are prepared (as very few people are) to spend time on it, and comment page by page with candour and tact, you will do better to imagine them than to enlist their aid in the flesh.

Clear Thinking Again

In Chapter Five we said that good written communication presupposes clear thinking. If you are not thinking clearly—either from the start, or after a sorting-out process as you get your ideas down on paper—you will not communicate satisfactorily to anyone else. Given a certain talent and vigour, you may still induce a state of mind in your reader; you may win a partial or temporary assent to your main message. With the spoken word such successes are easier and often serve their purpose. A skilful demagogue thrives on them. But, as always, the written word is different because of the absence of direct contact. Hitler himself would never have attained power if his crazy book *Mein Kampf* had been his only means of reaching the public.

To help you clarify your ideas, and keep them clarified as you go along, Reader No. 1—the lively-minded critic—can be very useful. Keep him constantly before you, both to open your eyes to major errors of thought and to sharpen the logic of individual phrases and sentences.

Errors of thought are fundamental, and we must now spend some time considering what they are, and how to avoid them. They can undermine a paragraph, an article, even a whole book. In a subtler way they can weaken the effect of fiction or drama, and sap its credibility. Hence they take priority over the hazards which 'rules of writing' are mainly concerned with, and which we shall look at afterwards. To learn to think accurately, indeed, is to go a long way towards a state of mind in which the hazards will take care of themselves.

Let us say that you are writing to make some serious point. Imagine Reader No. 1 in sceptical mood, taking the opposition in a friendly debate, querying your statements, challenging your arguments. There are two main types of faulty thinking which he might pounce upon. Your words may reflect (or seem to reflect) a basic failure of grasp in your own mind. Or they may be open to criticism because of an air of falsity or unfairness, confusing your audience rather than yourself. In either event Reader No. 1 will catch you, given half a chance. He will make you think again and write differently.

Here are some specimens of the dangers you should guard against. First, the potential shortcomings of your own thought, whether applied directly to a factual theme, or worked out in the plot of a novel or a play.

1. When you make or imply a broad general statement, have you enough grounds for it? Are you basing it on too few instances, too casual observation, too little research?

Every serious author deals in statements of this kind. He makes them as starting-points of discussion ('Crime is on the increase'); as conclusions of his argument, or part of it ('Hence it is obvious that the Beatles were a disaster to music'); as advice ('Divorce ought to be easier'); and in other ways, badly or by implication. Generalizations like this are the lifeblood of all coherent discourse. Failure to put them on a firm basis is one of the commonest of faults. It comes out, for example, in attitudes to nationalities. 'Italians are thieves' may mean no more than 'I once lived next door to some Italians who stole my clothes-line'. A person with that idea in his head might never express it outright, might well deny indignantly that he had it, yet might still show his prejudice by (for example) his choice of incidents in a travel book. Prejudice is an error even when it is kind. It is said that in G. K. Chesterton's detective stories, if an Irishman is suspected, you know he won't be the criminal.

You may believe, yourself, that you would never write anything as silly as 'Italians are thieves'. Perhaps you wouldn't. But beware of thinking in ready-made stereotypes which are hardly more sensible; beware of generalizing and dogmatizing from scanty data, or too narrow a range of data. Where such basic errors exist, elegant writing and stylistic correctness are worthless. They become vices instead of virtues; they paper over the crack.

If you do slip into poorly-grounded assertions or arguments, the image of Reader No. 1 puncturing your case ought to correct you. Confronted with an old man who said, 'I belong to a club that's gone swimming daily for forty years, even in the coldest weather, and look at me now,' he would reply, 'Right enough—but what about the others?'

Could Reader No. 1 deflate you by a parody? There is a kind of popular-science item which sins by concentrating on hand-picked facts while ignoring other facts that tell against it. One of the neatest criticisms ever made of it took the form of a deadpan article entitled 'Your Pants Could Kill' (supposedly from the *Reader's Digest*), which described a 'survey' revealing that of all the American soldiers who had died of a certain illness, every single one had worn trousers—therefore . . .

Reader No. 1, I can assure you, has read that article.

2. When you say or imply that something follows from something else, does it?

Here we pass from statement to reasoning. The technical term for a thing which purports to follow and doesn't is a *non-sequitur*—Latin for 'it doesn't follow'.

Chekhov, in a short story, conveys the atmosphere of a small-town circle by a single exchange of remarks. A doctor urges the abolition of capital punishment. Back comes the retort, 'Then you think everybody should be free to murder anybody he pleases.' This absurdity makes you form an impression of the speaker, even if you agree with him about capital punishment. But when you are determined to take a certain view —or rebut someone else's—you may jump to conclusions just as illogically.

Take special care in the realm of cause and effect. When A is followed by B, or when A and B often go together, we are all apt to jump to the conclusion that A causes B. Yet it may well be a *non-sequitur*, in the logical sense. The fatal trousers apply here too. Doubtful reasoning on cause and effect is common in the discussion of big, complex, emotional public issues. Political issues, for example: Jones was Prime Minister or President during such-and-such a period, the country was prosperous, therefore Jones was a good Prime Minister—or President. And social issues: children and teenagers see violence on television, they behave violently in real life, therefore television has affected them. Well, has it? Not necessarily. A fatal flaw in any reasoned argument is to say that one factor out of many is the sole cause of a given effect.

Another frequent *non-sequitur* is the analogy that is pressed too far: the argument (or assumption) that because a thing is true in some cases it is true in all, or that because a thing is happening now it will go on happening. The latter error appears in the form of 'trend' thinking. Here again political pundits have often been the worst offenders. Before 1914 most of them took it for granted that because the English-speaking countries were the richest and most advanced, and other countries were evolving towards their type of democracy, the whole world would eventually become like them. Between the wars came a phase when the triumphs of Hitler and his allies convinced many people that dictatorship instead of democracy would soon be the rule everywhere. After 1945 the rise of Russia and China led to much the same expectations about Communism. All the way along, trend-minded political commentators were pouring out wasted words by the million, and conspicuously failing to foresee the next trend. Their books, however brilliant, died after very short lives.

A few pages back I cited G. K. Chesterton as illustrating a certain kind of bias. In recompense to a very great author, it is fair to point out that he also wrote one of the wittiest, most far-sighted of satires on 'trend' thinking and the *non-sequitur* underlying it—the first chapter of his fantasy *The Napoleon of Notting Hill*, published in 1904.

3. Are you begging the question or arguing in a circle?

If you are writing to prove some point, then make sure you are proving it; not slipping it in as an assumption, open or concealed. Even unconsciously and in good faith. You may really be stating the issue, or defining the terms, in such a way that your intended conclusion must emerge whether it is right or not. An acute critic would expose the fallacy and blow you to pieces.

The classic example of question-begging is 'Have you ceased beating your wife?' Whether the husband answers 'yes' or 'no' he confesses to having beaten her, so the confession has no value as evidence. In France, where the laws governing the press are not as strict as in England, a newspaper reporting a murder trial kept referring to the accused as 'The Monster Assassin'. This went on till the trial ended with a verdict of Not Guilty. Next day the paper reported this result under the headline 'Monster Assassin Acquitted'.

Believers in any doctrine, religious or otherwise, are prone to this error. If you have strong convictions, watch yourself. Suppose a churchgoer is arguing that Christians are better than other people. An opponent retorts with examples of the bad behaviour of a great many Christians—Spanish inquisitors, for instance. The advocate replies, in effect: 'Oh, but people like that aren't true Christians'. What he has done is to define a Christian in his own mind as somebody who *is* better. From that axiom he goes on to 'prove' that Christians are better. He could hardly fail. In fact he has proved nothing.

Orwell, in *Nineteen Eighty-Four*, portrayed the regime of Big Brother preventing revolt by changing the language so as to turn it into one vast system of question-begging. 'Newspeak' is a strictly utilitarian English with many words re-defined, so that it can only be used to say conformist things, and dangerous thoughts cannot be expressed. Big Brother is good by definition, and 'good' has no meaning at all apart from his will. To a child taught Newspeak from the beginning, nothing opposed to Big Brother could ever be 'good'. The word 'equal' refers only to physical measurements such as height and weight. To this child, the sentence 'All men are equal' would mean that all men were the same size and would start no subversive notions. It would just be silly.

Newspeak is a literary invention for showing up the fraudulent logic by which a doctrine or dogma can impose itself. It makes the fraud blatant and obvious. With the English we actually employ, such fraud can be camouflaged, and concealed even from the user himself. If an author begins by tacitly assuming what he pretends to prove, he may build up arguments that go round in a circle. He is still only demonstrating that Big Brother is good because Big Brother is good.

Challenge your own assumptions. And imagine Reader No. 1 doing it, more probingly than you might care to yourself.

4. Are you making guesses and then letting them harden into facts?

This is a common fault among historians, biographers, and kindred writers who deal with matters that are partially known and partially unknown. When some event is not fully recorded, the author tries to fill out the picture with a credible guess or reconstruction. At the time he plays fair and doesn't pretend that it is anything more. A few pages later, however, or even sooner, you find he is treating his conjecture as a plain fact, and perhaps inferring other facts from it. Historical novelists, of course, are entitled to do this within reason. But even they go too far if they set up their own fancies or interpretations in defiance of the evidence.

Among famous non-fiction authors, a major offender is Lytton Strachey. His irreverent lives of *Eminent Victorians*, published in 1918, brought freshness into the art of biography. But their impact depends too much on the trick of making opinionated or prejudiced guesses, and then following these up as if they were facts, on the same level as documented facts. Strachey has a beautiful style, and any writer can learn from him. But the style has an insidious power to carry a sort of propaganda, which is sincere in its way, yet often misleading and not to be imitated.

Writing of Cardinal Manning, who started his career as an Anglican clergyman and went over to Rome, Strachey mentions an interview which Manning had with Pope Pius IX before his conversion. No record of it exists, but Strachey supplies the lack most adroitly.

> It is at least possible that the authorities in Rome had their eye on Manning; they may well have felt that the Archdeacon of Chichester would be a great catch. What did Pio Nono say? It is easy to imagine the persuasive innocence of his Italian voice. 'Ah, dear Signor Manning, why don't you come over to us? Do you suppose that we should not look after you?'
>
> At any rate, when he did go over, Manning *was* looked after very thoroughly . . .

And so on to an account of his rapid advancement as a Catholic. The idea of a gentlemen's agreement appealing to Manning's careerism begins as a fantasy. By the end of the next paragraph the unwary reader has probably swallowed it as a fact, with Strachey's blessing. The extreme case was confessed by Strachey himself. In his life of Dr. Arnold, the reforming headmaster of Rugby, we read the following:

> His legs, perhaps, were shorter than they should have been; but the sturdy athletic frame, especially when it was swathed (as it usually was) in the flowing robes of a Doctor of Divinity, was full of an imposing vigour.

Afterwards, when the book was an established classic, Strachey admitted that he had not known how long Dr. Arnold's legs were. He had just felt that they must have been short. Here the feeling became an instant fact, with no transition at all. Strachey's 'perhaps' is not sufficient excuse.

The motive behind this surreptitious promotion of guesses is wishful thinking. When you hit on a notion which you like, and would find handy to buttress an argument or reinforce an impression, tread carefully. You may get too fond of it, and give it a status which it doesn't deserve.

More Deviations from Logic

Further species of mental warpage and blocking may well occur to you. They are primarily ways of deceiving yourself. Always be aware of that reader, imaginary or real, whom they won't deceive: Reader No. 1.

If he can expose errors in the author's own mind, then, more surely, he will expose those tricks of style which nearly everybody with something to say is tempted to fall into—tricks which are not exactly dishonest yet prompt the audience to think wrong. Here are a few.

(a) *Trying to put a point across by assertion instead of reason:* e.g. by appealing to an alleged common consent ('Everybody agrees . . .'); or to an authority, preferably vague ('Science teaches . . .'); or even to your own prestige ('Speaking as a driver of thirty years' experience . . .').

(b) *Using slanted language or special pleading:* e.g. calling your own side's case 'information' and the other side's 'propaganda'; denouncing A for doing what you condone, or keep quiet about, when B does it (the occupational disease of the politically indignant).

(c) *Confusing the issue:* e.g. drawing red herrings across the trail, or appealing to emotions that are beside the point. One recalls Gilbert's parody of a mushy humanitarianism in *The Pirates of Penzance:*

> *When a felon's not engaged in his employment,*
> *Or maturing his felonious little plans,*
> *His capacity for innocent enjoyment*
> *Is just as great as any honest man's . . .*

When the enterprising burglar's not a-burgling,
  When the cut-throat isn't occupied in crime,
He loves to hear the little brook a-gurgling
  And listen to the merry village chime.
When the coster's finished jumping on his mother,
  He loves to lie a-basking in the sun;
Ah, take one consideration with another,
  The policeman's lot is not a happy one.

(*d*) *Trying to crush opposition by discrediting the person you are arguing against, or misrepresenting him, or imputing motives.* During the 1960s, when there was much talk about 'permissiveness' in conduct, some people attacked its advocates as Communist agents seeking to undermine western society by debasing its morals. This sort of thing can work, for a time, with some audiences. But don't do it.

The Key to it All

More variations on the theme of What Not To Do may occur to you, and don't delude yourself into supposing you are exempt. I have said, 'Write about what you know and care for.' But you will now see that this principle of good writing carries built-in risks. The more you know and care, the stronger your convictions are apt to be; the more determined you will be to persuade others; the more impatient you will feel with those who think differently; and hence, the greater the danger of putting your case wrong, or slipping into unfairness, or exploiting prejudice and emotion.

The final, positive rule is this. *Know, and care*; and if knowing and caring mislead you into wishful thinking or injustice or any other error, then the remedy is to know and care more. As with so many problems, the solution is to be reached by going through, not by turning back. Truth matters. Rightness matters. They can serve a good cause more potently than any deception of yourself or your readers. Only learn to love them enough, and then write as you please. Sooner or later you will cease to need advice under specific heads. All these warnings will take root at subconscious levels.

Exercises

1. Suggest what sort of facts would be needed to substantiate the 'broad statements' given as specimens on page 63:

(*a*) 'Crime is on the increase.'
(*b*) 'It is obvious that the Beatles were a disaster to music.'
(*c*) 'Divorce ought to be easier.'

You may disagree with a statement, or think it ought to be qualified. But show what a writer would need to do to support whatever case there is.

2. Criticize these arguments.

(*a*) 'It is a striking proof of Divine Providence that almost every great city has a river running throught it.'

(*b*) In the early days of aerial warfare, a woman explained that she always ran about during an air raid, 'because it's harder to hit a moving target'.

(*c*) A very old man told a visitor: 'I've noticed a funny thing—if I don't die in March, I don't die at all that year.'

3. Expose a major instance of illogical or misleading argument which you feel strongly about—in politics, religion, or some other public sphere.

CHAPTER EIGHT

THE CUTTING EDGES OF PROSE

Criticism in Close-up

When you come to the details of composition, the critical Reader No. 1 is still a helpful person to keep before you. But now his colleagues join him: No. 2 who won't make an effort, and No. 3 who has an eye for the comic or incongruous. Most of the rules laid down by authorities can be reduced to making sure that none of the trio would react undesirably to the way you put things. Prose should be sharp; every such reaction (or non-reaction) tends to blunt it.

Your imagined readers might not state their reactions in plain terms. But if they did, they could make any one of a number of disconcerting comments. Your job is to write so that no such comment can ever be made. The most destructive might be expressed like this:

(1) *'Wait, I'm not quite there yet.'*
(2) *'How's that again?'*
(3) *'Have I missed something?'* or *'But what about . . .?'*
(4) *'How do these things relate?'*
(5) *'What does all that amount to?'*
(6) *'That's a bit off-key.'*
(7) *'There he goes again.'*
(8) *'Oh, dear!'*

Some of these are more especially Reader No. 2's comments; some, No. 3's. Let us see how they can be provoked, and how avoided.

Clarity and Momentum

The first three comments reflect a single fact: that a great deal of the efficiency of writing consists simply in ensuring that no one will stumble because of an outright mental query over the message. If such a query arises, it may lead not merely to disquiet but to misunderstanding—as with Cardigan's error over the order at Balaclava.

(1) 'Wait, I'm not quite there yet.'

This is a reader's mental reaction when you create a feeling of bewilderment, perhaps only slight, perhaps really obstructive. Many sorts of confusion and imprecision can cause that feeling. To guard against it, ask yourself whether you are following such guidelines as these.

(a) *Make it clear, all the time,* **what** *you are talking about*

Here, as in other parts of this chapter, we are picking up again on points already covered in a general way—in this case, on pages 30–1. But now they will be examined in closer detail so that their application will become clearer.

An article (let us say) begins like this:

> Cats fascinate me, and I have always kept at least two. The other day I was sitting with Miauler, a current favourite, on my lap. The telephone rang. I got up to answer it, putting Miauler on the floor. It was Aunt Lucy. She asked how I was, and said she had called to check whether it was on Tuesday or Wednesday that she was to visit me. Aunt Lucy wears skirts too short for her age. When our conversation was over I looked out of the window and noticed that a boy on a bicycle had stopped near my gate. I wondered why. Presently, however, he went on. Meanwhile the cat had vanished. I took out my diary and noted down Aunt Lucy . . .

Here, approximately, the reader begins to feel that he isn't with the author. He pauses, baffled. Is the article meant to be about a cat, an aunt or a cyclist? He may go back and read the passage again; or he may give up and turn to another page.

Conceivably most of the details could be brought in—but not thus. The following might pass:

> Cats fascinate me. I have owned many, but Miauler, who lives with me now, is the most gifted. The other day he was sitting on my lap when the telephone rang. To answer it, I had to deposit him on the floor, where he sat looking affronted. The caller was only Aunt Lucy with a brief inquiry (she has a knack of ringing up inopportunely about trivia), but the damage was done, Miauler had been unsettled. After replacing the receiver I was going to take him up again, but was detained for a fatal further moment. I saw that a cyclist had stopped near the gate and I wondered why. Anyhow, by the time the false alarm (whatever it was) had passed, Miauler was no longer in the room . . .

Not the most inspired prose, but now, at least, the cat is clearly the main topic, and the function of the other details is just to strike a gossipy, personal note.

(b) *Be sure that your text answers the basic questions that come into a reader's mind: especially* **who, when, where**

This means, in effect, 'Study news stories written by good journalists, and do (more or less) likewise.' If you skip ahead for a moment to the section of this book beginning on page 198, you will find the point enlarged upon and illustrated; after which, you can pick out as many examples as you want from the press. Meanwhile, ponder a splendid illustration of what not to do. From Henry Cecil's novel *Friends at Court*, it is part of the cross-examination of a witness by Mr. Crabtree, a barrister.

'Very well then, Mr. Sanders—you remember that meeting, the one I was referring to, not the one in January—that was a mistake on my part—the one in February, the meeting which is referred to in the correspondence. You know the one I'm talking about, there's no mistake about it, is there? Now, at that meeting there were three of you present. You, Mrs. Bole, Mr. and Mrs. Meadowes—no, that makes four, I'm sorry. There were four people present and what I want to ask you, Mr. Sanders, is did any of you at that meeting—any one or more of you, I mean you or Mrs. Bole or Mr. and Mrs. Meadowes—I think there was no one else present—that's been admitted—your Lordship will see that in the particulars delivered on the 14th January last—no, I'm sorry, my Lord, it's in the defence itself under paragraph 7—oh, no, my Lord, I'm so very sorry—it *is* in the particulars of the 14th January after all—I had them in the wrong order in my bundle—I'm so sorry, my Lord. Now, Mr. Sanders, this is very important, I shall make a note of your answer— did you, or Mrs. Bole or Mr. and Mrs. Meadowes—any one of you, I mean—say anything like this—I don't mean the actual words—no one expects you to remember the exact words of a conversation all that time ago, but anything of the kind, I mean. I'm waiting for your answer, Mr. Sanders.'

'Did who say what?' intervenes the judge.

'Oh, my Lord,' says Crabtree, 'I'm so sorry. I thought I'd asked the witness. Well, Mr. Sanders, so that there may be no doubt at all about it I'll ask you again.'

(c) *Be careful that the reader won't be in danger of losing the thread in your longer sentences*

We have taken note of sentence-length as one of the major factors affecting prose clarity (page 55). It is perfectly possible to write long sentences without being obscure. But they have to be kept under control. The danger is that if a sentence does get long, you will start back-tracking, qualifying, putting in second thoughts and amplifications, even forgetting the structure, so that the sentence comes unstuck before it is finished.

Mr. Crabtree illustrates this hazard as well. But he has the excuse that he is trying to think on his feet. In the following sentence by John Ruskin, supposedly a master of style, there is no such excuse.[1]

---

[1] The example, like one or two others in this chapter, is taken from Waldhorn and Zeiger, *English Made Simple*.

If there be—we do not say there is—but if there be in painting anything which operates as words do, not by resembling anything, but by being taken as a symbol and substitute for it, and thus inducing the effect of it, then this channel of communication can convey uncorrupted truth, though it does not in any degree resemble the facts whose conception it induces.

I once came across a nineteenth-century account of a poltergeist, written by the owner of the house, who believed in the mysterious agency. Here is one of his sentences.

But what matters?—neither I, nor the servants—singly or together —nor any one—be he whom he may, could or can, I aver, work the wonderment, that I, and more than half a score of others, saw.

This sentence in twelve small bits is not enormously long, nor is it grammatically faulty, apart from the 'whom'; yet around the seventh bit, you begin to feel unhappy.

Don't avoid long sentences too rigidly. But if you feel impelled to write one, see if you can break it up into shorter ones, and if not, then be sure that you do have it under firm control.

(d) *Take care not to put unnecessary strains on the reader's memory*

Keep him adequately reminded of everything he needs to remember in order to stay with you. As another illustration of what not to do, careless writers of fiction are apt to give long stretches of dialogue in which the reader loses track, and suddenly finds that he isn't sure who is speaking. By inserting 'said Mary' or 'roared John' at intervals, a better writer will maintain contact.

There is a popular novel in which the author describes a man having breakfast on a hotel terrace. He doesn't want all his bacon, and gives a piece to a wire-haired terrier which is sitting near by. The dog hasn't been mentioned before and seems to fade out. Various events occur, and then, several pages later, comes the sentence: 'He gave the wire another strip of bacon'. To my knowledge, that sentence has pulled readers up with a round turn.

(e) *Follow a natural, logical, decisive order in every passage, and in your work as a whole. Don't make the reader grope uncertainly back and forth, rearrange ideas in his mind, and sort out what you should have sorted out for him*

Read again what was said about the difference between spoken and written English on page 45. You should find that it comes in here also, with new force.

One of the soundest maxims for writers is the advice of the King of Hearts in *Alice in Wonderland:* 'Begin at the beginning, and go on till you come to the end; then stop.' Granted, a few geniuses such as Joseph Conrad have done otherwise with success; granted, the flashback has a legitimate role; but never lose sight of the King's advice as the norm. If you observe it fully, both with the whole and with the parts, you will have taken a long step towards ensuring that your readers will stay with you and always know where they are.

Even in a single sentence, the natural order is generally best. A reader will stumble, if only for an instant, over such a sentence as 'He turned and looked back after rushing madly to the end of the path'. Better, 'He rushed madly to the end of the path, then turned and looked back'.

(2) 'How's that again?'

This is a reaction to ambiguity, or to the simultaneous presentation of ideas that don't fit together. A reader may feel, not that the text pulls him up, but that it pulls him on in more directions than one. So . . .

(a) *Be careful that your sentences are **not** ambiguous*

Once again, re-read—this time, the passage on pages 40–2 about 'foolproofification', and the examples given there. It isn't enough to say, 'Oh well, it's perfectly obvious what I mean.' You can still upset communication by the mere hint of another meaning. And remember, if it's a silly meaning, Reader No. 3 will spot it.

(b) *In particular, be careful with tricky words such as pronouns*

It is specially easy to get into a muddle with 'he' and 'his'. Gowers cites the sentence 'John told Robert's son that he must help him,' which could have, not merely two, but six different meanings. An old hymn contains the couplet:

> Satan trembles when he sees
> The feeblest saint upon his knees.

A child asked, 'Why does Satan let the saint sit on his knees, if it makes him tremble?'

(c) *Be careful not to write phrases that seem to dangle, or point in the wrong direction*

One reason for keeping sentences under strict control, and for following a 'natural, logical order', is that if you are trying to connect several ideas, you must make sure that they get connected properly; and looseness of thinking or construction can interfere.

Handbooks of grammar and syntax warn against 'dangling modifiers' —phrases that relate, or can relate, to the wrong word. In the sentence 'Having reached home, the door closed behind him,' the first three words apparently go with 'door' . . . only they don't. This objection may sound like a purist's quibble. However, it ceases to be a quibble when we consider such sentences as 'Hanging from the bell tower, crowds watched as the fanatic prepared to jump,' or 'Listening to the concert with rapt attention, Beethoven seemed more than ever a magnificent composer.' The crowds were not hanging, Beethoven was not listening—yet strictly speaking, the sentences say they were. The result can be even worse if the fatal phrase comes in the middle: 'The policeman approached the gate, and as he came in, barking furiously, the dog retreated.'

(d) *Be sure that your phrases and sentences link up, so that a reader passes from one to the next with no unnecessary jolt*

Sheer disjointed incoherence has, I hope, been sufficiently illustrated in the first specimen under heading (1). The 'jolt' is slighter and subtler. A reader may be going along smoothly, and then have a sudden flash of uncertainty because of an awkward transition. There is an unexplained change of standpoint, or a parallelism that breaks down. 'I will go to Bristol, I will see my solicitor, and the question of the property will be sorted out.' The natural form of the third phrase would be 'I will sort out the question of the property'. The shift causes a little uneasiness. It hints at a shift of focus—will the sorting-out be done by somebody else? But by whom? The reader will probably dismiss the idea of a third person, but the jolt has occurred.

A similar jolt, perhaps more violent, can result from the *non-sequitur* on a small scale, or any similar connection that fails to connect. Chesterton has a journalist in one of his novels who was nicknamed 'Hibbs However'. A typical Hibbs gaffe was in a news item about an assassination attempt. He wrote: 'The Minister is now out of danger. The assassin, however, is not, as was previously thought, a German.'

(3) 'Have I missed something?' or 'But what about . . .?'

This is the reader's reaction if you confront him with a passage which is clear and logical, and cannot be faulted under heading (1) or (2), but leaves out something which its logic would lead him to expect. The guideline is simply:

Make sure that you include every vital point, and satisfy every expectation which your words raise.

Suppose you were to begin a story:

> Four men were paddling a canoe up a remote Brazilian river. Their names were Jack Stevens, Bill Kubelik, Charles Anthony, and Alphonsus Meade. Jack was a tall red-haired Australian aged about forty. Bill, small and dark and taciturn, had come all the way from New York to join him, accompanied by Charles, an accountant who had quit his job in the hope of bigger rewards from this expedition. The sun blazed down . . .

A reader is now going to worry about Alphonsus, perhaps for pages.

Acceptability to the Mind

Next, while all of your three test-readers might grasp the sense of a passage and not feel it to be exactly wrong or confusing, they might still query its content and organization. Thus:

(4) 'How do these things relate?'

You may convey an impression that while everything you have written is technically sound in itself, you are darting about inconsequentially, or putting items in the package that don't belong.

(a) *When you associate X and Y, be certain that they do go together logically*

If, for example, Y is supposed to illustrate X, make sure that it does: unlike the boy who wrote, 'All birds come out of eggs. There are many kinds of eggs, for instance, frogs' eggs.' Here the mind's eye has wandered from the ball.

(b) *See that each paragraph coheres, and deals with a single topic*

Don't press this so far as to be pendantic. There is a notion that every paragraph ought to have a 'topic sentence', usually at the beginning—a sort of headline stating what the whole paragraph is about. For example: 'The President was gravely ill. Four eminent doctors were at his bedside but could not agree on the proper treatment'—and so on, with further details for ten lines or so, to the conclusion 'Meanwhile the patient grew weaker'. That opening, 'The President was gravely ill', does set the scene and make for unity, but you need not regard the topic sentence as an absolute 'must'. What does matter is the coherence of the paragraph. It would be wrong to turn away from the President, mention a docker in Baltimore unloading a crate of bananas, and then go back to the sickroom.

(c) *Watch your punctuation and sentence division, and see that they fit the general logic*[1]

Suppose you were to write, 'I am left-handed and my car is a Vauxhall'. On the face of it, you have two separate statements, and they should go in separate sentences. If you do combine them, Reader No. 2 may be puzzled, and Reader No. 1 will want to know what the connection is: whether, for instance, you are leading up to the news that the police are looking for a left-handed thief driving a Vauxhall. If you aren't, don't arouse the suspicion that you are.

(5) 'What does all that amount to?'

This mental comment expresses the insidious feeling that the writer

[1] On the detailed technique of punctuation, and allied matters, see *English Made Simple*, and Gowers, *The Complete Plain Words*.

hasn't as much to say as he pretends, and that he is trying the reader's patience with needless reiteration, empty verbiage, evasion of issues, or flogging of the obvious. A most undesirable reaction. Therefore:

(a) *Be concise, and make every sentence tell; every word, in fact*

Churchill remarked of an opponent that he had a rare talent for compressing the maximum of words into the minimum of meaning. It is not a talent to emulate. Consider this as the opening of a story:

It was a fine spring day. The sun shone in a blue sky. The air was warm. Several floors up in an office block, higher than most of the buildings round, Alf sat at his desk. It was covered with sheets of paper, and he had, as usual, plenty of work to get on with, but at this particular moment of time he was not getting on with any of it. He was looking out of the window at the buildings in the spring sunshine, and he was reflecting that he hated his job. All he ever did was copy information, deadly dull information, from one kind of form to other kinds. And the seemingly endless details which he transcribed daily from nine to five were useless anyhow. He was sure that nobody would ever want them again . . .

Faced with prose as slack and bumbling as this, a critical reader will soon notice the slovenly waste of words, and be disinclined to take trouble with a writer whose style consists largely in disguising a shortage of ideas. A less critical reader may not do that, but he will gradually get a feeling of slow progress and frustration, and become bored.

The content of the specimen is not very exciting, but it could at least be tightened up. The second and third sentences, for instance, add nothing of value to the first. Throughout, many of the words have no real function at all. Experiment suggests that less than half the number would be enough.

It was a fine spring day. High up in an office block, Alf sat at a desk by the window and looked out at the sunlit buildings. It struck him that he hated his job. All he ever did was copy information from one kind of form to other kinds. Useless information, at that, which nobody would ever want.

There is no short cut to economy in prose, but there are exercises which you may find helpful. One is précis-writing. Take a sample passage of two or three hundred words out of an article or book (preferably not fiction, and not technical material). Try composing a paragraph of your own, giving the entire substance of the passage in less than one hundred words. Such a summary is called a précis. It will not, of course, be a model of literary prose if the original itself was well written. It will sacrifice the style, the nuances, the elaborations and elucidations. A book written entirely in précis English would be intolerable; it would be lifeless, and would require too much unrelieved concentration. But précis-writing can give you a sense of relative importance, an awareness of issues, an understanding of how to compress and re-word so as to reduce long sentences without fatal loss. Then, in your own writing, you will be better able to distinguish what you should prune away altogether; what you should consider cutting down or rephrasing; and what you must say fully, explicitly, without compromise. You will also be better equipped to do these things.

Another technique for the same purpose is to imagine, when launching out on a piece of writing, that you are sending your message by cable at so much a word, and will have to account for every penny to a tough employer. What are the absolute bare essentials which you *must* transmit, and how can you state them as lucidly and concisely as possible? Having decided, drop the 'cable' game and proceed with the real writing, but organize it around those essentials which the game highlighted for you.

(b) *Stay on firm ground; avoid padding out your text with semi-irrelevancies, or idle remarks and fancies*

Historians and biographers tend to speculate when they are short of facts. One warning sign is the phrase 'must have', or its equivalent. 'As he rode into London for the first time, Shakespeare must have looked at the Palace of Whitehall and conjured up Elizabeth's court in his imagination.' Must he? and so what, anyhow? Has the author really said anything?

The Right Sort of Dignity

Lastly, watch out for Reader No. 3's detection of the jarring note, the awkward, the ludicrous. He can help you to maintain dignity in the right way and not slip up. There are several potential comments which are more especially his.

(6) 'That's a bit off-key.'

A reaction that reflects a feeling of discord, often comic discord.

(a) *Bear in mind the pitfalls in the connotations of words*
It is enough here to re-read page 28.

(b) *Satisfy yourself that your language is appropriate to the subject at every point, and all of a piece*

This is a matter of taste and judgment. The only way to acquire them is by varied reading. You should not (unless for conscious comic effect) tell a fairy-tale in the language of a *New Statesman* article, or report on a Board meeting in the manner of D. H. Lawrence. This may be obvious. The subtler kind of lapse is inconsistency: writing generally in one way, doubtless the proper way, but slipping from time to time into another.

Even eminent authors are known to do it. Kipling, for instance, notoriously drops into archaic phrasing—often biblical—for no good reason.

Clergymen and scholars, when trying to sound human for the man in the street, are apt to flounder among several kinds of language. At one moment they are unconvincingly colloquial, then they switch to old-fashioned pomposity, then they echo the Bible or some other classic. Consistency is best.

(7) 'There he goes again.'

One mental comment which can badly impede communication, and weaken respect for you, is the reaction to ill-advised repetition that obtrudes—repetition of ideas, of sounds, or of individual words. But the adjective 'ill-advised' is crucial. Repetition in itself may be allowable and even impressive, especially for emphasis, as in the Gettysburg Address (page 31). There are two guidelines here which may seem to lead you in contrary directions. Actually they don't; but you must learn to choose, and strike a balance in your choice.

(a) *Avoid repetition which, with no special function, forces itself on a reader's notice and distracts from the meaning*

Don't labour the same idea and revert to it often without developing it or showing fresh aspects of it.

Don't put words together that scan like verse with a recurrent beat, or rhyme or jingle. The sentence 'She listened relatively silently to the introductory summary' rams home the final '-y' sound with an ugly effect, even in such a brief space.

Don't use the same word over and over again, *unless* for special emphasis. There is no such motive in the following: 'I admire the man who is courageous enough to go up to a man whom he sees bullying a child or a weaker man and tell him, as man to man, that he must lay off.' The repetition of 'man' is aimless; it just happens.

In all such cases the reader very quickly reaches a point where, half-consciously, he is almost counting rather than reading.

(b) *But now the converse. Have the courage to repeat without scruple, if the alternative is to go through even more distracting struggles in order not to repeat*

Quiller-Couch supplies the classic example. In his own words:

> An undergraduate brings me an essay on Byron. In an essay on Byron, Byron is (or ought to be) mentioned many times. I expect, nay exact, that Byron shall be mentioned again and again. But my undergraduate has a blushing sense that to call Byron Byron twice on one page is indelicate. So Byron, after starting bravely as Byron, in the second sentence turns into 'that great but unequal poet' and

thenceforward I have as much trouble with Byron as ever Telemachus with Proteus to hold and pin him back to his proper self. Half-way down the page he becomes 'the gloomy master of Newstead': overleaf he is reincarnated into 'the meteoric darling of society': and so proceeds through successive avatars—'this arch-rebel', 'the author of *Childe Harold*', 'the apostle of scorn', 'the ex-Harrovian, proud, but abnormally sensitive of his club-foot', 'the martyr of Missolonghi', 'the pageant-monger of a bleeding heart'.

A reader's ability to take in this essay would soon have been overshadowed by curiosity as to how Byron would be described next. Strained avoidance of repetition becomes a kind of repetition itself.

(8) 'Oh, dear!'

This is Reader No. 3's amused recoil from worn clichés like 'leaving no stone unturned'; also, from unfortunate images.

(a) *Be careful with metaphors and figures of speech*

Beware of the kind which we held up to scrutiny on page 42. Ask yourself what would happen if somebody tried to draw the picture which a metaphorical sentence conjures up. 'We must nip this octopus in the bud, before it spreads like a miasma over the whole area.' Or the sentence which was once believed—wrongly—to have killed the expression 'bottleneck': 'The economy of the Ruhr is bound to move within a vicious circle of interdependent bottlenecks.'

(b) *Even where an image is acceptable, be sure that it is felicitous and not liable to raise a laugh*

The Times, June 18th, 1971, quoted an allusion to the Queen in a speech at a literary luncheon:

> At certain times of grave national stress, when that ragbag called the British constitution is in danger of coming unstuck, thank heavens for the big safety pin at the top that keeps it together.

(c) *Take care not to mix figurative and literal phrases*

It would not do to write: 'She sat with her head in her hands and her eyes on the floor.'

(d) *Always restrain your imagery from getting out of hand*

Graves and Hodge—from whom the previous example is also taken—give a ghastly paragraph from a sermon, genuine or invented:

> Our struggle against sin resembles a cricket-match. Just as the batsman strides out to the wicket, armed with pads, gloves and bat, and manfully stands up to demon bowling, with an adversary behind

him always ready to stump him or catch him out . . . and when the sun sets, and stumps are drawn, he modestly carries his bat back to the pavilion, amid plaudits. So likewise the Christian . . . And when, finally, safe in the celestial pavilion, he lays aside the bat of the spirit, unbuckles the pads of faith, removes the gloves of doctrine and casts down the cap of sanctity upon the scoring-table—lo, inside, is the name of The Maker!

By the end of this effusion Reader No. 1 would have a wry smile on his face, Reader No. 2 would be looking distressed, and Reader No. 3 would be shaking with laughter.

And on that note we may take our leave of them.

Exercises

1. The confusing paragraph beginning 'Cats fascinate me' (page 71) was re-written so as to make the cat the main topic. Re-write it again so as to make Aunt Lucy the main topic. You can say more about her, and less about the cat and the cyclist, but you must keep the main points, just as they were kept in the original re-write.

2. Make a précis of the opening passage of this book, from 'Here at the start' to 'by any other method'. Your précis should be approximately one-third the length.

3. Collect a few examples of speeches, lectures, etc., from papers such as *The Times* and *The Listener* which quote them in full, or at any rate copiously. Examine these in the light of the warnings given in Chapters Seven and Eight.

CHAPTER NINE

TOWARDS MASTERY

The Higher Virtues of Style

With practice, you can make your prose clear and right and persuasive. Can you also give it distinction? What about beauty and individuality, and where do they come from?

Of course there are no sharp dividing lines. The higher virtues of style are not optional accessories fitted on afterwards. Nor are they confined to special, 'creative' classes of writing, such as fiction. Outside these classes the scope for them may be less. But even if you write as a chore only—an unwelcome part of a work routine—you can at least hope to please and arrest attention, rather than repel. We are still in the field of Writing in General, though admittedly close, at last, to the point where paths diverge.

The Wealth of English

Let us begin by standing back, and looking again at the English language, in a longer perspective. It is a rich language. To compare it with French or German, or even with its Scandinavian cousins, is to see a difference in quality. English is simpler in some ways, harder and more complex to handle in others.

It is rooted in Anglo-Saxon, the speech of certain Teutonic tribes that crossed the North Sea and conquered most of Britain, during the four centuries after the fall of Rome. The first English word on record is 'keel', meaning one of the boats that brought them over. This is embedded in a Latin history written about the year 545. The word is still with us. 'Keel' can still mean a boat—a flat-bottomed craft used on the rivers Tyne and Humber. English as a whole shows the same continuity. Much of the vocabulary of everyday talk is Anglo-Saxon, if you trace it back far enough. We are dealing with a language that is Teutonic rather than Latin. But because of later influences, it has a variety which its European relatives cannot match.

Norsemen overran a large part of England during the ninth century, and left their mark. The Norman conquest in 1066, and three hundred years of dominance by French-speaking nobles, brought a massive infusion of French words—especially words reflecting upper-class life: thus farm animals kept their Anglo-Saxon names ('pig', 'cow', 'sheep'), but when cooked for the tables of the gentry they became French ('pork', 'beef', 'mutton'). Meanwhile the use of Latin for serious writing also made a deep imprint. The revival of Greek studies in the sixteenth century gave a new set of terms to the arts and sciences. Contact with the Celtic fringe led to other linguistic imports (though not many) from Welsh and Gaelic. More recently, commerce, exploration, and empire-building have drawn in words from farther afield.

Quiller-Couch, in his *Art of Writing*, suggests that the growth and enrichment of English in its formative ages was a process that fed on itself. There was purpose in it, or at least aspiration, as well as chance. Needs were felt and then met. Though Anglo-Saxon supplied a firm basis from the beginning, the Old English of the early Middle Ages was limited as a medium. It was narrow in range, and curiously shapeless. Even its poets wrote without rhyme and usually without regular metre. But during the long French cultural paramountcy, pioneers such as Chaucer made English versions of French originals. They transplanted continental verse-forms; they acclimatized the spirit of a more mature literature. While the poet Langland was keeping an Anglo-Saxon style meandering on in *Piers Plowman*, Chaucer was composing the crisp rhymed couplets of *The Canterbury Tales*. The innovator's work was a springboard as the conservative's was not. Chaucer, and after him Malory (most of whose prose romances of King Arthur are adapted from French originals), handed on a language that could do many things which the old insular English could not. Furthermore, it gave those who used it a feeling of larger potentialities. They would no longer rest content. Inevitably they would reach out after fresh conquests.

In the early Tudor era (Quiller-Couch goes on) English prose was still rather flat and unwieldy. It had trouble in rising to emotional heights, and expressing ideas with energy. The next major advance was the advent of the New Learning, which made ancient Greek literature known again. Besides adding to the actual store of words, Greek writers showed English ones how to think more precisely and give their thoughts articulate form. In 1611 came the translation of the Bible from Greek and Hebrew under King James I, an amazing piece of inspired teamwork by forty-seven scholars. Through public exposure to this masterpiece, which, for religious reasons, every literate person read, English was finally launched on a career that would fit it for any task.

Attempts to 'Purify'

We may or may not accept all of Quiller-Couch's history. However, there is wisdom in his stress on the way the language expanded its powers by feeding on foreign literatures and foreign vocabularies. This manifest gain has defeated several attempts to simplify, and reverse the movement.

In the Victoran age a number of authors (William Morris was the most eminent) tried to prune away the alien graftings, especially those from Latin sources, and make English as purely Anglo-Saxon as possible. When they could find no Teutonic replacement for a rejected Latinism, they sometimes made one up. The only such coinage that survives today is 'foreword' for 'preface', invented in 1842; and even this, although it survives, has not killed 'preface'. Readers saw that however many words were found or invented, a reduced Pure English would not and could not do the same things. Altering the medium, even in this restricted sense, would alter the message. A critic pointed out that the scientific phrase 'the impenetrability of matter' would become 'the ungothroughsomeness of stuff'. Despite Morris's unquestioned stature, writers preferred to go on undeflected to the point where we took up their story previously, in the early twentieth century.

A more recent proposition was Basic English, devised during the 1930s by C. K. Ogden and I. A. Richards. It consisted of 850 carefully chosen words, with a few hundred extra for technical requirements. By combining these, it was claimed, you could say anything. What the claim actually meant was that you could define anything, and then employ definitions, where necessary, to replace words. For example, if not allowed the word 'tell', you could turn the sentence 'Tell me something' into 'Give me some knowledge'. A critic (doubtless descended from the impenetrability-of-matter critic) asserted that in Basic, 'roast chicken' would become 'the fowl from which we get eggs cooked to a good brown in the oven'.

Enthusiasts urged that Basic English ought to be spread abroad as an international medium—the Esperanto dream in a new guise. H. G. Wells voiced his hopes in *The Shape of Things to Come*. The British Government acquired the copyright. Books, including the Bible, were translated into Basic. By exploiting the simpler aspects of English, and removing the complex ones, Ogden and Richards had indeed produced a very easy, logical language. But an attempt to turn, say, a scene of Shakespeare or a story of Henry James into Basic ought to convince anyone that it cannot do everything that English can do.

Language—The Craftsman's Workshop

To revert to the English language and its rare wealth. A couple of pages of the *Concise Oxford Dictionary* supply the words *tableau* (French), *taboo* (Polynesian), *tabular* (Latin), *tacamahac* (Aztec via Spanish), *tachometer* (Greek), *tackle* (Teutonic), *tael* (Malay via Portuguese), *taffeta* (Persian via French), *Taffy* (Welsh). If you speak of 're-macadamizing' a road, you employ a term that is made up of a French prefix, 're', followed by the Gaelic 'mac', the Hebrew 'adam', the Greek '-ize' and the purely English '-ing'.

Through varied regional interactions, and changes in pronunciation and usage, English has evolved into the language we know. Pronunciation has sometimes drifted away from spelling. That is why English spelling is so irregular and therefore so difficult. But another trend has made for ease. The passage of time has rubbed many grammatical complexities smooth. English retains few of the inflections, case-endings and conjugations that make Greek and Latin so rigorous and daunting, and linger on to this day in languages such as Russian and German.

Latin gives a noun different endings according to the context. Thus 'king', as the subject of a sentence, is *rex*. But as the object, it is *regem*. In the phrase 'of a king' it is *regis*. 'To a king' makes it *regi*, 'with a king' makes it (*cum*) *rege*. With more variations in the plural. In modern English, the pronouns are still inflected a little (as when 'he' becomes 'him' if used as the object of a sentence, or after a preposition), but nouns have only one singular form, and generally only one plural. Likewise, English verbs change a little with the way they are used (we say 'I sweep, she sweeps'), but far less than verbs in Latin or French. Context and function, not form, determine meaning.

As Robert Graves put it, English is fluid. It does not fit into mechanical patterns. You cannot make it 'good' just by setting up approved models and academic standards. Beside French it looks illogical and chaotic. Somerset Maugham once alleged that an author can get closer to perfection in French, because the rules of French grammar are bound up with felicity of language and never oppose it, whereas the rules of English grammar (such as they are) sometimes do.

But as Robert Graves further said, this untidiness of English is largely an optical illusion. It is like 'the untidiness of a busy workshop,' where a skilful craftsman is more at home, and better able to work, than he is in a highly regulated factory. The language is capable of the utmost precision, the most exquisite effects, if you employ it well. Its words are versatile, many-faceted. One result of the long process of eroding complexities is that ever since the Elizabethan era, the parts of speech have been more nearly interchangeable than they are in other languages. Outside English a noun is usually a noun, a verb is a verb, a conjunction is a conjunction. Here, however, is Scott:

> 'I heartily wish I could, but—'
> 'Nay, but me no buts—I have set my heart upon it.'

A conjunction does duty as a verb and a noun, very forcefully, and the sentence does not sound contrived. Latin of course has its conjunction 'but', which is *sed*. However, translation would compel you to coin words and say, approximately, 'Noli mihi sedere sedia'. In Latin the 'buts', to be grammatical, would have to acquire suffixes to define their meaning, and the sentence would turn into a verbal stunt out of key with the dialogue. In English the 'buts' can perform acrobatics and still sound natural.

This freedom in using one part of speech as another has conjured up a vast array of nouns-used-as-adjectives ('*school* life', '*taxi* rank'), and nouns-used-as-verbs, with various effect. In the sentence 'The boy coloured the drawing,' the noun 'colour' has become a verb that simply preserves the literal meaning. In the sentence 'The man towered over the boy,' the noun 'tower' has become a verb with a new, figurative meaning.

Writers who care for beauty and correctness have complained that in modern times the process is out of hand. For instance, we have too many unwanted and ugly noun-verbs such as 'to service', 'to contact', 'to author'. Yet even with some of these, there can be a correct, functional use if we care to insist on it. 'To author' should not be made a synonym for 'to write'; T. S. Eliot did not author *The Waste Land*; but the verb might properly denote doing a prescribed writing job to order—'Who authored the scripts for these commercials?'[1]

Again, a word can retain its normal grammatical status, yet undergo subtle shifts of alignment and enlargements of connotation. Often the accuracy of good English is a matter of nuance. To illustrate how English differs from German, Coleridge quoted the line 'The pomp and prodigality of heaven,' referring to the inspiration showered on such poets as Milton. You could not turn this directly into German, he argued, because it would become 'The pomp and spendthriftness of heaven.' In the setting of a rich composite language, 'prodigality' has acquired shades of meaning which its German counterpart has not.

Or, to take a case with much wider applications—does any other language (except, conceivably, Chinese) possess an equivalent of 'gentleman'? Only by etymology is it the French *gentilhomme*. 'Gentleman' is *gentilhomme* after a long, almost indescribable chemical change. Neither moral nor social definitions exhaust its content. This noun, which prissily replaces 'Men' over lavatory doors, is also, in cricket, a snobbish synonym for 'amateur'. It is also the key word in one of the few great epitaphs. Captain Oates, the sick member of Scott's polar expedition who walked off into the blizzard rather than be a drag on the party, is for ever 'a very gallant gentleman'. Step outside English and it is doubtful whether you could say that.

Two Non-rules

In Chapter Seven I suggested that you can, to some extent, soft-pedal 'rules of writing', by cultivating habits of thought that keep them in their

---

[1] Thomas Hardy told an amusing story. A critic reproached him with having coined a spurious adjective-verb, in the sentence 'His shape smalled in the distance.' To rebut this and similar charges, Hardy looked up a few of his more dubious words—including the verb 'to small'—in the *Oxford English Dictionary*. They were there, sure enough. But his relief was short-lived. The only quotations given in support were from his own books!

place. It should now be clear that this method is peculiarly well suited to English, because English actually is less subject to rules, and harder to pin down, than most languages. At the copybook level, in fact, it is so free by contrast that it has made pedantic experts uneasy. Feeling that there simply must be more rules than appear on the surface, they have invented several of their own, which are pointless and best forgotten.

Thus, generations of children used to be taught that you must avoid ending sentences with prepositions . . . or, in the words of the ancient classroom joke, that a preposition is a word which you mustn't end a sentence with. The no-preposition idea is said to have begun with John Dryden in the seventeenth century. No one need dispute that Dryden himself wrote excellent prose. But other writers of excellent prose have seldom bothered about the rule which grammarians based on Dryden's practice. Winston Churchill deflated it in a famous sentence, 'This is the sort of English up with which I will not put.'

Another hoary non-rule asserts that you must always avoid splitting an infinitive, as in 'to openly declare'. Yet it may be difficult to express your meaning otherwise, except by a roundabout paraphrase. How else would you say, 'He made a loss by the first investment, but hoped to more than retrieve it by the second'? Even where the split can be avoided without awkwardness, the sense may suffer in the process. The following, cited by Sir Ernest Gowers, is a clear sentence: 'The hailstones were so big that they failed to completely melt before they reached the ground.' If, in obedience to the split-infinitive rule, you were to say 'they failed completely to melt,' it would become ambiguous. Avoid splitting if you can; but don't be afraid to if you must. (Lincoln wasn't. Look carefully at page 31.)

Organic, Not Mechanic

Once more: at the plain, practical level, and on the more rarefied heights also, English is a language not easily constrained or brought to perfection by abstract definitions and principles. One corollary is that it had unrivalled possibilities for the slipshod and muddled. Bad English may well be worse than bad French. Good English is superb: but the precision, power and splendour which it so amply offers depend on qualities in the writer himself—on his feeling for words and phrases, for logic and impact. You will attain such sensitivities best through a bias towards the self-training we have discussed; and through steady, resolute, painstaking application.

Your writing should be organic, not mechanic. It should grow out of you, the writer. Don't try to synthesize your text by fitting pieces together with a handbook beside you, or with preconceived, undigested notions about 'the sort of thing that should go in here'. Certainly there are handbooks which can help—I have listed a few in Appendix One—

but only as aids to an activity with its own momentum, driven on from within. The same continues to be true as you attempt to pass beyond bare competence, and write with distinction. The goodness of good writing is not a coat of paint daubed over a colourless text. It comes, if it ever does, through a refinement of the same imaginative watchfulness and care for detail that produce competence. You cannot shirk your responsibilities by talking lazily of overall effect. Details and overall effect are too closely related. As Michelangelo put it, 'Trifles make perfection, and perfection is no trifle.'

It is by reflecting on these issues that you can best approach the habits of mind which will carry any writer to the peak of his powers, and especially a writer in English. There is a balance, a perspective to look for. Michelangelo's epigram might seem to clash with what was said a moment before about the 'mechanic' writer. Surely this laborious person who fits pieces together is, precisely, giving due weight to points of detail? Not quite. The trouble with him, or part of it, is that the trifles have taken over.

Like many writers he keeps a notebook, or its mental equivalent; this is a good practice, in itself; but he contrives his text with the notebook too much in mind, straining to bring in what he conceives to be his brilliancies. A few may actually be brilliant, yet even these will only shine in their proper setting, if any. An 'organic' writer will not allow his jottings to dictate to him. If the larger scheme provides logical places for them, he will put them in—not otherwise.

Poetry might appear more amenable to a fitting-together technique than prose. Yet the greatest poets, however enraptured they may be with a phrase or image, still know how to bring it in where it belongs, not force it in where it doesn't. Keats surpassed all his contemporaries in his love for 'jewels five words long' and his genius for creating them. Keats's rough copies, however, show how meticulously he could plan. While composing *The Eve of St. Agnes*, where the action happens in a castle on a cold, rough night, he hit on the phrase 'the besieging wind'. His draft reveals that he tried several times to work it in, crossed out each variant as incorrect *at that point*, then went on a little further to a place where he saw that it did belong, and put it there.

In prose, too, though great writers work lovingly on the minutest parts, they keep a grip on the all-pervading logic, the character of the whole, from which the perfection of the parts should follow with grace and fitness. The classic instance of the laboured perfectionist-in-detail is Gustave Flaubert. His reputation as a novelist is of course secure. But Somerset Maugham rightly criticized his failure to 'develop a story line', as we might now say, that would hold and direct the reader's attention. Maugham compared Flaubert's novel *L'Éducation Sentimentale* with Jane Austen's *Sense and Sensibility*. Jane Austen leads her readers along so firmly that although the novel has weaknesses, they do not disturb. Flaubert directs his readers' interest so feebly that they hardly care what is going on. 'This makes the novel very difficult to read,' said Maugham. 'I cannot think of another that has so many merits and leaves so shadowy an impression.'

Even in *Madame Bovary*, which does have a fairly definite movement, Flaubert could slip into curiously off-putting lapses. For example, while he stresses Madame Bovary's beautiful eyes, he leaves a doubt as to what colour they are. They seem to be brown when her future husband first meets her, black when he takes her to a party, blue when she is on the brink of surrender to her lover Léon. Léon's hair changes colour too. Translators have smoothed over the discrepancies, but the original is more specific, and thus confusing. It seems—not often, but often enough to cause disquiet—as if the novelist's obsession with each portion of his work in turn made him forget other portions, and lose sight of the whole.

A compatriot of Flaubert's, Paul Valéry, asked how you could tell a masterpiece. He suggested that a true masterpiece is a work in which nothing can be changed without loss. There is a complete, powerful organic conception, which extends to all the details, so that the work is an inviolable pattern. This is a French rather than an English definition, appropriate to a nation which has an Academy to define its language and taste; the nation of Shakespeare and Dickens might perhaps query it, being familiar with masterpieces which could be changed a good deal; yet you would be unwise to lean on Shakespeare or Dickens as excuses for ignoring the truth in Valéry's remark.

Prefabricated Prose and its Dangers

You should know what you want to say, as a whole and at each stage of composition, and say it resolutely. *You must be master of your medium, consciously and deliberately and all the time, if you are to make the most of it.* One reason for guarding against the 'mechanic' use of phrases or notebook items is that if you succumb to that temptation, you are losing control; the medium is mastering you.

This will be adverse enough to your intents if the phrases are your own. It can be catastrophic if they are not. A special vice of twentieth-century style, denounced by all the major authorities, is the habitual surrender to ready-made forms of words. The writer allows them to do his writing for him, and sometimes, far worse, to do his thinking for him, even to a point where he no longer realizes what he is saying. It is a vice of the age of mass-production. To face these would-be invaders squarely, and repel them from your own sector, is one of the most valuable victories you can win.

Organization style—whether in business, politics, or administration —must bear a large share of the blame. It has stuffed millions of minds with formulae and indirections, a worn verbal currency. It has opened the way to infiltration by the set phrase—the word-combination that undermines the word.

Take, for instance, the abuse of adjectives. Some teachers of English lay it down as a rule that you should be sparing with them. Put like that, without qualification, the rule is too sweeping. But the adjective does indeed become a plague, and the enemy of the noun, when it is coupled with the noun as a familiar companion. If you yield to the habit of saying things like 'the true facts', you raise queries as to what you mean if you say 'facts' without 'true'. If every crisis is acute, and every emergency is grave, what can the words 'crisis' and 'grave' do by themselves?

The motive, in this mechanical, propping-up use of stock adjectives, is emphasis. People realize that a word which is frequently employed becomes devalued. They try to restore it by adding another word. The devaluation is real, but no simple remedy will cure it if the remedy goes the same way.

That applies to more drastic measures than merely adding a qualifier. The head of a Washington government department, under war-time pressure, tried to get special treatment for priority items by having EXPEDITE stamped on them. For a while, they went through his department more rapidly. But the EXPEDITE stamp came to be used so freely that the staff ceased to pay any attention to it. Stamped items many weeks old accumulated in wire baskets alongside others. The head now introduced a new stamp, URGENT. Again it worked for a time. But the cycle was repeated; presently URGENT items were found lying neglected. Next came a stamp saying RUSH, with the same result. According to rumour, only the end of the war averted the introduction of a stamp saying FRANTIC.

When a capitulation of mind and will has taken place, and ready-made verbal forms are relied on to do the work, they do it poorly. You cannot refurbish a worn word by replacing it with another and letting that get equally worn; or by attaching an adjective which soon has no more effect than the URGENT stamp replacing the EXPEDITE stamp. A combination of words, fresh and well-conceived, will be more than the sum of its parts; but if it declines into a formula the result is weakness, not strength. An air of staleness hovers round it. The reader gets no feeling of a definite person talking to him, because so many others have used the same formula before. This is true of stock verbal couplings, and also of stock phrases, often more elaborate.

Clichés

These stock phrases are known as clichés. *Cliché* originally meant a printer's stereotype plate. If he would be requiring the same bit of text often, he set it up and kept it in one piece, ready for instant insertion. A cliché, in speech or writing, is a phrase of a kind we already noted as provoking the reader's comment 'Oh, dear!'—a phrase once apt, now blunted through coming too readily to too many hands. The classic and senior example is 'leave no stone unturned,' so widely recognized as a cliché that it has become a joke. It dates from 477 BC, when a Greek officer, searching for treasure hidden by a defeated enemy, consulted the oracle at Delphi and was told to 'leave no stone unturned'. Similar clichés, not so ancient, are 'explore every avenue' and 'put your shoulder to the wheel'.

But there are other types of cliché. Wellington was nicknamed the Iron Duke, Gladstone the Grand Old Man; the capital of England was Swinging London; such phrases, however vivid once, have no vitality now. Many quotations, too, have been quoted till threadbare. *Hamlet* is full of them, from 'For this relief much thanks' in the first scene to 'The rest is silence' in the last. Police jargon provides clichés all its own, such as 'behaving in a suspicious manner' and the notorious 'helping the police with their inquiries'.

The point here is not that you should never employ a cliché at all, but that you should never become so slack mentally as to let the ready-made phrase come in uncontested. It may do the job you want done, but is most unlikely to do it well. More probably it will put the reader off, or slither through his mind as it slithered through yours, without getting a purchase.

Allied to clichés, and more insidious, are standard forms ('to say the least', 'far be it from me to . . .'), and the synthetic verbs and prepositional phrases that clog modern English—'give rise to' and 'make contact with' and 'militate against', and 'with regard to' and 'in connection with' and 'in respect of' and 'relative to' . . . and so on.

Such expressions are crutches for the writer who is unwilling, perhaps unable, to think clearly and speak out plainly for himself. They blur outlines, they obscure visibility. People who rely on them are apt to have other habits which enhance the effect. They insert qualifying phrases like 'shall I say', because they won't take the trouble to be exact. They put things in inverted commas, with the implication 'I know this isn't quite right, but I can't be bothered to think of anything better.' Their verbs tend to be passive rather than active; their nouns, to be abstract rather than concrete; their adjectives, to have the edge taken off by mealy-mouthed adverbs ('somewhat', 'rather') or by the prefix 'Not un-' ('not unreasonable').

All writing of this kind, with its lack of affirmative vigour, betrays the same poor-spiritedness. The writer is not confident. He is not in control. At heart he does not want to be lucid or impressive, or to come through as himself rather than a faceless phantom. He fears responsibility. We have already glanced at the hazards of involvement with long words and ponderous, abstract terms (pages 53–5). Sometimes these are symptoms of the same weakness. After their fashion, they too are clichés, and take command. Ironically they often turn up in reports and letters and technical papers, the work of practical, efficient men who have no literary pretensions and aim only to communicate— the irony being that this is precisely where they fail. Their mass-produced jargon is not efficient. It wastes time while the reader sorts out the meaning.

Long Words, Short Words and Straightforwardness

This perhaps is the one serious issue in the debate about 'Latin' versus 'Anglo-Saxon' vocabulary. The Victorian anti-Latinists, though unsuccessful in changing the language, had more success than they deserved in convincing the public that every writer's invariable duty is to use short Anglo-Saxon words whenever he can, and steer clear of the usually longer ones with a Latin or 'Romance' derivation. Fowler agreed,[1] but not everyone. The objection to long words (as we have seen) and to Latin-derived words (as we may now add) is not that they will *necessarily* spoil your English. Aptly introduced, in moderate numbers, they won't. But unless you are firm and careful in handling them, they may dominate you with a bogus allure, and thereby obstruct the message. Gunning's term 'Fog Index' is well chosen to underline that fact.

George Orwell parodied a certain type of bad writing by making a modern version of a passage in the King James Bible. The original is:

> I returned and saw under the sun, that the race is not to the swift, nor the battle to the strong, neither yet bread to the wise, nor yet riches to men of understanding, nor yet favour to men of skill; but time and chance happeneth to them all.

Now for the modern version:

> Objective consideration of contemporary phenomena suggests that success or failure in competitive activities exhibits no tendency to be commensurate with innate capacity, but that a considerable element of the unpredictable must invariably be taken into account.

Here it is obvious that the clumsy, stereotyped abstractions enfeeble the thought. Even when long words are used more skilfully, they are liable to cause the same trouble. Boswell, in his life of Dr. Johnson, tells how Johnson went to the theatre and said afterwards of the play: 'It has not wit enough to keep it sweet.' Then, yielding to his addiction to Latinism, he translated: 'It has not vitality enough to preserve it from putrefaction.' Anyone can see that he said it better the first time, and ought to have stopped. Gowers notes that another well-known though fictitious literary figure does the same in reverse. Mr. Micawber,

[1] 'Prefer the Saxon word to the Romance.' Fowler: *The King's English*, Chapter 1.

in *David Copperfield*, repeatedly succumbs to the lure of the long word and pompous cliché . . . only, he has second thoughts. 'Under the impression,' he says, 'that your peregrinations in this metropolis have not as yet been extensive, and that you might have some difficulty in penetrating the arcana of the Modern Babylon . . . in short, that you might lose your way . . .' Micawber's second thoughts are wiser than Johnson's.

With both, however, the forceful version is not forceful purely because the words are short. It is forceful because the speaker is firm, specific, straightforward. The short words help the effect, they do not cause it. The best proof is that you can stick conscientiously to short words and still produce a thoroughly flaccid jargon. Routine verbal counters such as 'case', 'instance', 'nature', 'degree', lend themselves to it. An accident report might read: 'In this instance the crash was due in some degree to the concealed nature of the lane.' All the words are short, yet the sentence is limp and unattractive. On 'case' (and observe the temptation to say 'in the case of "case" ') purists have made hatchet attacks which, though overdone, are more nearly right than wrong. To say 'Summers don't seem as hot as used to be the case' is slipshod and ugly. To say 'Water for drinking purposes is carried by hand in many cases from an outside source' is to be in real trouble.

Orwell's parody was aimed at the disease of long words. But a less famous, yet equally deadly parody shows how prose can be simple, with only a moderate sprinkling of long words, yet still muffled, shapeless and cliché-ridden, because of a failure of the essential mastery in the person behind it. Here is part of Lincoln's Gettysburg Address (see page 31) as it might have been if delivered by President Eisenhower. The author is Oliver Jensen.

I haven't checked these figures but 87 years ago, I think it was, a number of individuals organized a governmental set-up here in this country, I believe it covered certain Eastern areas, with this idea they were following up based on a sort of national independence arrangement and the program that every individual is just as good as every other individual. Well, now, of course, we are dealing with this big difference of opinion, civil disturbance you might say, although I don't like to appear to take sides or name any individuals, and the point is naturally to check up, by actual experience in the field, to see whether any governmental set-up with a basis like the one I was mentioning has any validity and find out whether that dedication by those early individuals will pay off in lasting values and things of that kind.

Eisenhower, the parodist implies, was the prisoner of a politicians' dialect meant for the mass audience. Orwell put his own parody in an essay entitled 'Politics and the English Language'. Though dated, it is still deeply interesting. Orwell argues that if a writer depends on mass-produced expressions that come to mind too easily, it is not only his readers who suffer. He may confuse himself. Verbal patterns take control, and if the theme is controversial, they are not neutral. They do his thinking for him, steer him away from objectivity, and stultify his judgment.

Thus, politicians are fond of euphemisms that camouflage evil. Phrases such as 'transfer of population', 'rectification of frontiers', 'police action', give a respectable gloss to tyranny and tragedy. A writer who adopts the phrase, rather than describe the facts in his own words, also adopts the estrangement from human realities that goes with it. If he perseveres, he may soon learn to condone or ignore the most hateful atrocities. Then his writing becomes special pleading, morally base and stylistically false.

Again, an emotionally-charged key word—'democracy' or 'socialism' or 'patriotism' or 'freedom'—can lead him on to all sorts of further ideas. But the content of the key word itself depends on his own creed. It will take him in a direction where a reader with a different creed will not follow, because, for that reader, the key word has other implications. Communication breaks down without the writer knowing why; he has let the magic word govern him without ever unpacking it. He and his reader remain shut up in closed systems, condemning each other as fools or knaves.

Three Sets of Rules that can Help

At the end of his essay, Orwell proposed six rules for writers. If you bear them in mind, he maintained, you can avoid getting trapped by ready-made language. You can preserve your ability to know what you are talking about, and realize when you are being stupid. Rules of this kind, taken in the context which we can now give them, are certainly better worth considering than non-rules about prepositions and split infinitives.

1. *Never use a metaphor, simile, or other figure of speech which you are used to seeing in print.*
2. *Never use a long word where a short one will do.*
3. *If it is possible to cut a word out, always cut it out.*
4. *Never use the passive where you can use the active.*
5. *Never use a foreign phrase, a scientific word, or a jargon word if you can think of an everyday English equivalent.*
6. *Break any of these rules sooner than say anything outright barbarous.*

Quiller-Couch suggested a few rules of the same sort. Here are his.

1. *Almost always prefer the concrete word to the abstract.*
2. *Almost always prefer the direct word to the circumlocution.*

3. *Generally use transitive verbs in the active voice.*
4. *Use adjectives with economy.*

Quiller-Couch decided that the 'rules' about short words and Anglo-Saxon words were non-rules, and left them out of his list. Here, finally, is the equivalent list offered by Gowers.

1. *Use no more words than are necessary to express your meaning. In particular, do not use superfluous adjectives and adverbs, or roundabout phrases where single words will serve.*
2. *Use familiar words rather than far-fetched, if they express your meaning equally well.*
3. *Use words with a precise meaning rather than a vague one; prefer the concrete to the abstract.*

These three lists overlap, but I will not try to combine them. Try it yourself—and critically, not slavishly. It will be clear that while agreeing in general, I have reservations myself about several. Orwell's first rule, against clichés, hardly goes far enough. Hackneyed figures of speech are not the only clichés. In another place, Gowers gives a hint towards a more comprehensive rule: 'Watch out when one word suggests another, as in "part and parcel", "intents and purposes".' That is not the whole story either, but it exposes the nature of the hazard. The facile verbal reaction and the conditioned verbal response are among your chief dangers, if you are to remain master of your medium—whether you let yourself be steered into officialese, or jargon, or ideological double-talk, or Micawberish inflation, or the spineless ordinary-guy chat of statesmen in their less inspired moments.

Style and Personality

To be in command—firmly, constantly, yet without undue effort—is the heart of style. But a reader may wonder: granted a certain writer is in command . . . still, who and what is he?

According to a famous remark of Buffon, a great author as well as a great scientist, 'The style is the man'. What personality comes through, in ideas or in language; and does it come through by any process that can be defined or learnt? Indeed, how is style individualized at all? How do you, the author, express *yourself* so as to achieve a result that is yours alone, stamped with your stamp and no one else's?

The soundest advice is simply not to try, but to let it happen. Striving after a brilliant personal effect is a beginners' failing. Individuality should come as a by-product of the way you achieve mastery and say whatever is in you to say.

In Chapter Two (page 16) I offered a warning against imitating the styles of other writers, however warmly you admire them. Yet while imitation is a practice to avoid if you can, it may be a better method of forming your style than the opposite error of straining to be original too soon. If your models are good, you can learn from the exercise and then outgrow them. Robert Louis Stevenson confessed that in his early years he imitated several established authors. He called this 'playing the sedulous ape'. His own style was slow in developing, but in the end it created such books as *Treasure Island* and *Dr. Jekyll and Mr. Hyde*, which combine superb quality with proved staying power as best-sellers.

As we saw (page 10), this imitative technique, in the pre-1914 era, was not confined to Stevenson; and with the less gifted writers it produced second-rate Edwardian 'pudding-stone'. Their mediocrity, however, was mainly due to Oxbridge conformism and a restricted public. They never really won free. Today, Stevenson's mode of self-training is still not to be recommended. But if you do imitate, you are better placed than the Edwardians to learn from the attempt, and break through uninhibitedly to the style that will be you alone.

However you arrive at this, your material will affect the process. Some classes of writing give more scope to character than others. But the difference is less than you might suppose. Even with a routine report in a vast impersonal organization, the executive who reads it may sometimes know, without being told, which member of his staff is responsible. He may know from its handling of the subject, its logic, its clarity. Conversely, even a book-length account of a personal experience may be flat, dead, faceless throughout.

Among English authors of the past century, three of the most intensely individual in style are Gerard Manley Hopkins, G. K. Chesterton, and P. G. Wodehouse (especially in the Jeeves stories). With these in their maturity, a quotation of a few lines, sometimes a few words, is enough to reveal the author. Nobody else could write like that without sounding merely imitative. Observe, however, that subject-matter fails to account for the facts. If authors can achieve such characteristic styles by writing poetry *or* essays *or* literary criticism *or* comic fiction, then they can do it in any more or less creative form.

Nor is there any reason to think that Wodehouse, (for instance) ever consciously tried to be different or distinctive. Authors with a marked style do occasionally begin to labour it, but only after prolonged success. Then they give the public what it expects from them, and sink into self-imitation or even self-parody. That, however, is a prospect too remote to concern us now.

Three Controversial Issues

If you attain the requisite command, you will stamp yourself on what you write; and because human beings vary so widely, there is not much more that can be said about style. But there is a little.

Figurative Writing

Debates have raged over several special topics—recently, for example, over 'plain' versus 'picturesque' language, and the right use of metaphors and images. Yet no general rules emerge. It depends on you. Some great authors have written with the severest plainness: Johnson is said to have remarked of Swift, 'The rogue never hazards a metaphor.' Others have soared in the contrary direction, becoming memorably colourful without undue floweriness. Oscar Wilde did it in *The Picture of Dorian Gray*.

While plain writing is safer, dogmatism on that point is certainly wrong. Rudolf Flesch, an American exponent of prose during the 1950s, attacked all figurative language. Quoting Churchill's 'I have nothing to offer but blood, toil, tears and sweat,' he made the astounding claim that Churchill could equally have said 'You must expect great suffering and hard work,' and nobody can tell which sentence is better. As a rival exponent of prose, William H. Whyte, Jr., retorted, the answer is so obvious that anybody who thinks it isn't has merely disqualified himself from pronouncing on style.

Still, two specific warnings are worth giving. Both arise from the recurring vital point, that you must be in control. If you employ figurative language, take care never to get mixed up, and never to let it run away with you. Getting mixed up can lead to results such as we have already twice deplored—'I smell a rat, I see him floating in the air,' or 'The Prime Minister literally exploded during the debate.' More subtle is the lure of the image that hardens into fact and throws your thinking askew. 'The constitution of this country has been built up over the years like a noble arch, stone by stone. Remove a single stone and the whole edifice may fall.' The arch might; it doesn't follow that the constitution would.

Humour

Another matter which some writers worry over, and misjudge, is humour. Should you try to amuse or not? The answer is the same. It depends on you. If you are serious by temperament, you won't improve your work by sticking in jokes to lighten it. On the other hand, if you have a natural bent towards humour, don't be timid. There is no eternal distinction between serious and frivolous topics. Bertrand Russell could be witty when dealing with abstruse problems of philosophy. Chesterton did as well or better with religion—and not as an opponent making fun of it, but as a man of profound and thoughtful religious faith. One result of television, especially since the wave of satire, has been a far wider realization that all subjects are open to a variety of treatments.

Rhythm

Yet a further aspect of prose which you will find discussed by the older authorities is rhythm. The difficulty here is to decide whether it actually is a topic, or only a pretentious non-topic. George Saintsbury, author of a vast history of English metre, also attempted a history of English prose rhythm. Opinions remain divided as to whether the book is, strictly speaking, about anything at all.

Take what is perhaps the most durable of doctrines under this heading —that the rhythm of English has been deeply influenced by the King James Bible. C. S. Lewis, in a lecture, exposed even this notion to criticism from which it has not recovered. At one point he told his audience, 'I am going to read a made-up sentence which has precisely the rhythm of a verse in the Bible. See if you can catch the echo. "At the regatta Madge avoided the river and the crowds."' This is a rhythmic replica of the very first verse in the Bible, 'In the beginning God created the heaven and the earth.' It is doubtful whether anyone in Lewis's audience did catch the echo.

Nevertheless, again, a few miscellaneous remarks are in order. Quiller-Couch rightly insisted that a sentence has logical points of stress. These should be few, and the wording should bring them out naturally. 'Whoever opposes me I will crush to pieces' carries a stronger impact than 'I will crush to pieces whoever opposes me'; the voice rises in the first sentence, and falls in the second. As a painful example of a sentence reduced to chaos by too many stresses with no pattern, Quiller-Couch quotes from a story:

> 'Are Japanese Aprils always as lovely as this?' asked the man in the light tweed suit of two others in immaculate flannels with crimson sashes round their waists and puggarees folded in cunning plaits round their broad Terai hats.

Quiller-Couch also urged his students to write verse as practice for writing prose. He meant verse in regular metres. The advice has an old-fashioned air, yet there is much to be said for it. Writing verse, however unpoetic, will help you to cultivate a feeling for correct emphasis, an ear for sound, an awareness of the music of English, especially its fine range of vowels.

The only warning (which ought to be obvious, but isn't) is that the techniques and habits of verse-writing must not be transferred bodily to prose. There may be no positive definition of prose rhythm, but there is a negative definition: it is not verse rhythm. A regular beat in prose very quickly becomes distracting. Emotion is liable to set it off. Dickens had a notorious trick of slipping into unrhymed metre when his own writing stirred him. Nell's death scene in *The Old Curiosity Shop* contains whole lines of blank verse, more regular than many of Shakespeare's. Few writers wander so far astray as to make their prose actually rhyme, but even that has happened. A Victorian mathematician wrote: 'And yet no force, however great, can stretch a cord, however fine, into a horizontal line that shall be absolutely straight.' He had composed, without noticing, a stanza that could have gone into Tennyson's *In Memoriam*.

Less blatant but more seductive is the device of alliteration—writing phrases and sentences in which several words begin with the same letter. This is often an enhancement to verse ('The fair breeze blew, the white foam flew. The furrow followed free'), less often in prose. It can be done sparingly for a rhetorical or comic effect, but it is easy to overdo. Nothing can excuse this, from the autobiography of the poet and self-proclaimed magician Aleister Crowley:

> The compiler . . . is not only the most ponderously platitudinous and priggishly prosaic of pretentiously pompous pork butchers of the language, but the most voluminously voluble. I cannot dig over the dreary deserts of his drivel in search of the passage which made me write to him.

Assessing Your Progress

You must learn by doing. No substitute exists. But how can you tell what progress you are making? What are the possibilities of self-criticism?

On the basic themes of logic, clarity, and the rest, Chapters Five to Seven have said enough. Imagine people at the receiving end. That applies to the text as it unfolds sentence by sentence, and I would add that it applies also to the overall conception, as a test of your being in full command. Suppose you are working on a book. Picture yourself meeting some intelligent but non-literary person (the grocer, for instance) who asks you what it's about. Could you explain to him, briefly and understandably? If not, reconsider. Your ideas may have got too complex, or recondite, or would-be-clever. You may not be wholly clear what you are driving at yourself. In that case, if you persist, your writing will be unsatisfactory.

But when you come to the deeper felicities and beauties of style, imaginary critics are less use. So, can you judge for yourself whether what you have written is good?

The record of authors' self-appraisal is discouraging. Sometimes, like the proverbial clown who yearns to play Hamlet, they go so far as to have delusions about the nature of their own talents. Robert Browning referred to himself as a 'writer of plays', yet he survives only as a poet; his plays are dead. When invited to pick their favourites from among their own works, some authors make highly unexpected choices.

Judging one's own merit seems a dubious operation in matters of detail also. Dr. Johnson and Quiller-Couch, in fact, both offered the aspiring writer the same maxim: when you think you have written a particularly good sentence, cross it out. 'Murder your darlings.' It is a hard saying, but more nearly right than wrong. Excellence does not come through ornamentation, or through deliberate fine writing of any kind, and for some reason a conscious effort to write finely is apt to distort the judgment.

The best advice is simply not to fret too much about self-assessment. Stick to the positive, creative side. Do the things which will make your work come out right. Above all, remember the first principle stated in Chapter Four: 'Write about what you know and care for.' Whatever important work you have it in you to do will be accomplished by *being yourself*, intensely, completely, fearlessly. That is not a precept of idealistic ethics, but a plain fact. One of its artfullest exploiters was Dale Carnegie, author of the best-seller *How to Win Friends and Influence People*. He used to run classes in public speaking. When a member of a class sat contributing nothing, Carnegie sometimes drew him out by discovering a subject on which he had strong convictions, and then privately asking another member to make a speech taking the opposite view. The silent member would be stung into a passionate rejoinder, and come to life as a speaker in the act of making it.

Be yourself; and—last of all—keep it up. Successful writing comes most surely through perseverance. The problems are most surely solved by pressing ahead, and getting to grips with them in practice. Don't be paralysed at the outset, or hesitate till your entire plan is complete in your mind. Once you are clear enough on the main ideas, get started. Your work should acquire its own momentum. Force yourself, if necessary, to keep it rolling by writing a certain amount each day, without waiting for moods and inspirations. And so long as your theme stays with you, coherent and alive, don't give up or lose confidence. Granted, some of what you have produced may not be as good as you think. But the advice about 'murdering your darlings' has a converse. Self-assessment can fail in the other direction. Some of what you have produced may be better than you think. So persist to the end. Carrying a fair-sized project right through is an immeasurable aid to morale; and the writer who has done it, and thus knows that he has the capacity to do it again, has taken a long stride towards final mastery of his medium.

Exercises

1. As suggested on page 95, draw up a list of rules combining the lists made by Orwell, Quiller-Couch, and Gowers. Re-phrase and expand as you see fit.

2. Four examples were given of emotionally-charged words that can have various implications according to who uses them: (*a*) 'democracy', (*b*) 'socialism', (*c*) 'patriotism', (*d*) 'freedom'. What are some of the different ideas which these words convey to different people? Can you think of another word which raises similar difficulties?

3. Discuss and illustrate Michelangelo's saying, 'Trifles make perfection, and perfection is no trifle.'

4. Whatever your own feelings about learning by imitation, which authors would you name as good models for the kind of writing you want to do? What do you specially like about them?

PART THREE: *WRITING AS A VOCATION*

CHAPTER TEN

THE ANATOMY OF COMPULSION

Are You a Born Author?

Turn back to page 3, and Sinclair Lewis's question to the students: 'How many of you actually want to write?' Whatever you may think of the sharper question that followed, most of those students did 'want to write', or thought they did. They had not come just to pick up tips on how to do next week's essay. Writing was an activity which they cared about. At least in theory, they dreamed of doing it themselves on a large scale (as novelists, dramatists, biographers, critics), or on a smaller scale but memorably (as poets, essayists, short-story writers). Disillusion might be close. For all but a handful of them, it probably was. But as they sat facing the celebrated Mr. Lewis at that first session, they could picture themselves spending exalted hours on literary pursuits, and even making literature their chief business in life.

If you 'want to write', in that most demanding sense, the persistent question of *attitude* recurs still more urgently. Recall what was said about it in Part One, but be prepared to go deeper. I suggested that if you write at all, for whatever reason, the proper attitude calls for an active awareness of society—the human context. If you see writing as your vocation (or possible vocation) there is a more selective awareness, which can help to form the more specialized attitude you need . . . or can disenchant you, supposing disenchantment to be your fate, with a minimum of grief and wastage.

This is an awareness of that small fraction of society which you are aspiring to join: the company of other authors, living and dead. The guidance that comes through knowing them and thinking about them is different, less direct, because you are not trying to establish direct contact with them as you are with the reading public. It is guidance nevertheless. What sort of people are they? Why do they write? How do they do it? Can you fit into that scene yourself, and behave likewise? Do you honestly belong in that company?

Authors vary endlessly, so you won't have to conform to a pattern. If you are indeed made for authorship, you will be one more unique variant, not a mass-produced unit. Yet there are ways in which authorship does, as a matter of experience, happen; and there are ways in which it does not.

To begin with, can we generalize about the main driving forces? Are there special qualities of character which make authors tick, which they all possess, and which you should look for in yourself?

Obviously they do all possess what the Roman satirist Juvenal called a *cacoethes scribendi*, an itch for writing. They suffer from a compulsion. But when Juvenal coined the phrase, he was complaining of a fact which must have been as evident in Rome as it is today: that while everyone who is made for authorship has the compulsion, far too many people have the compulsion who are not made for authorship. They waste their time, and bore others, with incurable scribbling. You must have the compulsion, yes, but it proves nothing without further definition.

Let us assume that you do have it. One question you can usefully ask is this: when did it start?

Beginning Young

Most authors begin young. That does not mean that they are all infant prodigies, or that many are. They may not publish for a long while. Their juvenile output may be very bad, showing no promise, and not foreshadowing what they produce later. All the same, they are apt to start trying in their schooldays, and usually their early schooldays.

To call somebody a 'born author' is not a mere complimentary cliché. As the poet Alexander Pope put it, 'I lisped in numbers' (that is, metre), 'for the numbers came.' At school the born author is not simply a pupil who enjoys essay-writing more than most, he is a pupil who launches out into literary ventures which his teachers haven't asked for —ventures which may conflict with his school work. Pat McGrath, the youngest of recent English novelists, drafted his first published story at the age of fourteen, in a neglected seat at the back of the class. While the born author may contribute to the school paper, it is more typical of him to start a paper himself and write it himself. Or he uses exercise books for wildly imaginative fiction instead of exercises. Evelyn Waugh, when established as a novelist by his mature work, finally published his first-ever story. It belongs to this type, and it is worth reading, though hardly for the reasons which the young Evelyn intended. The Brontë children composed romances about invented countries, influenced by the poems of Byron, which they precociously read.

The junior author is liable to be scrappy, to lack staying power, to make innumerable false starts. He may fill up his exercise books, but very likely with fragments: bits of abortive self-written magazines, carefully lettered headings followed by only a single sentence, fifty-line openings of epics which could scarcely be completed in less than five thousand. He may not know what he wants to write. He may grow up to write something quite different. But the compulsion grips him, and it goes on.

Probably an immense majority of authors begin thus, even more than the evidence would suggest, because most of the material is destroyed. Juvenile efforts seldom get hoarded. Admittedly some authors make a late start on the work which they become known for. Walt Whitman's characteristic poetry was all written after the age of thirty-five. Tolkien's 'Hobbit' trilogy *The Lord of the Rings* began coming out when he was sixty-two. But Whitman had been writing journalism and conventional verse, now forgotten, long before he struck his own vein in *Leaves of Grass*; and the *Lord of the Rings* trilogy was the product of many years' unpublicized labour, with other books—including the original *Hobbit*— appearing on the way. Occasionally a publisher announces a new author as breaking into print at an advanced age, sometimes as a centenarian. But if you examine such a case, you will usually find that the author did not begin writing at the time when the publisher showed a belated interest, but much earlier.

How old, or how young were you when you began writing yourself— that is, of your own accord? It is only a dubious recommendation to say that you always enjoyed doing school essays, and it is no recommendation whatever to say that you got good marks for them. Your school record has no trustworthy meaning unless you scribbled outside the line of duty, driven on by an urge that wouldn't let you alone. If nothing of that kind happened then, and if you are now an adult and it has shown no sign of happening yet, think carefully. You may still be the exception, the really late starter. Be *very* sure, however, before you expend too much time and effort.

The Fundamental Drives

Where does the born author's compulsion come from, and what keeps it active in adult life?

As a child he does what many other children do, and with no less zest than himself. He uses his imagination. But he may show an unusual bias towards one type of imaginative game: playing at being grown up. His fantasies may be based more often on adult activities. Also (and here he does diverge) they have a vividness and interest which impel him to write them down, work at them, and preserve them. The will to do this, to go on doing it, to move presently from fantasy towards truth, and to grow and develop in the process, is the heart of his literary calling.

There is no single cause for it which applies to every author. However, a maladjustment to life is a frequent factor. Many authors have had an unhappy childhood, oppressed by parent trouble or poverty or delicacy. Ill health often seems to act as a spur, not only then, but after they grow up. From their earliest days they have problems which they cannot solve by direct action.

Recognizing this fact, Freud suggested that authorship is, at bottom, indirect action. The author wants the same things as most people— pleasure, power, sex. These are the common stuff of dreams and day-dreams. He is normal, too, in being largely frustrated. But his maladjustments combine with his talents to endow him with a peculiar gift. He can dream others' dreams for them, better than they can for themselves.

They pay him to do it, by buying his novels or going to his plays; they take notice of him and value his friendship; and so, in due course, he gets what he could not get by straightforward methods—pleasure, power, sex.

Like many of Freud's ideas, this theory has some truth in it, but it can hardly be the whole truth, even if we leave non-fiction out of account. It may fit the fashionable best-seller. It fails to explain many authors' willingness to forego well-paid jobs, to live quietly, and to press on year after year with no prospect of popular success. While Freud may often be right about the unconscious hope, it is probably not universal, and the compulsion can survive when the hope fades. Ardour and determination, a conviction of something wrong in the world or of something that needs saying—these can endure alone.

The nearest thing to a significant common factor, in the lives of authors who leave their mark, is probably suffering. It may be personal, or it may be outward-looking, a sense of the burden of evil weighing down others. Dickens was stung to creative energy by mental stresses of both kinds—memories of his squalid childhood, distress over his unfortunate marriage, and alongside these, anguish at the injustice and cruelty round him.

Suffering, it may be said, is the common lot of humanity. True. But a high proportion of authors suffer exceptionally. They are unusually frail in body (Keats, Proust), unusually handicapped (Milton, Byron), unusually grief-stricken (Tennyson), unusually exasperated (H. G. Wells, John Osborne), unusually sensitive to falsehood and wrong (Tolstoy, Orwell), unusually horrified (Siegfried Sassoon, and many like him who have protested at war). Also, the author copes differently. Most people react to tribulations by grumbling at them, or learning to put up with them, or trying to pretend that they don't exist. Authorship reacts by a mental quest for definition and diagnosis, for compensations, for remedies. The results may be no more sensible or moral than those which other people arrive at, but they are, or can be, literature.

Beware of Explicit Egotism

Is your life like that, and do you react to its unhappinesses in that way? Nobody but you can decide. Observe, however, another fact about the author of stature. Despite his intensities of feeling, whatever form they take, you will seldom catch him simply 'expressing himself'. Even when he writes poetry, his self-expression is generally only one aspect of his theme. It used to be a stock joke that ageing actresses always imagined there would be a public for 'The Story of my Life', and poured out reminiscences in that spirit. As a rule, there wasn't. This is a false trail.

A rapid survey of European literature will pick out one great work which is indeed a 'Story of my Life', an undiluted personal outpouring

—Rousseau's *Confessions*. However, it is much less easy to go on and think of a second, unless Casanova qualifies; and Rousseau himself did not compose his memoirs till he had become famous through comparatively impersonal works. There is a widespread belief that everybody has at least one good book in him, based on his own experience or special knowledge. Perhaps. But that book is most unlikely to be a literal record of his actions and thoughts. Written out, say, as a novel, it will probably involve much selection and re-arrangement, and its value will lie in something larger than a revelation of one person.

If you suspect you have a vocation for authorship, and it prompts you to tell the story of your life, *mistrust it*—however interesting your life may have been. Unless it offers other ideas as well, you are almost certainly mistaken. Mistrust it, likewise, if it urges you to write with the main object of expressing yourself. The mere fact that 'this all actually happened', or 'this honestly *is* the way I feel', has no literary weight whatsoever.

One of the clearest warnings against explicit egotism, one of the strongest hints that this is no symptom of a vocation but (if anything) an anti-symptom, is a fact of literary history: that the greatest English author is, as a person, the most elusive. We can draw inferences about Shakespeare from his plays and poems, but hardly any can be directly supported from the known data on his life. In other words, we can hardly ever prove that he is expressing *himself*. Even his sonnets may have been composed as a poetic fiction, in an assumed character. It may not be likely; it is conceivable.

However, if Shakespeare was far from egotistic in that sense, he was profoundly so in another. Here too he sheds light on the literary calling in general. So far as we can judge, he had no doubts about priorities. He virtually deserted his wife and children to work in London, sometimes neglecting to pay Anne's debts when he was prospering himself. If we do accept the sonnets as autobiography, his authorship got him into involvements most unfitting for a burgher of Stratford . . . but in these he found further themes for authorship. Meanwhile, Anne and the children stayed at home, scarcely seeing him except when he came to buy some more local property with his theatrical profits.

The born author is not necessarily callous. Nor is he necessarily harder to get on with than others, or more likely to be disloyal to a spouse or a friend. He may raise children successfully, and provide for them well. He may live long and happily with the same partner, and even salute that partner in all sincerity as an inspiration to him—Browning did.

But he has his priorities. If any relationship is liable to prevent him from writing, that relationship will be altered or ended. If the pursuit of his vocation means imposing hardship on somebody else, then, in the last resort, hardship will be imposed; minimized perhaps, but imposed. This may not be ethical. It is the fact.

Ask yourself: 'Am I ruthless enough to be an author?' Don't take that question too literally, of course, or allow it to lure you into the seductive delusion that art is above ordinary morality. Yet if you can picture any person on earth—however dear, however important—persuading you to give up *for a non-literary reason*, then pause. I don't absolutely say 'Give up now', but I do say *'Think, before you get too deeply committed'*.

Inspiration and Perspiration

Whatever the ultimate promptings that make a person an author, they are probably so deep-seated that he could hardly be certain what they are. Those that induce him to write in a particular form, on a particular theme or series of themes, are apt to be almost as obscure. Still, we can see roughly how they operate.

Inspiration—Muse or Maladjustment?

Ancient myth-makers recognized the mystery here. The Greeks regarded poets, and other creative artists, as being visited by unseen goddesses called the Muses. There were nine Muses, each with her own department. Erato inspired love-songs, Thalia inspired comedy, and so forth. Homer opens his epics with a prayer to the epic Muse, Calliope. The Hindus had a single goddess of literature named Sarasvati, and Indian epic poets began, like Homer, with a polite glance in her direction. The poet-prophets of Israel believed, more earnestly, that their messages were dictated by God himself. Amos, Isaiah and the rest relate how the word of the Lord came to them.

But pure inspiration, however accounted for, slowly went out of favour. Even in Homer, as far back as the eighth century BC, we may suspect that the invocation is more a hallowed formula than an act of faith. The poet does not really wish us to think that his Muse ought to get the whole credit for all the thousands of lines that follow. Four centuries later, the philosopher Plato makes fun openly of poets' claims to be enlightened by a divine spark, and expounds his own more intellectual theory of inspiration.

Romantic notions about an all-explaining 'genius', itself unexplainable, were still fairly potent in the Victorian era. When Anthony Trollope disclosed his cool, businesslike methods of writing novels, an affronted public ceased buying them. Yet Trollope was symptomatic of the same trend as in ancient Greece. Edgar Allan Poe had already broken new ground as the first poet to reveal candidly how he had composed a poem (*The Raven*) in a cold-blooded step-by-step procedure. Edison, the inventor, was soon to analyse genius as 'one per cent inspiration and ninety-nine per cent perspiration'. This was a healthy tendency, and today the point should not need any further labouring.

Inspiration, in itself, is not what gets the work done, and the processes which do get it done can often be described in detail without bringing inspiration in.

Yet . . . it happens, and it governs the rest. Edison's figures may be correct, in terms of anything we can measure; time, for instance. They are meaningless in terms of importance. Without that mysterious one per cent, the perspiration will not add up to ninety-nine-per-cent genius, but to no genius at all—only hack work or pot-boiling. And while an author may be less than a genius, he needs at least a dash of inspiration to be more than a mediocrity.

Inspiration is the emergence of a conception out of subconscious depths. We will not discuss how it may have taken shape in those depths before it rose. If you wish to believe that a Muse put it there, by all means do. When it does emerge, it may still be dimly outlined, but it has a compelling quality. Somehow the author is seized by the idea of a unique experience, worth living through, worth re-living, and worth communicating to others in the most effective way possible. An adventure, actual or imaginary; a quest for the solution of a problem; an illumination of spirit or intellect; an exploration of the career of a famous person; a love, a hate, an indignation, a nightmare—all these experiences, and many more, can present themselves clamorously as topics and demand to be communicated in a certain form.

The roots are far down and strangely interwoven, with a life of their own. An author may write several books, each on a different subject, each set off by a different impulse, and realize only afterwards that all were related to a single issue: to some private preoccupation which he never raised far enough into consciousness to tackle at that level. Indeed he may never realize it for himself. It may take the insight of a biographer to show what his actual inspiration was.

Never resist such probings, into your own subconscious depths or anyone else's. The only thing to resist is what Jung called the 'nothing-but fallacy'—the notion that explaining a mental fact is explaining it away, so that if an author's original motives are revealed, there is no longer any reason to take him seriously. For example, a critic might argue that most of the major poems of Shelley can be traced to his quarrel with his father, which they symbolize or dramatize under various masks. Maybe they can. But Shelley's visions of liberty and love, his revolt against authority and official creeds, have the same value which they had before the explanation. To say that the poet was steered towards these grand permanent themes by his parental trouble, with all it implied, is not to reduce the themes to mere variations on his parental trouble. In fact, it is part of the character of the born author that he is a person for whom this debunking does not work; a person who can make his private problems a springboard, and leap into more important and interesting surroundings.

The Trigger

An author's *immediate* motive, the trigger that releases an inspiration and brings it into action, is more likely to be conscious. He starts writing a book, play, or whatever, for one or more reasons in a wide spectrum, ranging from free creative energy to overpowering external pressure.

A strong, sustained personal interest in a subject may drive him finally to write about it. This motive is simple and obvious, and no more need be said. Chance and circumstance, however, may also play their part. Robert Louis Stevenson amused his stepson during a rainy spell by drawing a map of an imaginary island. They began making up a story about it, and *Treasure Island* was the result. W. S. Gilbert is said to have hit on the idea for *The Mikado* when a Japanese sword, insecurely hung on the wall, fell down. (In both cases there is evidence of a prior gestation.)

Not quite so spontaneous, but still more or less freely creative, is the impulse for a work which follows on from previous works, or extends an existing scheme. Balzac intended his novels to build up a complete picture of French society, and accordingly planned them as 'scenes of political life', 'scenes of army life', 'scenes of life in Paris', and so on. Galsworthy invented the Forsyte family, and then produced story after story tracing the Forsytes through several generations.

Such instances still fit into a traditional view of authorship. What you may need to un-learn is an illusion which would blot out the rest of the motivational spectrum—the illusion that true authorship is necessarily free and creative, that work written to order or mainly for money is necessarily second-rate.

This is quite mistaken. What, in practice, are the outside causes that exert pressure? An author may be prodded by public events, or the perception of a lack, without anyone else's prompting. He may say to himself, 'A book on so-and-so would be topical,' or 'There is no satisfactory book on so-and-so, I'll write one.' Then again, a publisher may commission him to write such a book, which he would not have thought of himself. And in these situations, a need for money may well have a decisive effect.

Work undertaken for such reasons is certainly in danger of falling below the author's highest standard. He may write hurriedly, carelessly, without feeling. If he is wise he will never let assignments encroach too far. But he does not have to be a rigidly pure fanatic, refusing all supposed prostitution. Nor are the results bound to be uninspired. Balzac himself was remorselessly squeezed by financial shortage, and, because of it, got much further towards completing his ambitious plan than he would otherwise have done. Dumas wrote many of his romances to recoup fortunes made by previous romances, and spent.

External factors can produce excellent work, adding to an author's solid achievement, *provided that they tap his own sources of inspiration and engage his best talents.* The important point is that when these factors impinge on him, he should respond, as far as he can, by taking on jobs which do fit in with his proper vocation, and which he might conceivably have done by his own free choice, if it had occurred to him. Dumas, whose genius was for adventure stories, rightly reacted to his financial crises by turning out more adventure stories.

The only real literary prostitution is the acceptance of assignments which do not suit you, for material reward alone. American novelists (Budd Schulberg, for instance) have drawn appalling pictures of splendid talents trapped and debased by Hollywood script-writing. The ability to stick to the Dumas response, if necessary at some cost, is a mark of the born author; not an invariable mark, but an eloquent one when it occurs. Have you got that ability yourself?

Perspiration—The Long Haul

So much for the inspiration. Now for the perspiration. I have already stressed the value of learning to push ahead regularly, to write something every day, to carry your projects through to completion. Here the author with a vocation—or what he thinks is a vocation—is more apt to fail than professional journalists and film-writers who work to order for a living, with no loftier dreams.

He can find endless methods of rationalizing laziness. He can tell himself (and others) that he has to have the right surroundings, the right company, the right weather; that, just at the moment, he is too much beset by distractions, or in an un-literary mood; that his inspiration has dried up. All such causes of inaction *can* be genuine, *can* inhibit output . . . but if you catch yourself dwelling on them, sit back and review the position. Are you being strictly honest? Somerset Maugham, in *The Summing Up*, gives a sad little sketch of a dilettante friend: 'For twenty years he amused himself with thinking what he would write when he really got down to it and for another twenty with what he could have written if the fates had been kinder.'

Of course the light of inspiration can fade. It usually does. Artistic creation in a continuous flame, at a headlong pace, is so rare that the classic cases of it are famous. (The best known are Handel's *Messiah* and Stevenson's *Dr. Jekyll and Mr. Hyde*.) As a statement of the norm, the sober verses of Matthew Arnold are closer to experience:

> We cannot kindle when we will
> > The fire which in the heart resides,
> The spirit bloweth and is still,
> > In mystery our soul abides.
> But tasks in hours of insight willed
> Can be through hours of gloom fulfilled.

The ways in which 'insight' does stay alive through 'gloom', not actually deserting an author, are hard to describe and doubtless vary from one to another. My own impression is that it may take the form of an unrest, nagging below the threshold of consciousness as the work proceeds, which bursts through—perhaps at intervals, perhaps only towards the end—and brings it out right. The author plods on, piling up chapter after chapter according to plan, yet with a feeling that he is not getting matters in quite the true perspective; that there is more than he is managing to express; even that he has not entirely grasped what his own book is about. A presence which escapes him is still waiting in the wings.

Cromwell is said to have remarked, 'No man travels so far as he who does not know where he is going.' That is an extreme way of putting it. But when an authentic inspiration is hovering behind the day-to-day labour, it is apt to make itself felt by upsetting the author's plans and re-aligning his energies. The book develops a kind of logic which is not as he thought. This may only become consciously clear to him at a late stage. It may then force him to reconsider, perhaps to rewrite heavily. But however subversive, it is a symptom of inner life—so long as the discords which it sets jangling are resolved in the end.

When you attempt authorship, don't be afraid of second and third and *nth* thoughts, or of multiple re-drafting; but do take a cool look at the final product. If the right sort of mental processes have been going on, it should read harmoniously and coherently, with no trace of the confusions that led up to it.

Keeping Alive

The born author is proof against discouragement. He needs to be. He is likely to collect dozens of rejection slips before he is fairly launched. Nor is publication equivalent to success. Publication does not mean that you have arrived. A resoundingly successful first book is uncommon, and when the phenomenon does occur, there is usually a history of unknown trial-and-error behind it. Let us assume that your first book has come out, and met with a favourable reception: you still haven't arrived. Notoriously, the test comes with the second book. Plenty of writers can do it once, by writing the 'one good book which everybody has in him,' based on personal experience or special knowledge. Plenty of writers then flounder miserably in the effort to do it again, and make several false starts before getting their second wind, if they ever do.

Meanwhile, how are you going to keep alive and pay the bills? Ideally, if you are made to write, you should live by writing. In practice you probably can't, and certainly not in the early stages, unless you have a private income or are one of the few who produce an instant best-seller. Be particularly on guard against the partial success, such as a single published story. This can silence doubts which it might be wiser to take seriously; it may raise false hopes which make you think you can do better than you actually can, or that you have found your proper line when you haven't, and drive you to waste time and effort trying vainly to follow up. In a later chapter we shall glance at the economic aspects again. For the moment it is enough to say that you will probably need a bread-and-butter job, and should not feel ashamed of this; but you should be careful what it is. The kind of writing we are concerned with now is a full-time pursuit, in the sense that it must be the chief purpose of the author's life. He should be engaged on it all the time. If he is not literally writing, he should be reading, reflecting, experiencing; even absorbing material from his wage-earning activities themselves. A job which interferes with his proper pursuit is dangerous to it.

Hence you may do better to live by some wholly un-literary job than by one of the half-literary jobs which authors drift into, such as journalism and teaching. The half-literary job will either involve writing, or make demands on that part of the mind where writing originates. When the person who does it has other literary ideas entirely, it splits and weakens. On the one hand, it can wear him down and blunt his individuality. On the other, his division of energies will handicap him as an employee. Unable to give his job the attention which the employer requires, and has a right to require, he may lose it. (Freelance journalism and part-time teaching are a different matter and less insidious.)

As with writing to order, so with the bread-and-butter job. You may have to accept both. Up to a point, there is no reason to demur. The test of your authorship is not whether you keep it 'pure' (which is nearly always pretentious nonsense) but whether it remains on top, exploiting everything else, never exploited. If it does, the rewards can make up for all the pain.

Exercises

1. A teacher who believes in encouraging literary talent invites her 12-year-olds to write free compositions on any subjects they please. She discusses the results with each child individually. What advice ought she to give in the following cases?

   (a) A dull-seeming, inarticulate boy hands in a brilliant but inaccurate crime story set in New York, where he has never been.
   (b) A boy who is good at most classwork hands in a muddled, ungrammatical, but heart-rending account of his broken home.
   (c) A demure, pretty girl hands in a first-person love story showing observant and precocious sexual awareness.

2. Biographical surveys reveal that until fairly modern times, most authors of importance began life with advantages, financial and educational. Very few authors with 'poor' or working-class backgrounds figure among the recognized great. How do you account for this fact?

3. Should authors and publishers have complete freedom? If you are in favour of censorship, what restrictions ought the law to impose, and who should make the decisions? If you oppose all censorship, give your reasons.

CHAPTER ELEVEN

NOVELS

The Growth of a Literary Form

The Muse of the Novel is young as goddesses go, an addition to the ancient Nine. Some other types of fiction, such as epic and legend, have a far longer history. But although a late-comer, the novel is the highest development of fiction as such. Careful reflection on it will take you over most of the ground you need to traverse, if you hope to make story-telling, of any kind, your literary pursuit.

As a distinct form in the sense that now concerns us, the novel dates from the eighteenth century—from the rise of the middle classes and the growth of a freer, more individualistic society. Long works of prose fiction were composed centuries before that, in Greece and Rome, in Japan and Spain and France. To some of them the term 'novel' might be loosely applied. Generally speaking, however, they were episodic tales with little organized plot and little study of character, wandering rather aimlessly from scene to scene.

Cervantes's *Don Quixote* (published in two parts, 1605 and 1615) stands out from the rest by its genius and human insight, its foreshadowing of the novels to come, and its inspiration to their authors. But Cervantes had no immediate followers of comparable stature. The meandering, not very profound kind of story, with slight literary pretensions, continued to be the norm for another century. Such tales often dealt with the adventures of rogues; the resultant term 'picaresque', from the Spanish *picaro*, a rogue, is employed by some critics to describe long disjointed stories in general. Picaresque romance verges on the novel in *Gil Blas*, by Le Sage, influenced by Spanish models, and published in instalments from 1715 onwards. But the true figure of transition is Daniel Defoe, best known for *Robinson Crusoe*, and also— among much else—the author of *Moll Flanders* (1722), the fictitious life story of a woman of questionable morals.

In 1740 Samuel Richardson, a printer, was told by bookseller friends that there would be a market for a volume of specimen letters showing how to conduct correspondence. He agreed to write one, and had the brilliant notion of making the letters tell a story. The result was *Pamela*, an instant best-seller. Richardson followed it up seven years later with the more ambitious *Clarissa Harlowe*, also told in letters. Meanwhile Henry Fielding had set out to parody *Pamela* in *Joseph Andrews*, and had then become so interested that he made it a story which could stand alone. Fielding, like Richardson, followed up with a book of larger scope, *Tom Jones* (1749). With *Tom Jones* the essential pattern is established.

The chief discoveries in the decades after Fielding were, first, that novels could be made out of everyday domestic and social life, with no adventures or dramatic departures from the norm—an art carried by Jane Austen to a perfection rarely equalled since; and second, that novels could be set in the distant past as well as the present, thereby becoming 'historical' and acquiring a different sort of interest—the leader here being Sir Walter Scott.

After Scott came the first high tide of mature novel-writing. England produced the Brontës, Dickens, Thackeray, George Eliot; France, Stendhal and Balzac and Flaubert; Russia, Dostoevsky and Tolstoy; America, Hawthorne and Melville; with many more in all these countries, and others. Their achievement was so vast that the experiments of more recent times should be viewed largely as conscious efforts to break new ground, in a medium where little more could be done till new ground was broken.

Thus James Joyce's *Ulysses* (1922) is a novel of unprecedented complexity written in several styles, some of which are themselves unprecedented, and make immense demands on the reader. It is based, as the title hints, on a symbolic use of Homeric legend. Joyce uses his new methods to explore the characters' thoughts with an intensiveness beyond the reach of orthodox fiction. Another technique for penetration in depth is the 'stream of consciousness', associated with Joyce and also Virginia Woolf, where everything that passes in a character's mind is poured out, supposedly unedited. Kindred motives inspire D. H. Lawrence's probings of the subconscious and irrational.

Worth noting also, and much less frequently noted, is Robert Graves's transformation of the historical novel. Scott and his imitators were content to tell mainly-invented stories in a 'period' setting, with real history supplying background and romantic colouring, rather than the chief interest. Graves, in *I. Claudius* (1934), took nearly all his characters and incidents straight from history, the novelist's contribution being to bring the dry facts to life and interpret them. Most historical fiction since Graves has followed his lead, even on the more popular level, as in Anya Seton's *Katherine*.

Novels of other kinds, since the Second World War, are not so easy to generalize about; and while there have been many successful novelists, it is hard to feel quite sure of the status of any one of them in the long term. England has produced its accomplished and often witty observers of society—Anthony Powell, Angus Wilson and others. America has gone further with ruthlessness, violence, protest: Norman Mailer is an author who would come at once to the minds of many readers. So far as there has been a trend in the most recent years, it is perhaps towards minute detail and total recall, as in some of the work of John Updike, the author of *Couples.*

In frankly popular fiction during the 1960s, the writers who had the strongest effect were probably Ian Fleming and Harold Robbins. Fleming's 'James Bond' books gave a new and controversial quality to what had been a pure entertainment, the spy-thriller. Robbins, having written several best-selling but unexceptional stories, suddenly broke through in *The Carpetbaggers* (1961) to a startlingly enlarged exploitation of sex and sadism. *The Carpetbaggers* influenced sensational fiction more than is always realized. Before it, the most notorious shocker was Grace Metalious's *Peyton Place* (1959). To read *Peyton Place* today is to wonder why it caused any fuss.

Meanwhile, throughout most of the twentieth century, various sub-species have grown up and changed and branched out—detective stories, science-fiction, novels of politics and ideas, novels about the business world. Films have had their effect, causing novelists (Hemingway, for example) to rely more on dialogue and on what can be visualized. They have also created curious interrelationships: first, by inspiring many novels written with one eye on a potential film-of-the book; later, by starting a reverse traffic, with synthetic paperbacks appearing to order as the book-of-the-film. Occasionally even, after the filming of a novel, a fictionalized version of the film has been issued that is not the original from which it was taken: the traffic has gone both ways, there and back.

It is still too soon to be sure whether the book-of-the-film (or book-of-the-TV-programme, another variant) will develop as a new sub-species. At least it suggests that the novel may still have powers of renewal, and that if you try your hand at it, you will not be entering—as some critics would have you fear—a worked-out field where there is no future.

Presenting 'Truths of Human Life' in Fiction

Where a literary form has such rich variety, most generalizations will be rash. It is hard even to define the term 'novel', in a phrase covering the work of all novelists. The best definition known to me is more successful in prompting fruitful thoughts than in actually fitting every case. *A novel is a narrative that presents certain truths of human life through a series of imagined facts.* A shade pretentious, and only vaguely relevant to the pure 'entertainment', but still helpful.

To begin with, consider the 'truths of human life' part. The world's major novels all undoubtedly *say something*, about real people, through the medium of fictitious ones. A novel is not a book of academic research, distilled from other books. It expresses (or should express) living human contact, living experience, and it communicates through this.

But the word 'truths' is the first crux. What sort of truths? Does this imply that a novel should have a moral or purpose?

Purpose in Fiction

The eighteenth-century pioneers made a show of edification at least. They depicted virtue rewarded, and vice punished or rebuked. Defoe does it, or professes to be doing it, in *Moll Flanders*, and so does Richardson in *Pamela*. Yet neither carries conviction. With Defoe, one feels that his alleged lesson in virtue is mainly an excuse for the fun he has with the vice. As for Pamela, she is a servant who resists her master's attempts at seduction. So far, so good. The trouble is that her reward calls in question the motives behind the chastity that led up to it: her baffled employer marries her. Even at the novel's birth, the naïve moral is already looking like a mistake, off-putting and with a bogus air. It has remained so. Novelists of stature have avoided it ever since, and there is no reason to ignore their example.

So again, what sort of truths? Akin to the moralizing novel, but more worth attention, is the novel with a purpose. Usually this is a reformist purpose. Dickens campaigned against social evils by writing stories exposing them. However, the amount of social purpose in a Dickens novel varies considerably. The attack on bad private schools, in *Nicholas Nickleby*, takes up only a fraction of the book and is not the main theme. *Bleak House* does depend on the Court of Chancery and its abuses, and would not work without them. Yet it is doubtful whether a reader ever feels that Dickens's social conscience entirely dominates a book, except perhaps in *Hard Times*; the iniquity, however rampant, is not what the story is *about*.

The best-known novel devoted frankly to rousing the public against an evil is *Uncle Tom's Cabin*. Harriet Beecher Stowe brought it out in 1851 as a tract against slavery in America. Its success, both as a fine piece of melodramatic fiction and as a serious influence on opinion, proves that the novel-with-a-purpose should not be dismissed. Very few, however, attain the same peaks. An *Uncle Tom's Cabin* of the early twentieth century was Upton Sinclair's *The Jungle*, a revelation of the callous treatment of immigrants in Chicago, especially those employed by the meat industry. *The Jungle*, though a savage and telling document, is also a warning to novelists. It caused a furore, but not on the immigrants' behalf, and not in favour of the remedies Sinclair urged. Americans were alarmed simply at the horrors of the meat industry itself—the dirt, disease, and ghastlier things which they discovered to be polluting their food—and the President set up a commission of inquiry. If the book's aim was to champion the immigrants, its success was very limited.

Ideas in Fiction

'Truths' of the sort that can be defined become more surely acceptable in the novel of ideas. One of the first great novelists of ideas is Dostoevsky. *Crime and Punishment*, though on one plane it is a detective story, sets out to examine a question in ethics: whether an exceptional person can ever be above good and evil, and what might happen if a man tried to prove that he was by committing a murder. In more recent times the novel of ideas has sometimes become ideological. André Malraux portrayed the Communist movement of the 1920s and 30s in *Man's Fate* and other books. A comparable classic by an ex-Communist is Arthur Koestler's *Darkness at Noon*. Koestler reconstructs the background of a Russian trial under Stalin, and tries to show how the dictator's victims, devoted Party leaders innocent of the charges against them, might have been induced to confess through an appeal to their own warped loyalties.

A philosophy or system of life can inspire fiction in a variety of ways. Aldous Huxley's *Brave New World* challenges the ideal of material progress: suppose all its goals were fully achieved in a world run by science, would the result be desirable? Orwell's *Nineteen Eighty-Four* imagines other trends pushed to logical and dreadful extremes. Evelyn Waugh in *Brideshead Revisited*, Graham Greene in *The Power and the Glory* and *The Heart of the Matter*, analyse the effects of Catholic faith on human beings in various crises.

When such novels come to mind—some of them being among the few modern books, in any class, that have perceptibly influenced the thinking of millions—it is plain that the novel of ideas is a serious proposition. It needs no defence. If you have an idea which could be expressed in a novel, go ahead without misgiving.

Yet notice that the most powerful effects are seldom achieved by direct rubbing-in of the entire message. Compare, for instance, the works of novelists who have speculated about the future. H. G. Wells made a splendid beginning as a pioneer in science-fiction. Afterwards, deciding that he had a mission, he wrote novels-with-a-purpose. Even when these are still scientific they are apt to be weighed down by discussion and pamphleteering, thinly disguised or not disguised at all. *The Time Machine*, his first long story, already has a most haunting idea going far beyond mere fantasy, but it carries this adroitly and beautifully. *Men Like Gods* (to pick one of his later Utopias) is a bore. It has no genuine story; the characters who stand for what Wells wants are remote and unattractive; the characters who stand for what he dislikes are puppets embodying attitudes, too artificial to make the reader share in the author's feelings.

Turn now to the infinitely stronger anti-Utopias, *Brave New World* and *Nineteen Eighty-Four*. Both have characters who rebel against the society round them; the latter is told from the rebel's viewpoint. But neither rebel is a mere mouthpiece of the author, and neither offers a reasoned case, or an alternative. While a rubbing-in of the point does take place on the negative side, no constructive advice for ourselves is ever offered.

Or consider the modern Catholic novelists. They make a clean break with the edifying religious fables of a past era. The aim is to show how Catholics are different because of their religion, rather than to persuade the reader directly that Catholics are better or that their religion is true. There the reader must decide for himself. He may well end up disagreeing with the author; but he will certainly have a deeper appreciation of what the issues are.

Major novelists, of course, seldom deal with explicit ideas even to this extent. Their 'truths of human life' concern individual psychology, or family or social relationships. Fielding, in the preface to *Tom Jones*, defines his subject-matter as 'human nature', and that statement is still as sound as any generalization about the novel can be. The great change since his time has been a change of approach. The abandonment of moralizing and spelt-out messages is only one aspect of it. There has been a shift away from all explicit comment, all explicit discussion. Fielding himself breaks in to lecture his readers quite unashamedly—on the characters, on human conduct in general, on the literary techniques for portraying it. A century later Dickens still makes his presence felt, and Tolstoy, in *War and Peace*, philosophizes between scenes. Today a good novelist will probably avoid speaking in his own person. He will be wary even of commenting through a character used as a mouthpiece. He will leave his 'truths of human life' to be inferred from the story.

Making Points through Characters

His problem is to ensure that his 'truths' are conveyed without misunderstanding. If he is not to state them outright, the question is how far he can and should drive them home by deliberate manipulation and highlighting. It used to be widely felt that a novelist should convey his message (or whatever one called it) by contriving a plain instructive battle between right and wrong, with a hero and villain. Or if that was too crude, he should at least make sure that some of his characters were recognizably 'goodies', with 'baddies', in however muted a sense, opposed to them. Again, tastes and standards have altered. D. H. Lawrence was one of the trail-blazers. Despite his moral fervour he puzzled readers, and confused them at first, by writing novels where the characters defied such classification. You couldn't see which side you were meant to take, or even that clear-cut sides existed.

As a writer of fiction yourself, never be afraid of sympathy, admiration or dislike; but be subtle, be tactful. To make statements about the human condition it is not always necessary to have goodies and baddies. It may be a mistake. A clash between different ideals, between different conceptions of what is right (as in the better parts of Galsworthy's Forsyte cycle), may be more eloquent than a clash between manifest right and wrong. Also more convincing. Graham Greene has pointed out that one reason why Dickens's stories sag at the end is his habit of setting up a conflict of good and evil, and then giving the wicked a vividness he cannot give to the virtuous. The final triumph of the right is therefore incredible. Another critic has claimed that among modern English novelists, only one, not generally counted a major figure, has succeeded in making virtue interesting. This is C. S. Lewis; and even Lewis's successes occur in science-fiction and fantasy remote from familiar life.

What you should be careful to do is not so much to embody your point in an opposition of good and bad characters, as to include at least one character whom readers can identify with and care about; also perhaps, in contrast, at least one who will be felt as alien. In this way attention can be held, whereas it is apt to wander if all the characters seem neutral or distant; and you can get the reader to absorb the point of the story, not from moral labels, but from the distribution of sympathy which takes shape as he reads it.

The character whom the reader 'feels with' need not be a hero. During the 1950s, in fact, a cult of the anti-hero came in, with such novels as Kingsley Amis's *Lucky Jim*. An anti-hero story is likely to be closer to life as the reader knows it. But if you attempt one, you must handle it well if you are to leave any positive impression. It is tricky to make a valid point through a character who is not very forceful, who does not stand for any cause that enlists partisanship, and whose opponents may have an obvious case.

Lucky Jim itself is a partial failure because of an oversight in that respect (at least, it looks like an oversight, and is thus a flaw even if intentional). Amis gives a clever and funny picture of class relationships at a small university in the 1950s. The plot turns on the prolonged uncertainty as to whether Jim's teaching appointment will be renewed by his snobbish superiors. Unfortunately, while we can sympathize with him, we can never feel quite committed or quite sure what the situation is, because there is no unequivocal indication whether he is or is not a good teacher. Hence the effect is weakened. The anti-hero's academic potential is left so uncertain that the professors' motives may not necessarily be as implied.

However artfully prompted, the reader's identification with people in the novel, and his drawing of conclusions to take away with him, should come from his own mind. Remember what we noted in Chapter Three, about the modern shift from explicit to less-explicit communication, from direct preaching or teaching to the evocation of response. We are now seeing how it applies to novels. A reader nowadays is likelier to take in a truth if the novelist lets him work it out, partly, for himself. Even the anti-Utopias, which do contain pages of undiluted discussion, only convey the positive warnings they are meant to convey when the reader looks round him, and relates their imaginary future to the actual present.

Plot and Conflict

To revert: what about that 'series of imagined facts'?

The word 'series' raises such issues as how far a novel should be unified by a plot in the traditional sense, and how much time it can cover and hold together, without breaking up into episodes. These two questions are connected. When the novel matured as a literary form, it tended at once to size, traversing long periods, and introducing dozens of characters. For stories on such a scale the old picaresque mode of writing, which simply wandered from episode to episode, was soon felt to lack cohesion.

As in several other respects, Fielding was the arch-pioneer. He intended *Tom Jones* to be a kind of comic epic in prose. An epic, however, requires unity and a firm direction. Having resolved to trace Tom's entire life from birth to marriage, Fielding devised what is still one of the most intricately-wrought plots in English fiction to bind it together. The full title, *The History of Tom Jones, a Foundling*, is significant in itself. The plot begins, not merely at the hero's birth, but before. It depends partly on his uncertain parentage, and is not wound up till his parents are identified and his station in life adjusted accordingly, at the end.

This plot, with all its ingenuities, can be swallowed. So can some of the plots of Fielding's successors. Only *some*, however. Emily Brontë's *Wuthering Heights* covers a stretch of thirty years, and though clumsy in places, is well enough organized to be in no danger of either falling apart or getting preposterous. But in the progress of Dickens, we can see reasons why later novelists veered away from tight plotting, and also from those vast sweeps of family history which seemed, in Dickens's hands, to need an elaborate internal structure to make them cohere. Dickens's first novel, *The Pickwick Papers*, is almost picaresque in its looseness of form—chiefly because it began as a collaboration with an artist, coming out in serial parts, with neither of the collaborators knowing where it was going. Afterwards Dickens's planning grew much more conscious, and he came under the influence of Wilkie Collins, the mystery-story writer. Bernard Shaw accused Collins of 'ruining Dickens with plots'—inaccurately; Dickens was inventing them for himself, before; but he now went further in tying up his novels with over-ingenious entanglements, which might be proper in mystery stories, but were harmful to his.

Often Dickens creates a superb character—sinister like Wackford Squeers, comic like Micawber—and then, for the sake of the plot, plunges this wonderful grotesque into action which cuts him down. Also, to fasten the loose ends which a long and crowded story inevitably leaves hanging, he resorts to blatant coincidences. The unravelling of *David Copperfield* requires half a dozen. Even the simpler *Great Expectations* has one which is so far-fetched that it had to be dropped in the film version.

The Waning of the Plot

With the passage of years, and the increasing sophistication of readers, such contrived events gradually grew less frequent in novels. Thomas Hardy still used them, if not with quite the same architectural purpose. Thus the crowning disaster in *The Return of the Native* results from a complicated and highly unlikely accident. A mother visits her estranged son and his wife, to make up the quarrel. When she knocks, he happens (for a reason planted farther back) to be dozing in the front room; he says 'Mother!' without fully waking; his wife, hearing, thinks he has answered the door; so it stays shut, and the mother, taking this as a refusal to let her in, goes off to collapse in despair. It is precisely Hardy's undoubted power that throws the difficulty into relief. If the 'series of imagined facts' depends on coincidences and chances that stick out painfully from a fine context, then its logic is inescapably faulty. We don't feel that things would have had to happen in that way; we may well feel that they would probably have turned out differently. The artificial plot, holding together a long sequence of events, or forcing a complex situation to come out right (in Hardy, wrong), is not like life.

We can still accept it with reservations in a novel about events which are abnormal to begin with. One reason why tight plotting has always been admitted in crime stories, from Wilkie Collins onward, is that a crime is itself contrived and planned. The word 'plot' has a double meaning here. Nobody would deny Agatha Christie a respected status. And Somerset Maugham's warning, that there is no substitute for the story line as an attention-holder, remains sound. But most novels in the twentieth century have freer, less elaborate plots than their precursors. Novelists make them cohere by other methods.

Often they do it by greater concentration. The same problems persist. The time factor, for instance, continues to play its part. A novel covering a long time still has to be unified somehow. But unification may come differently—perhaps through a more exclusive focus on one character (as in Joyce's *Portrait of the Artist as a Young Man*), or through a starkly dominant theme (as in Dos Passos's *USA* trilogy, where all the loosely-linked episodes portray human debasement through acquisitiveness). Observe how Scott Fitzgerald, in *The Beautiful and Damned*, handles a drawn-out tragedy resembling that of *Bleak House*. However, the twentieth century has also produced more novels that overcome the time sprawl by dealing only with a short period, or several short periods with gaps between. The whole of *Ulysses* takes place on the same day. Though very highly wrought after its own fashion, it requires no plot in the Dickensian sense, and could hardly carry one.

In your own thoughts on prospective novel-writing, do not worry too much over plots. You will need them, but not as the Victorians did. Aim at unity and organization of a more profound kind. Remember that the strength of a good story (with a few exceptions such as whodunits) is not so much in the ingenuity of its battle-plan as in the clash itself— the conflict which runs all through.

Conflict really is essential. It may be between persons, or between persons and environment, or between rival forces in one person's soul. It may be any combination of these, and it may be multiple. Conflict, however, there must be, and here, not in superficial plotting, the main-spring should be found. You need a certain toughness to be a good novelist. If you prefer not to think of unpleasant people, or trouble, or inharmonious relationships, you had better write something else. The clash, as we saw, does not have to be a crude combat of goodies and baddies. Nor, as Jane Austen proves, does it have to involve frantic passions or crushing calamities or death. But there has to be darkness somewhere, from enmity, failure, prejudice, ignorance, or whatever cause your thoughts may suggest; and unhappy situations, alas, are more fertile and interesting than happy ones.

In practice your plot may have more value for carrying the story along than for knitting it together. It can keep the reader curious to know what comes next—what is the next term in the series, when the logic (let us hope) is not so obvious as to make it predictable. At any rate the story must be carried along.

You must give the story momentum, and without delay, getting it off the ground quickly and defining the conflict that will determine it.

Beginnings

Beware of leisurely beginnings. Only the rare genius Marcel Proust could get away with an introductory passage consisting of several pages of rumination on how he lay in his bed at night (alone). The reader should have at least some notion of what the opening theme is, and where the situation is tending, as soon as possible.

Here is the beginning of Aldous Huxley's *Point Counter Point:*

'You won't be late?' There was anxiety in Marjorie Carling's voice, there was something like entreaty.

'No, I won't be late,' said Walter, unhappily and guiltily certain that he would be. Her voice annoyed him. It drawled a little, it was too refined—even in misery.

'Not later than midnight.' She might have reminded him of the time when he never went out in the evenings without her. She might have done so; but she wouldn't; it was against her principles; she didn't want to force his love in any way.

'Well, call it one. You know what these parties are.' But as a matter of fact, she didn't know, for the good reason that, not being his wife, she wasn't invited to them.

A clear-cut statement is not strictly necessary. In *Crime and Punishment* it is some time before we learn the exact nature of the dreadful-thing-that's-going-to-happen. But we know very soon indeed that something dreadful is on the way; suspense is rapidly established and we are hooked. Hooking the reader is important, because there is nothing to prevent him from putting the book down if he isn't. Never, in a novel, or indeed in any other form of writing, assume that you have a captive audience. Readers can always stop if you bore them.

Endings

The beginning of the 'series of imagined facts' is one problem, the ending is another, and difficult. In a more naïve age, readers expected —and were uncritically happy to get—a last chapter that dispensed justice and tidied up the whole situation. Often it was a marrying-off chapter.[1] Once again, a modern reader is less easily satisfied. We can accept the lovely and final diminuendo of *Wuthering Heights*, because it is not contrived; the chief characters are dead.

I sought, and soon discovered, the three headstones on the slope next the moor; the middle one grey, and half buried in heath; Edgar Linton's only harmonized by the turf, and moss creeping up its foot; Heathcliff's still bare.

I lingered round them, under that benign sky: watched the moths fluttering among the heath and hare-bells; listened to the soft wind breathing through the grass; and wondered how any one could ever imagine unquiet slumbers for the sleepers in that quiet earth.

But if all or most of the chief characters are alive, is is unsatisfying to have a neat winding-up and conclusion of the entire imbroglio, with everyone getting his deserts or at least a suitable dismissal. Life isn't like that. It is unfair, and it goes on.

Finality can be conveyed best through some event or speech which shows that the conflict we have been reading about, the conflict which gave the novel its unity and direction, is over. Life will go on, yes, but henceforth the characters will have other concerns. To manage this controlled halt is an art which the earlier novelists could not always master. If they did not wind matters up with a marrying-off chapter,

---

[1] This was such a norm of fiction that when the French biblical scholar Renan published his popular and imaginative *Life of Jesus*, one young lady commented: 'What a pity it couldn't have ended with a wedding.'

or its equivalent, they were apt to be hesitant when and how to stop. Scott, notoriously, has a trick of hanging about after the story is finished; and Dickens felt so little confidence in his first, negative ending of *Great Expectations* that he let himself be persuaded to make it 'happy', by a change which leaves readers with misgivings, and a suspicion that all would not be over.

Sinclair Lewis closed *Main Street* with one of the classic modern endings. Carol Kennicott, the heroine, goes through several years of erratic revolt against her humdrum lot as the wife of a small-town doctor. At last she settles down, insisting, however, that she has made an honourable protest.

> She patted his pillows, turned down his sheets, as she reflected.
> 'But I have won in this: I've never excused my failures by sneering at my aspirations, by pretending to have gone beyond them. I do not admit that Main Street is as beautiful as it should be! I do not admit that Gopher Prairie is greater or more generous than Europe! I do not admit that dish-washing is enough to satisfy all women! I may not have fought the good fight, but I have kept the faith.'
> 'Sure. You bet you have,' said Kennicott. 'Well, good night. Sort of feels like it might snow tomorrow. Have to be thinking about putting up the storm-windows pretty soon. Say, did you notice whether the girl put that screwdriver back?'

With her husband's affectionate lack of interest, and his query about the implement to do a household chore, we know we are back on Main Street for keeps.

Or take the two great anti-Utopias, where the whole point is that the horror is not defeated or even checked, and that everything *will* go on. In *Brave New World* the end is marked by the protester's suicide, in *Nineteen Eighty-Four* by his surrender. Both events make it plain that the conflict we have been reading about is over, and that is enough. The series of imagined facts is completed and closed.

Obviously, anything as final as a leading character's death can always make a conclusion. But not all themes allow such an ending, and even where it can occur, it still has to be timed correctly. What matters is not so much the mere halting of action as the feeling that the struggle is finished and the situation no longer exists. Conrad could have ended *Lord Jim* at an earlier point by having the hero killed sooner. It is only by happening when it does and as it does, with his long torment of spirit resolved, that his death gives the novel a conclusion.

Imagination: the Inescapable Need

So, lastly, to the phrase 'imagined facts'. All that must be stressed here is the meaning of 'imagined'—the relation between a novel and actuality. You are not likely to produce fiction of much value by writing a slightly camouflaged version of what actually happened. Nor is it a defence of a poor story to plead that it actually did happen. 'Imagined' *does* mean 'imagined'.

As with most rules, there are exceptions. A few distinguished modern novels are, in effect, dramatized documentaries, re-telling actual events with the names altered. A fine example is Meyer Levin's *Compulsion*, which reconstructs the Leopold–Loeb murder case in 1924. Even here, however, the main impact of the novel comes from its author's bold attempt to get inside the murderers' minds, and explain dark matters which the transcript of actuality, in the trial records, does not reveal.

Before these documentaries arrived on the scene, a hybrid called the *roman à clef* was a recognized form. The principal characters were all real people under different names, and the story, though invented, bore some resemblance to what these people did in real life. Disraeli, the only English novelist who was also Prime Minister, introduced various well-known figures into such stories as *Lothair*. Readers had a good deal of fun spotting them, and composing 'keys' to the Conservative leader's books. When Disraeli died he was working on a new one intended to pillory the Liberal leader, Mr. Gladstone, as 'Falconet' (the name of a noisy antique gun, and also a near-anagram of 'Gladstone'). But Disraeli's formula has produced few memorable novels in other hands.

Undigested reality will never make a story, and it will seldom help one. A supreme masterpiece of fiction, Stendhal's *Le Rouge et le Noir*, was suggested in part by a report of an actual murder. Yet many readers have felt that when Stendhal's hero at last commits the murder, it strikes a discord. By intruding with stark literalness, instead of hovering in the author's mind as a hint, the reality mars the novel. If you draw on literal facts for your fiction, you will probably find that you must at least distort them to make your point, as sculptors in medieval cathedrals carved statues that were out of proportion, so that they would look right in high niches seen from below. Even in historical novels of the type launched by Graves, where all the main characters and incidents come from history, the novel itself is not history but imaginative interpretation, with events and thoughts and an inbuilt logic which the author has added, out of his own mind, to what he found in his sources.

Symbolism and Allegory

Before passing on, we must take note of a special case. Without transcribing reality directly, a story may blend it with imagination in a sort of counterpoint, through a symbolic or allegorical meaning. This cuts deeper than the mere parlour game of a *roman à clef*. Sometimes the story's veiled meaning is not literal, not easily pinned down, and yet it generalizes the facts of our own experience or our feelings about it. Herman Melville's *Moby Dick* has this subtle reference to real life, and so have Kafka's stories *The Trial* and *The Castle*. The same technique appears, with a reference that is far more overt and specific, in allegories. Swift's Lilliput is England; the Lilliputians' religious and political factions are parodies of English ones. Orwell's Animal Farm is Russia; several of the animals stand for actual Communist leaders, and the story of the uprising and its aftermath corresponds, in a selective way, to the story of Russia between 1917 and 1945.

When a literary technique can exploit actuality with such potent results, its use must not be discouraged. However, it is extremely difficult to succeed with. If you attempt it, you may have trouble in striking a correct balance. On the one hand there is the risk that the dictates of your inner meaning will deprive the characters of life, dominate the action, and prevent the story from developing in its own right. A story that *depends on* symbol or allegory—to such an extent that it has no logic of its own, and cannot be enjoyed even superficially without the key—has something wrong with it. One test of an allegory is whether it stands up as a good story for a reader who doesn't know what it is about. Children can enjoy *Gulliver* and *Animal Farm* in that spirit. They cannot enjoy, say, Anatole France's *Penguin Island*, much of which is pointless if the allusions to French politics are not grasped.

But having settled that the story must be a good story, you face the contrary hazard: that if it works by itself too successfully, readers may miss the symbolism entirely. For many years *Moby Dick* was read, if at all, simply as an adventure yarn; the 1897 edition of *Chambers's Biographical Dictionary* has a ten-line article on Melville which does not mention it.

Between the two chasms you may be skilful enough to find a safe path. If you are, your chances of doing work of distinction will be above average. But tread warily.

Characters: Giving Them Substance

Outside science-fiction, where an idea or situation may be sufficient, no novel can possess much vitality unless it has characters who stand out, engage a reader's interest, and differ sharply from one another.

Poets and dramatists were creating characters long before novelists existed. The size and scope of the novel, however, brought two immense advances, foreshadowed only by Shakespeare and a few other rare spirits. These advances are part of the modern novelist's heritage, and affect all characterization.

Depth in Characters: Making them Three-dimensional

First, with amplitude came a new depth and complexity. Most of the characters in older literature are simpler than human beings usually are, and more homogeneous. They have well-marked qualities and display them constantly. In Greek and Roman epics, some of the heroes have epithets tacked on to their names, which they almost invariably live up to. Virgil's Aeneas is always *pius*, that is, inspired by duty towards his gods and kinsfolk, and even when he succumbs to the charms of Dido he starts being *pius* again very soon afterwards. In Malory's romances of the Round Table, Galahad is always pure, Mark is always mean and underhand, and so forth. Only the chief lovers are divided enough in spirit to break out of the pattern by fits and starts. Ben Jonson, who was contemporary with Shakespeare, based several comedies on one-dimensional characters ruled by 'humours' or obsessions—as did Molière in *The Miser*.

The figures in eighteenth-century novels are still rather like this. Soon after meeting them, you know them. They will never surprise you and you will never learn much more about them. The realization of how many facets an individual can have came fairly late. Maugham suggested that the first fictitious character with anything like the diversity of a real person is Julien Sorel, Stendhal's hero in *Le Rouge et le Noir*. However that may be, a novelist today should be able to conceive characters who have depth and diversity and are not too predictable. At the same time he must be able to make them act according to their own natures without coming unstuck, and without straining probability. For instance, it is perhaps straining probability a shade too hard for us to believe in Julien Sorel, at the end of the story in which we have come to know him, committing the crime which his creator insists upon.

You should aim at having at least a few three-dimensional, boldly contrasted characters who give an illusion of life. These must carry the plot and deploy the conflict. Where does the idea for a character come from? In historical novels, some of the characters are real people; so also, it must be confessed, are some of the characters in non-historical novels. Publishers print disclaimers as a legal safeguard ('any resemblance to actual persons living or dead is purely coincidental'), but these are not to be taken at face value. Quite apart from full-fledged *romans à clef*, the real-person-under-an-alias is a recurrent phenomenon in fiction.

Can this portraiture ever be defended? One living original whom any novelist has a right to copy from is, of course, himself. Much of Dickens went into David Copperfield, and more of Joyce into Stephen Dedalus. But Dickens also portrayed—or cartooned—his own father as Micawber, and Leigh Hunt as Harold Skimpole. Maugham put the magician Aleister Crowley into a novel, entitled (frankly enough) *The Magician*, and his fellow-author Hugh Walpole into another novel entitled *Cakes and Ale*—both under aliases, but easily recognized. Crowley was amused, Walpole hurt. Among more recent writers, Harold Robbins introduces a recognizable Jean Harlow as the film star in *The Carpetbaggers*, calling her Rina Marlowe.

It can be done—especially if the victim is dead—and I will not say absolutely, 'Don't do it'. But, setting aside moral and legal issues, it is a practice that implies lack of creative power as soon as it goes beyond isolated cases. To draw one of your characters from life may be excusable. To draw most of them from life means one of two things: either you are concocting a *roman à clef*, which will be second-rate unless you are another Disraeli, or you can't invent characters for yourself and should stop trying to write novels. Invention, moreover, means more than simply taking a real person and altering details. That is neither creative nor precautionary. W. S. Gilbert, a lawyer himself, showed an odd naiveté when friends warned him that the silly, ill-qualified First Lord of the Admiralty in *Pinafore*, Sir Joseph Porter, might give offence to the real First Lord, W. H. Smith: Gilbert replied that there was nothing to worry about, because Smith was a Conservative, and he had made Sir Joseph a Liberal. An inadequate defence.

Depth in Characters: Making them Alive
Apart from a few skilful self-portraits like Stephen Dedalus, a few inspired caricatures like Micawber, the best characters are composite. Undoubtedly they have traits of people known to the novelist—real humanity, after all, is his raw material—but he has always added and subtracted, rearranged and combined. Some of the most impressive seem to bear out a philosophic theory of Plato, that art aspires to a vision of prototypes or archetypes. Long John Silver is so marvellously composed that he is not merely a pirate, but a sort of quintessential pirate. Likewise Sherlock Holmes is a sort of quintessential private detective. Neither, probably, bears much resemblance to any reality; yet you can suggest a pirate by drawing a man with a peg-leg and a parrot on his shoulder, or a detective by drawing a man with a deer-stalker cap and magnifying glass.[1]

While several classic figures in fiction have this quality of representing a class, or outlook, or mode of living, you must take care not to portray characters who are simply types or mouthpieces and nothing else. They should be individual as well as universal, and individual first. The converse hazard—as usual, a converse hazard exists—is the effort to build an imaginary individual too laboriously. You can seldom improve a character by piling up masses of biographical detail with no clear bearing on the story. When fiction-writing and fiction-reading were more leisurely pursuits, with less competition, a talented novelist could sometimes carry this off. Samuel Butler, in *The Way of All Flesh*, goes further. He gives a long account of the hero's family and does not get him born

[1] For the record, Holmes's deer-stalker is never mentioned in the stories; but the illustrator supplied it and Conan Doyle acquiesced. As for Long John Silver, there is much to ponder in Stevenson's confession that the nucleus of the character (no more than that) was a real person, and that this person was a magazine editor.

till the seventeenth chapter. Today it would be hard to hold attention through such a preface. Butler's readers persevere, partly because he is an exceptionally felicitous writer, partly because the merits of the story (when it at last gets moving) are well known in advance. You may possess the first asset. You cannot, until you actually *are* a classic, possess the second.

By all means supply a character with a detailed background. It will make him more alive, both for your readers and for yourself. Work it up thoroughly and at leisure. Keep a notebook, if you like, and jot down ideas for the character. Live close to him in your imagination till you have a detailed conception of him—what he is, how he came to be so, how he might react in various situations. But don't pour all this out when you introduce him. Feed it in piecemeal. Bring it to light naturally, through dialogue or inquiries or reminiscences, at points in the story where it is apposite. Flashbacks are acceptable, but the flashback device has been overworked and you should be sparing with it.

Ideally this problem of disclosure should solve itself. Strongly-imagined characters acquire a life of their own. They are not puppets. They will reveal themselves through significant acts and speeches which they almost force on their creator; they will generate situations that show what they are, and how they have come to be so. It is a test of your characters (as it is a test of your inspiration) to note whether you ever feel any unease or dissatisfaction, any sense of something actively struggling. Docile characters are apt to be dead characters. You should find your imaginary people wanting to say and do things you didn't envisage, and sometimes resisting the demands of the plot, so that if you push them, you can no longer make them sound convincing.

Change and Development of Characters

This matter of inner vitality brings us to the second way in which novel-writing has advanced the art of characterization.

In epic and drama and romance, before the eighteenth century, characters were usually static. They did not alter much. A story might turn on a change in a person's knowledge or attitude: on a disillusionment, for instance, or a delayed falling in love. Only rarely, however, in occasional master-works like the tragedies of Shakespeare, do we feel that a character has really developed at the end, into something he was not at the beginning.

In novels, by contrast, development does occur and is often the substance of the story. A useful descriptive term in German is *Bildungsroman*, education-novel—the novel of growing up, or settling down, or realizing one's vocation. There are plenty of them. Admittedly we still meet fictitious figures who go on through every vicissitude without changing; often in a popular series, where the hero keeps behaving as his public expects him to. Ian Fleming's James Bond is an example.

Sometimes, again, a character develops only because the author becomes more deeply involved and takes him more seriously. Mr. Pickwick begins as an improbable buffoon, then matures into an interesting and lovable elderly gentleman. Dorothy Sayers's detective Lord Peter Wimsey, almost a Bertie Wooster in the first book, is a well-read, sensitive and intelligent man, able to hold his own among scholars, in the later ones. (Both authors tried to rationalize the change. Neither succeeded.) However, many characters in novels develop more genuinely, and with conscious design.

They grapple with problems, altering in the process; they shed delusions; they discover the truth about themselves. The motif of dawning enlightenment has perennial potency. But whatever theme you have in mind when you conceive characters in a situation, ask yourself whether you can picture them *going* anywhere, becoming different from what they are now. You can write a story without their doing either, but it will almost certainly be better if they do. At the very least they should have a built-in logic, a dynamism driving them to behave in an intelligible way, even if they remain unaltered.

Points of View

A story can be told, characters and their logic can be revealed, from several angles. Having chosen one, take care not to shift from it, unless you know how to make the shift smooth and plausible.

You can tell a story entirely in the third person, 'he' and 'she', from the point of view of a superhuman observer—a god, so to speak—who sees all, including thoughts. This is Tolstoy's method in *War and Peace*, and Galsworthy's in the Forsyte novels, with the famous deliberate exception that Soames's wife Irene is always seen through the eyes of other characters and not from within, a modification intended to give her an air of mystery. A more recent practitioner of the method is Angus Wilson. Once adopted, with or without limits, the 'god's-eye-view' must be followed with consistent impersonality. A modern author should not intrude with comments or explanations that break the spell. Among the classic novelists of the past, there are a few who managed it quite agreeably. When Fielding's own voice interrupts *Tom Jones*, his disarming exuberance makes it bearable. This is not purely a matter of different literary conventions, as might appear. Thackeray's intrusions in *Vanity Fair* are surely beyond bearing in any age. For example:

If, a few pages back, the present writer claims the privilege of peeping into Miss Amelia Sedley's bedroom and understanding with the omniscience of the novelist all the gentle pains and passions which were tossing upon that innocent pillow, why should he not declare himself to be Rebecca's confidant too, master of her secrets and seal-keeper of that young woman's conscience?

Write from the omniscient standpoint if it suits you, though the method is somewhat out of favour today, but conceal yourself more than Fielding, and never imitate Thackeray.

At the opposite extreme, you can tell a story in the first person through a narrator, an 'I' who is one of the characters—perhaps the chief one, perhaps not. *Robinson Crusoe* has long stretches where the narrator is the only character. *Jane Eyre* and *David Copperfield* are novels told by the principal figure. Evelyn Waugh's *Brideshead Revisited* is told by someone who is part of the story, very much so, but not a member of the family which the story concerns.

The 'I' technique has advantages as a method of giving immediacy, colour, a sense of authenticity. It suffers from the drawback that except in peculiar situations, the narrator cannot know everything. This limitation can be made a source of strength. *Brideshead Revisited*, and Graham Greene's *The End of the Affair*, convey a poignant sense of spiritual mystery in the everyday world, precisely because their narrators cannot get 'inside' the Catholic characters and grasp why they behave as they do—why, in particular, religion should defeat love. But the inconvenience of the 'I' method remains. It is at its most acute when you come down to the sheer mechanics of factual knowledge. A narrator cannot be made to witness every event, and if you arrange for him to be told everything by other people, or to eavesdrop on them and read their letters, the reader's willingness to accept and sympathize will soon fade.

One of the earliest 'I' novels in English, Laurence Sterne's *Tristram Shandy*, reduces the technique to an absurdity never surpassed. Tristram is unborn for a large part of the story, and still a child at the end, so that he could not have known more than a tiny fraction of the events he relates in enormous detail. The absurdity is of course an intentional joke, yet a warning to novelists is wrapped up in it.

Between the extremes is the story told in the third person, but wholly from the point of view of a single character. Stories of this kind are much like 'I' stories, and the technique has much the same qualities of strength and weakness. It is capable, however, of subtler pathetic or ironic effects. The author can describe scenes which the character, as direct narrator, could not describe without becoming implausible (too literate, too observant); and in such a scene he can show the character plainly not understanding what he and the reader do understand. Several novels about children belong to this class, such as Carson McCullers's *The Member of the Wedding*, in which a girl begins painfully adjusting herself to the adult world. Her last purely childish act is to ask a couple to take her on their honeymoon; we see the wedding party both as it is and through her eyes, as a nightmare of rejection.

There are further variants. You can write in the first person, but with several different 'I' figures in turn, as Wilkie Collins does in *The Moon-*

stone. One way of doing this is to tell the story through letters written by several people (though in an age of telephones and fast travel, it is hard to make long, informative letters believable). Similarly, you can write in the third person, and shift at intervals from one character to another. If the shifts are frequent and the characters numerous, this technique may approximate in practice to the god's-eye-view. You may feel able to switch from the first person to the third. In *Bleak House* Dickens alternates between god's-eye-view chapters—told in the present tense like a sports commentary, a device Dickens learned from Thomas Carlyle—and 'I' chapters narrated by Esther Summerson, whose tone is in sharp contrast. A modern exploiter of the same switch is Harold Robbins (who, unlike Dickens, traps himself once into making a narrator describe his own death).

Dialogue

However you decide to exhibit your people, let them tell their own tale in action as far as possible. In particular, let them speak for themselves and speak in character, so that the reader comes to know the accents of each, and can tell them apart. This goes far beyond merely inventing verbal mannerisms. Admittedly we evoke Uriah Heep (for instance) by saying "umble'; but even such figures as these, when they occur in novels of any stature, are marked off by subtler touches. They may speak with a special vocabulary, reflecting, perhaps, their place of origin (as with an Irishman), or their profession (as with an army officer), or their social class (as with a titled lady). But if they are vividly conceived they will be personal as well as generic. Try giving their lines to other characters and you will often find that the words ring false. The other character wouldn't say that.

In a best-seller with no great literary pretensions, Margaret Mitchell's *Gone with the Wind*, the hero Rhett Butler acquires individuality almost entirely through his style of speech. A Southern gentleman, he is courteous in his own fashion, but with a bold freedom and honesty which defy Southern etiquette. When he appears, therefore, he stands out from the conventional company round him, offending yet attracting, and he soon begins to stand out for the reader.

Dialogue should be, on the whole, realistic, but not a mere transcript of the way people talk. As C. P. Snow has remarked, actual talk, read back from a shorthand record, tends to have a curious flatness. Also it is repetitive, imprecise, tedious. Nineteenth-century novelists, knowing this and aware that a novel needs more, often gave their characters speeches which make no pretence of literal realism. Nobody ever talked like the whalers in *Moby Dick*, except in snatches. We accept the literary convention for the sake of effects which ordinary speech could not give. Today, readers expect dialogue that is like reality; but it still needs to be more pointed and more selective. Even wholly realistic speeches can and should be given a greater weight of implication than they usually carry. They should be more significant.

Evelyn Waugh's Helena, a British princess, marries the Roman general Constantius and goes to live on the continent. A society lady visits her.

'My dear, you bite your nails.'
'Only lately; never before I left home.'

In an instant we infer more about the marriage, and Constantius, than she ever says. And if she did say more, the effect might well be less convincing. We might feel that the author was putting words in her mouth just to inform the reader.

Consistency and Exactitude

Your characters, like the acts they perform, must be credible and consistent . . . or consistently-inconsistent. You must give them an air of rightness, based on knowledge. If you want to portray a bishop falling into disgrace, you can do it in a number of ways, but hardly by making him conduct divine service in shirt-sleeves hopelessly drunk, because a bishop does not suddenly disgrace himself like that, and would be forestalled if he showed signs of doing so. Again, no character should have a career which is impossible or self-contradictory. You can say that a woman served in the Navy in 1940, but not that she commanded a battleship; you can say that a man was in prison throughout 1963, but not that he climbed the Eiger in the same year. Nor should you let your characters do what their personal limitations would prevent them from doing (as a fictionalized Nelson, in a novel which I will not name, uses both arms long after losing one of them).

Such advice may sound trivial. Yet authors find it strangely easy to go wrong. Even eminent ones have been guilty of such astounding lapses as changing a character's name in the course of the story. Muddles over dates and durations are surprisingly common.

As with people, as with events, so with their context. Get it right: the places, the scenes, the objects. Stevenson, after his *Treasure Island* experience, urged all story-tellers to make the fullest use of maps and plans, and to keep a calendar handy. A reader alert enough to ask 'where' and 'when' should never be allowed to conclude 'but it couldn't have been'. Authenticity is multiple. Consult pictures and books and old newspapers to give your context substance and accuracy. Visit the scenes yourself, if you can. And when you come down to detail, your readers should be able to see, hear, touch, smell, and taste, and to think always. 'Yes, this is how it would have been.' Search for the best descriptive word or phrase, in all cases; there probably is one; don't settle for second best.

By what seems a paradox, this process of getting everything right becomes more vital the further a story moves from familiar ground, the more fantastic it grows. Here was the secret of Ian Fleming's sustained triumph as a thriller-writer. Nearly all his Bond stories are absurd, often glaringly so. It is the tireless care for minute detail about weapons, about cars, about the local colour and customs of distant places, about how precisely a thing is done—how (for instance) Bond stacked the cards to outwit Drax in *Moonraker*, and how the hand was played—it is that quality which gives the stories their momentum. Not the sex and violence so much denounced at the time. Others have written of sex and violence without Fleming's success. To enter vicariously into the thrills of Bond's world, a reader had to be able to believe in it while the story lasted. Fleming made this possible, and the decline of Bond as a modish hero-figure does not detract from the achievement.

Science-fiction and Fantasy

This need for rightness, when the subject-matter is strange or remote, arises most pressingly of all in science-fiction and outright fantasy. The best fantasy is never merely fantastic, and never imprecise or inaccurate. From *Gulliver's Travels* onward, the masters in this field have placed the action in settings which may be weird, non-human, grotesque in the last degree, but are worked out with unswerving consistency and attention to detail. Tolkien has coined the term 'sub-creation' for the kind of imaginary realm which these books evoke. The author projects a world of his own devising, and he must make it convincing. Tolkien's own Middle Earth illustrates his point (and he, like Stevenson, has a map).

Historical Fiction

The same considerations apply to another class of fiction that deals with the unfamiliar and far-off—historical fiction. The author sets out to evoke a past era. Again, accuracy is manifestly essential. But the emphasis is not quite the same as in fantasy. The author cannot play tricks with people or human nature; psychological rightness matters too. He faces special difficulties in picturing the way people thought, in recapturing a different atmosphere, in conjuring up a vanished society which he cannot invent as he goes along. He has the problem of doing this through dialogue which is 'period' on the right level, neither jarringly modern nor spoilt by bogus gadzookery.

Because these obstacles are so daunting, second-rate historical novelists sometimes rely on getting the externals right, and burden the story with an excess of elaborately researched facts about costume, buildings, food, and irrelevant happenings. Such research is praiseworthy, but if you are attempting historical novels, you should appreciate that it cannot carry the story alone; not if realization of the inwardness of a past age fails to accompany it.

A Parting Challenge

There is no formula for success in novel-writing, whether literary or popular. We can note the obvious virtues—insight, imagination, humour, brilliance of style. We can also note factors in success which are more doubtfully admirable, such as sex; though that one has been devalued. Anyhow you must decide for yourself what sort of success you want.

Rather than close with empty maxims, I prefer to offer a challenge. G. K. Chesterton once defined, and Orwell in due course enlarged upon, a genre which they described as the Good Bad Book. The good bad book is one that 'makes no serious literary pretensions but remains readable when more serious productions have perished': a book that can be faulted by any academic standard, yet undeniably 'has something'. Orwell cited *Uncle Tom's Cabin* (fairly or otherwise), and *Dracula* and *King Solomon's Mines*. We might add *The Prisoner of Zenda* and *Tarzan of the Apes*.

Now the supreme instance—as already hinted—is not strictly a single book, but a series of stories long and short: the Sherlock Holmes saga. It is one of the most colossal successes in all fiction, and Holmes is one of the most stubbornly alive of all characters, in defiance of his creator, who disliked him and tried to kill him. Holmes has inspired countless translations and adaptations, apocryphal adventures by later hands, books and essays discussing him as if he were real. Indeed many people still believe that he was, including children born decades after his last exploit.

Let us be quite clear. The Sherlock Holmes tales are not 'good' by established academic or critical standards. Certainly they flout a great deal of the advice in this chapter. They are melodramatic. They are grossly careless; Holmes devotees play an endless game of reconciling the contradictions. They lack Ian Fleming's authenticity in detail; even the house in Baker Street cannot confidently be located. Holmes's vaunted reasoning is often preposterous. You may see nothing in him yourself. And yet . . .!

Literary critics who ignore Sherlock Holmes have written far more on The Novel, and its major practitioners and what you can learn from them, than there is room for here. Read their books. But don't despise a suggestion which you will not find in any of them, so far as I know. Account for the spell of Sherlock Holmes. Then use your insight to produce stories of your own with an equal spell. If you can do that, it will put you on the road to a safe immortality.

Exercises

1. Read three of the following novels (and more if you can): Jane Austen, *Pride and Prejudice*; Anthony Trollope, *Barchester Towers*; George Eliot,

The Mill on the Floss; H. G. Wells, *Kipps*; Sinclair Lewis, *Babbitt*; Muriel Spark, *Memento Mori*; Angus Wilson, *Anglo-Saxon Attitudes*; Meyer Levin, *Compulsion*.

(*a*) Decide which you like best. Write three pages saying why. Pick out things the author has done which supply useful hints to other novelists.

(*b*) Decide which you like least. Write three pages saying why you don't like it. Pick out things the author has done which, in your opinion, warn other novelists what *not* to do. (Make allowances for changes in taste and reading habits. Thus it would be unfair to condemn Dickens as 'long-winded' by modern standards; he wrote for a more leisurely public.)

2. You are writing a novel about (*a*) crime, or (*b*) sport, or (*c*) life in industry, or (*d*) life among professional people such as doctors. It is told by a narrator, an 'I', who is not the chief character. Write the scene in which the narrator first meets the chief character; in other words, the scene which introduces that character to the reader.

3. Do as in Exercise 2, but with a historical novel. Write the scene in which your narrator meets an important character (not necessarily the chief one), who must be a real person of past times—somebody whom many readers will already know a good deal about.

4. Conan Doyle, in *Rodney Stone*, has two long accounts of boxing matches. Read these and compare them with the fights in Budd Schulberg's *The Harder They Fall*. Which author do you think is more successful in holding the reader and making the fights vivid? How does he do it?

5. Write the first three pages or so of a novel, narrated by the chief character. There is only one restriction: the character must be of the opposite sex from yourself. What problems do you find? Do you think novelists often have difficulty with their characters of the opposite sex?

CHAPTER TWELVE

SHORT STORIES

The Difference

Our survey of the novel may have seemed disproportionately long. But the reason was stated at the beginning, and the case of Sherlock Holmes underlines it. The novel is fiction at its highest pitch of development. To grasp all that it involves is to grasp most of the essentials of any fiction. Holmes, I repeat, flourishes in short stories as well as long ones, with much the same spell. When we turn to the short story as a distinct form, our major concern must be to ask *how* it differs, and what special adaptations it calls for.

It is not a compressed or mini novel. If it were, the art of producing it would resemble précis-writing; and since a short story by definition is so very much smaller (usually under ten thousand words, instead of sixty, eighty, a hundred thousand or over), the result would be more like a summary than a story.

In its modern character, the short story arose with the medium that furnished a market for it—the magazine. Some critics name Edgar Allan Poe as its first exponent. Certainly he was the first person to take it seriously and try to define it. His own stories—some of them superb, some incredibly bad—appeared in the *Southern Literary Messenger* and other American magazines from 1835 onward.

Poe's theory of the short story was on the rigid side, and he did not always live up to it himself, but the guiding principle which he laid down is as good as any. A short story is not only smaller than a novel, not only simpler and more compact, it is *single* with a more intense concentration. It should work out a single idea; make a single point; close with a single 'punch'; convey a single effect. For Poe, at his best a highly atmospheric writer, the last requirement was vital. The opening paragraph—ideally, the opening sentence—should strike the keynote. Everything should follow on in the same spirit, and be strictly relevant to the theme. Anything out of key or inessential, any mere luxury, should be excluded. There is no room for extra episodes or characters, superfluous description, or sub-plots branching from the main one.

If we concur with Poe, as in principle I think we must, the short story will raise a problem raised by the novel also, and will make it far more acute. Life isn't like that. It doesn't come in neat parcels. So how can you write a story with beginning, middle, and end, unified and neatly packaged, as if it did?

The answer is that while a short story is a piece of imagined life taken out of the flow, so to speak, and given a special cut and polish, a reader can still be made aware of the flow. The story can be seen to fit into life-as-a-whole. It can and normally should imply a before-and-after, and also, perhaps, a context. Admittedly it may not present 'truths of human life' in a general way; it can seldom hold enough material for generalization. This is why it falls outside our rough definition of the novel. The partial exception (rare in modern fiction of any stature) is the parable with a moral, like Wells's *The Country of the Blind*. Such a story may communicate one 'truth of human life', though hardly more than one. But a short story can establish its own kind of relationship to things-in-general—and does, far more often—by simply dropping hints at some larger truth, illustrating it, turning a momentary spotlight on it, so as to set the reader thinking about general issues, although the story cannot state them.

O. Henry's stories of the New York working class are not social documents like *The Jungle*, with its carefully constructed immigrant family suffering every blow which immigrants suffered, and its explicit comments at the end. Yet the little crises which his characters go through, and their style in coping and enduring, are reminders of a broader reality. He published a collection under the title *The Four Million* (the population of New York at the time) to imply this relationship to the whole life of the city.

But whatever a short story may hint at, it must never wander. This is a form of fiction that demands self-discipline, economy, a readiness to cut without mercy. Moreover, because it must make its point in comparatively few pages, it needs to be sharper than a novel, and more vividly defined. Except in the hands of an author of rare genius, it has very little scope for digression, or hesitations, or fine shades and muted effects which a reader will be slow to appreciate.

The Plot and Where it Comes From

Plot, in the tighter sense, is more frequently central to the short story than to the novel. It is felt to be more acceptable here. Part of the explanation lies in the nature of the market. An ingenious twist, a crime committed and solved, a clever surprise ending, above all a clear-cut outcome with no loose ends—these are things which a busy editor can take in quickly, and he knows, usually, that they will please his readers. However, that is no excuse for patronizing remarks about commercialism or popular taste. The difference from the novel in this respect is due to other factors as well. A close-knit plot obviously belongs better to a close-knit type of story; where unity is vital, it is such a natural unifier that it is more likely to *be* the story; and since there is no room for the long-drawn interweavings of a Dickens, the feeling of artificiality has less time to obtrude, and the plot is a less dubious device.

Early in the twentieth century, the periodical market for short stories was much larger than it is now. As a result immense numbers were written. Mediocre authors could mass-produce them by developing a knack for plots, with little besides. This art is by no means dead today. But its vaster scope in the inter-war period caused a spate of 'formula' stories, undistinguished and sometimes almost indistinguishable. A theory arose that there were only a few basic plots, and hence that the short story was a limited form, doomed to mechanization and decline. Critics tried to list all the plots; inventors advertised plotting-machines, to help hack writers to ring the changes on them.

It was an overdone and cynical notion which we can safely ignore. Good writers of short stories, and many of the less pretentious as well, defy such patterning in any but the most general sense. The only plot-lists that work are lists of classes rather than formulae. The 'eternal triangle plot', the 'mistaken identity plot', the 'love story', the 'mystery story' . . . fair enough, they exist, and myriads of stories have been published under each heading. But you can't get anywhere just by saying to yourself. 'I'll write a mystery story,' or even by mixing the ingredients and saying, 'I'll write a mystery story based on a triangle situation.' All your work will still lie ahead.

A classic 'formula', once mentioned so often as to become a cliché and a joke, is 'boy meets girl, boy loses girl, boy gets girl'. The emptiness of any such set of words, as the explanation or summing-up of an actual story, was brought out by a cartoonist. When the film of *Gone with the Wind* was released, he drew a man coming out of the theatre saying, 'Nothing to it—just "boy meets girl" . . .' Granted, *Gone with the Wind* had more in it than a short story. The cartoonist's *reductio ad absurdum* is still worth remembering.

A formula, in fact, can never be more than a hint. A short-story plot of any value will always be the author's own. With that firmly in mind we may concede that the 'formula' notion, however inadequate, does reflect a genuine difference from the novel—a different relationship between concept and execution. A short story has a much more definite mental existence prior to actual writing. If you undertake a novel you cannot plan it completely in advance. You might try, but with a theme of any vitality you would find that the plan grew and altered as you progressed. If you undertake a short story, the need for singleness does require that the scheme should be clear in your head before you start. Your story should, mentally, be finished before it is begun; indeed it may happen that the end occurs to you first, and you then invent a plot leading up to it. You should not start writing as soon as an idea strikes you, except to the extent of jotting down notes. You should sit back, let the idea turn over, take it for a walk (perhaps literally), till it matures.

Point of Origin

Before any connected writing, you should have pictured a situation, built up before the story opens; and the characters who are in this situation; and a setting (which may be important, even dominant, as in Poe's *The Pit and the Pendulum*, or more subtle as in Stevenson's *The Merry Men*); and a sequence of scenes that will work out the situation logically to a climax.

Take Aldous Huxley's *The Gioconda Smile*, from the collection entitled *Mortal Coils*. This is a black comedy, close enough to a murder mystery to figure in detective anthologies. The basic situation is the extra-marital tangle of Henry Hutton, a sensual, successful, wealthy man, no longer young, but not old. He lives in Sussex with Emily, his wife. Hutton makes business journeys, Emily stays at home, most of the time complaining about her poor health. Such a relationship would suggest that Hutton has probably acquired a girl-friend; and indeed he has. Doris is silly and trivial, and he has turned to her (the latest in a series) for relief and amusement rather than love.

Thus far the situation is obvious and commonplace. But Huxley adds another woman who turns the triangle into a quadrilateral, and he leads into the story by way of her, not the two obvious ones. Janet Spence has aspirations to culture and seriousness. She is not Hutton's mistress, but would like to be, and she throws herself at him—thus providing him with a further diversion. Huxley does not rush into these complications too quickly. He takes several pages to unfold all the nuances. When they have emerged, however, the reader sees with interest that Hutton's irresponsible conduct is getting him into a muddle where something is certain to go wrong. Then piquancy becomes tragedy when his wife dies. Hutton is accused of killing her . . . but what has actually happened? In a four-sided situation, what is the answer?

Characters: Keeping the Pattern Simple

An instance like *The Gioconda Smile* underlines the fact that your characters must be firmly outlined and easily understood. Only a very few principals must carry the plot. Plenty of good short stories have only one, and beyond four the ground becomes dangerous. Hence, the central and determining conflict, whatever it is, may be more directly polarized than in a novel. Something closer to a naïve goodie–baddie clash may be admissible.

Conversely, the unheroic anti-hero is even trickier to manage, because in the limits of the short story he is apt to make such a negative impression. Possibly he stands the best chance as a comic figure. Wodehouse's Bertie Wooster is an anti-hero of a sort, with odd upper-class foretastes of Lucky Jim. But the durability of even the Bertie–Jeeves saga depends on the fact that it *is* a saga. None of its component short stories would have much impact alone, or be more than mildly funny alone.

In short stories, the enriched characterization which the novel gave to literature can occur only sketchily. There is no time to make characters complex, no time to show them developing. As the action progresses, the reader may learn unexpected things about them, and they may learn unexpected things themselves, which alter their lives. But the unfolding of characters must not go so far as to leave the reader wondering how he is meant to take them; and the utmost a short story can do in portraying change is to *catch it at the point of transition*, first indicating a long previous build-up, then describing the final push. Roald Dahl's *The Way up to Heaven*[1] tells how an elderly woman at last frees herself from an appalling husband. Hitchcock based a television film on the method, but the original story is a sick comedy of character, of a worm turning and being transformed in the process.

While the people must be presented simply, that is no reason to make them shallow, or to write stories devoid of insight, sympathy, charity, a sense of values. A short story can be a character study primarily. James Joyce called his own collection *Dubliners*, not *Scenes of Dublin Life*. Thurber's whimsical family sketches have no plot at all.

But even where character revelation is the chief aim, the rule of singleness still applies. A short story can reveal only one dominant trait in a person. It cannot paint a portrait. Muriel Spark's *You should have seen the Mess* is about a girl obsessed with tidiness and cleanliness, who misses endless opportunities for fruitful human relationships, because her attention is always taken up by the slightest sign of dirt or disorder. This is all we really know of her, and it would have been a mistake to say any more.

Beginnings

One at least of Edgar Allan Poe's precepts is better than his practice. *The beginning of the story should strike the keynote.* A reader should know quickly whether it is going to be grave, funny, satiric. He should also care. The opening sentences should hook him.

Today there is seldom justification for the slow run-in. Nor is there justification for a type of run-in which might, in an old-fashioned phrase, be called the General Enunciation—a preface that states the theme abstractly, or hovers round it. Poe himself started his extraordinary *Murders in the Rue Morgue* (in which he invented the detective story at one swoop) very unpromisingly indeed, but this was in an age when readers were used to the lengthy, leisurely approach.

> The mental features discoursed of as the analytical are, in themselves, but little susceptible of analysis. We know of them, among other things, that they are always to their possessor, when inordinately possessed, a source of the liveliest enjoyment . . .

He goes on like this for several pages before he comes to the point—that

---

[1] Published in the collection *Kiss Kiss*.

he is going to relate a feat of the analytic mind. Even then we do not immediately grasp that the story will concern the solution of a crime.

General prefaces of this abstract kind, if not always so daunting, remained in favour for many years. Their decline dates from about the turn of the twentieth century, when an author who wrote one was liable to feel self-conscious about it. Arthur Morrison, author of grimly realistic *Tales of Mean Streets* counted as one of the literary vanguard in his day. He could still begin with a preface, but he did it like this:

> It is a terribly easy thing to fall into—imperceptibly to glide into—evil-doing, and once embarked on the slippery descent, there is no telling how low one may descend. This, the moral of the story of Mr. Bostock, is, in accordance with modern practice, placed at the beginning of the story instead of at the end . . . Nowadays we get the moral over and out of the way as soon as possible and find it good riddance.

Nowadays, in the latter part of the century, we don't often put the moral in at all, and if we do put it in (possibly disguised as a remark by one of the characters), the opening is seldom the place.

The first line of the text which confronts the reader should usually be the first line of the story proper. It is best, as a rule, to start with a brief bit of stage-setting description, or instant narrative, or instant dialogue. Some authors like to hook the reader by giving the opening an epigrammatic or shock quality. 'Saki', for instance, in *Reginald on Besetting Sins*:

> There was once (said Reginald) a woman who told the truth. Not all at once, of course, but the habit grew upon her gradually, like lichen on an apparently healthy tree.

However, it is not necessary to be always as sharp as that. Here are three openings by Roald Dahl:

> Without in any way wishing to blow my own trumpet, I think that I can claim to being in most respects a moderately well-matured and rounded individual. I have travelled a good deal. I am adequately read. I speak Greek and Latin. I dabble in science. I have compiled a volume of notes upon the evolution of the madrigal in the fifteenth century. I have witnessed the death of a large number of persons in their beds; and in addition, I have influenced, at least I hope I have, the lives of quite a few others by the spoken word delivered from the pulpit.
>
> Yet in spite of all this, I must confess that I have never in my life—well, how shall I put it?—I have never really had anything much to do with women.
>
> (*Georgy Porgy*)

All day, in between serving customers, we had been crouching over the table in the office of the filling-station, preparing the raisins. They were plump and soft and swollen from being soaked in water, and when you nicked them with a razor-blade the skin sprang open and the jelly stuff inside squeezed out as easily as you could wish.

But we had a hundred and ninety-six of them to do altogether and the evening was nearly upon us before we had finished.

(The Champion of the World)

'Everything is normal,' the doctor was saying. 'Just lie back and relax.' His voice was miles away in the distance and he seemed to be shouting at her. 'You have a son.'

'What?'

'You have a fine son. You understand that, don't you? A fine son. Did you hear him crying?'

(Genesis and Catastrophe)

The first opening is a serio-comic self-disclosure by the narrator, partly intentional, partly not; it tells us plenty about him, and suggests what the atmosphere of the story is going to be. The second arouses curiosity: what is happening? The third simply establishes a situation in a few words, entirely through the characters. It seems a very familiar situation, and ordinary . . . but we shall soon know better.

Whatever else the first paragraphs do, they should convey information. The reader should be given answers to a few elementary questions —'what', 'where', 'when', and so forth—in enough detail to get his bearings. By all means hold something back to create curiosity and suspense, so long as you are sure that you are holding the reader too. But as soon as feasible he should know at least the main situation, and the state of play: how far it has gone.

How far should it have gone in order to get you smoothly on to the next stage? On that issue the safest guideline in plot construction— guideline, not rule—is to *begin with the situation as far advanced as you can manage* and still have a story that flows naturally and understandably. There may have been years of boiling-up beforehand, but don't attempt to cover the entire period. Reveal what has gone before in the course of the story. If that drives you into an excess of flashback or reminiscence, reconsider; you may have started *too* far on. But flashback has its legitimate uses. Maugham's *The Door of Opportunity* begins with a wife on the brink of leaving her husband. Most of the story is a flashback to events that led up to her decision. We return to the present and the showdown only in the last pages. Clumsy as the scheme may look, Maugham is right. The plot requires a long phase of happiness, evoked with a variety of details, and the ruin of this by a crisis, exposing an unsuspected flaw in the husband's character. If we did not know from the outset that the marriage was doomed, the story would be too slow in acquiring direction.

Movement Towards Story Climax

It is not actually impossible for a short story to move through as long a time as this marriage covers and longer, creeping towards an unforeseeable climax, without losing the reader. Where this can be done at all, selectivity is the key. If you accept the risk, you must traverse your period picking out only the few incidents that are strictly relevant to the theme. May Sinclair's psychological fantasy *Where their Fire is not Quenched* covers nearly the whole life of a woman, in chronological order, and pursues her beyond death. But it is not a compressed biography. We skip through the years from a youthful disappointed love, to a second disappointed love, to a sordid and stupid affair with a married man, to death and a hereafter where she reaps the results of self-devaluation. While an unprepared reader would go most of the way with only the dimmest foreshadowings, the selection of the three sexual passages in the woman's life makes it clear what the story is about. There is a definite clue that can be followed. Maugham could not have done the same with his doomed marriage, because he could not have been selective enough; it had to be described from too many aspects, with no pointers to the coming disaster.

One way or another, you must establish your situation and characters firmly. You must take them through a series of scenes which reveal them more fully, and develop, or disclose, the conflict you have set up. *The story must move.* You cannot afford to linger in paragraphs of description or reflection that take it no farther. As with the novel, so with the short story, only more so: the characters should tell their own tale *through action and dialogue.* If it is vital that John should have a red Volkswagen, it is better to say at some appropriate juncture, 'John's red Volkswagen drew up at the gate and he climbed out' than to say at some more or less arbitrary point, 'John had a red Volkswagen.'

To an extent rarely paralleled in novels, most short stories depend on suspense. The main impetus comes from a continuous, mounting tension in the mind of the reader. It may be acute, it may be gentle. He is led to expect that something interesting is going to happen; at the same time he is unable to guess what it will be. The extreme case is the straight whodunit, which is no story at all without the fulfilment of two conditions: (1) that we know the criminal will be unmasked, and (2) that we can't feel sure who he is in advance. But suspense, even in a detective story, can be created more subtly. Take *The Sign of the Broken Sword*, the best, though not the best-known, of Chesterton's Father Brown series. It poses the question 'What?' rather than 'Who?' and has an atmosphere rather than a plot. Yet Father Brown's gradual piecing-together of a hideous, unprovable crime is as charged with suspense as any process of detection.

A short story builds up to a climax which is the reason for its existence. This breaks the suspense, and ends the conflict we have been reading about, or at any rate shows how it is going to end. The remainder (if any) of the story is *dénouement* or unwinding.

The climax is generally more precise than it is in a novel. We know it when it happens. It may take the form of a revelation, as when a crime is solved. It may bring matters to a head with a 'punch line'. In Hugh Walpole's *The Silver Mask* a plausible young man with a hard-luck yarn insinuates himself into a rich woman's house, gets control of her affairs, takes advantage of her heart trouble to shut her up in a bedroom, and finally announces: 'You're too ill, I'm afraid, ever to leave this room again.'

Endings

A story can end on the note of climax, with no subsequent unwinding. It can stop short with a speech or incident that leaves a reader to imagine the rest. One that came out in a newspaper many years ago (I forget the author) consisted entirely of a monologue by a husband just home from work. The wife said nothing, except for a few implied monosyllables, but the husband's last line was: 'Whatever are you doing with that bread-knife, darling?' End of story.

Another type of abrupt conclusion, with less of the what-came-next implication, is the 'surprise' ending. This is a matter of degree rather than kind. Every ending should be a surprise in the sense that the reader cannot anticipate it. A twist or jolt of some sort is practically essential. In Ray Bradbury's science-fiction story *The Rocket Man* we follow the comings and goings of an astronaut, and the vague anxieties of his wife, with no sense of a plot taking shape. At last he is killed by falling into the sun. We are a few sentences from the end; what can possibly emerge? Then the wife realizes that henceforth, on every fine day, she will have to endure the sight of the sun.

However, an ending has the true 'surprise' quality when the reader is either puzzled or actively (though fairly) misled, and then, at the last moment, learns what has really been going on. O. Henry was famous for his surprise endings. They are pure plot-twists, of very unequal strength. Some remain models of their kind, unpretentious, but adroit and amusing. Others are anti-climactic. We either see them coming or don't get excited when they come. In one of his stories, a young man gets an unhoped-for chance to propose to a girl when their cab is held up in a traffic jam. After sundry romantic comments, it transpires that his father paid the drivers of several other vehicles to cause the jam. Not only is the surprise feeble in itself (we know all along that the father is rich and crafty), O. Henry drags it out through a ponderous paragraph of details on how much was paid to whom. The story is a warning: if you can't pull it off slickly and quickly and with a genuine sparkle, don't try. A more profound surprise ending is the surprise explanation. Ambrose Bierce's *An Occurrence at Owl Creek Bridge* describes an experience which sounds more and more bizarre until we realize, in the last sentence, that it is a series of images flashing through a hanged man's mind, in the moment between falling and dying. Angus Wilson's *Mummy to the Rescue*[1] appears to be about a child. At the end the character turns out to be adult, and everything takes a new complexion.

To withhold the crucial fact, and finally release it so that the reader goes back and reconsiders—this technique can give surprise a literary function going deeper than entertainment. It is difficult to handle. If the withheld fact is big enough to cause a shock and transform the picture, the story may be hard to make intelligible without it, even in a deceptive way. If it is trivial, and deferred solely for the sake of a trick ending, the reader may feel let down. Thus it might be possible to invert Angus Wilson's idea of the 'child' being revealed as an adult, but it would be merely tiresome to do this by describing a 'he' and 'she' apparently piloting an aircraft, and revealing at the end that they are children playing with a toy one.[2]

When the climax and resolution are reached, whether surprising or not, the reader must be clear what has happened. The outcome need not always be as clear-cut as it is (for example) in a detective story. There may be a residual speculation, a feeling that the situation has further kicks in it. The characters may be left in a state of doubt or delusion. Even so, the further potentialities must be easy to infer; the nature of the doubt or delusion must be plain. A story must not close in utter bafflement. One of the few exceptions is the horror story. Semi-rational 'explanations' of hauntings or kindred matters are apt to irritate. The finest stories—such as Algernon Blackwood's *The Wendigo*, John Metcalfe's *The Double Admiral*—run their whole course in a deepening ambiguity which is never dispelled. The climax is the dawning realization that there is no answer, a realization which the rest of the story confirms. It might be argued, however, that this absence of an answer has a horrible clarity of its own.

The resolution itself—the unravelling, if any, after the climax—is best kept brief. A mystery story may require an explanation, a confession, or a sorting-out or epilogue of some other kind. As a rule, however, the signing-off should be rapid. The story may close with an echo of the beginning; perhaps a return to the setting of the first scene, or a remark that strikes the opening note with a difference. A character may

---

[1] Published in the collection *Such Darling Dodos*.
[2] As a matter of fact, the trick of the person-who-turns-out-to-be-a-child has been used at least twice in successful popular songs. But the verbal jokes (so far as they mattered at all) depended on knowing, not on being surprised.

make a comment that relates the action to life-as-a-whole—a general observation, a hint at the future.

At the end of Hemingway's *Fifty Grand*, a boxer, by unaccustomed quick-wittedness during a fight, has thwarted a lucrative scheme to fix the result.

> He lies there, his eyes are open now. His face has still got that awful drawn look.
> 'It's funny how fast you think when it means that much money.' Jack says.
> 'You're some boy, Jack,' John says.
> 'No,' Jack says, 'it was nothing.'

Or the end may be a gesture or speech that clinches the climax, drives the point home, sets the seal on what has passed. After the sinister young man in *The Silver Mask* has told his victim that she is trapped in the room for keeps, he goes out, 'gently closing the door behind him'.

At any rate the last lines should be functional. The story may leave the reader with something to ponder, but it must not seek to convey this through an added miniature essay, tailing off into anti-climax. Nor should it expire slowly with an equivalent of the old marrying-off chapter, verbosely disposing of all the characters. A diminuendo or atmospheric fade-out will sometimes work, but it is most likely to succeed, if at all, in the ampler kind of story bordering on the 'long–short,' such as Walter de la Mare's *All Hallows*.

Reading and Practice

General advice on models to study is not easily given. Everyone who has read a fair number of short stories will have favourite authors of his own. Still, in the pre-1914 period there are names that stand out beyond all challenge. Here are a few . . .

Guy de Maupassant and Anton Chekhov are among the indisputable great. It is de Maupassant, rather than Poe, who first strikes the modern note. Chekhov is the subtler of the two. His stories have an air of vagueness and indecision which is deceptive.

O. Henry, old-fashioned in his manner, remains admirable for skill in plotting and sympathetic humour. He shows how an attitude of mind can go far to make an author attractive. Often he has a touch of that intriguing, elusive 'good bad' quality.

Rudyard Kipling is a far more interesting and offbeat writer than people who never read him are apt to think: sometimes marvellous, sometimes opaque, sometimes frankly bad, and strong in fields not always associated with him, such as terror and nightmare.

H. G. Wells wrote numerous short stories in his early career. Most of these are pioneer science-fiction. The science is out of date, the best of the stories have an evergreen verve. Incidentally Wells's own favourite among them was *The Man who could Work Miracles*, which is pure light-hearted fantasy. He may have been proud of its ingenious twist; if so, justifiably.

'Saki' (H. H. Munro) resembles O. Henry in being a short-story writer predominantly, and also in making his impression partly through a sustained attitude, though his own is almost the opposite of O. Henry's. His stories are masterpieces of compact statement, sardonic, and often cruelly funny.

Since the First World War the flood of stories has been so copious that it is hardly practicable to pick out a few authors and call them classics. Aldous Huxley, Somerset Maugham, Ernest Hemingway, Angus Wilson, Sean O'Faolain, Muriel Spark, Roald Dahl, Ray Bradbury—these (a most arbitrary choice) will do to go on with. You must find your own way. Among the best writers there are anti-models as well as models: that is, there are some whose effect depends so much on a personal style that you can't learn from them except in the most general way, because the only learning would be attempted imitation. Two outstanding anti-models are Wodehouse and Chesterton. Read them for delight rather than instruction.

Short-story writing can be approached more systematically than novel-writing. The unit of composition is so much smaller and easier to think about. When you read a short story, study its construction: how the author gets it moving, how he gives information, how the suspense builds up, when precisely the climax comes. Criticize it. Does it flag anywhere? Are all the details relevant? Does it start where it ought, and stop where it ought? Is the end unpredictable, but clear and satisfactory when you get to it? Can you accept the characters? If you feel industrious, keep a notebook and summarize the stories you read.

In writing your own, remember the importance of having the whole scheme in your head before you begin. You may then find that the actual writing comes in a rush. That is well enough, but beware of supposing that the job is done when the last word is on paper. Put the script away for a week or so, then take it out, read it again, revise. Try reading it aloud to a friendly but critical hearer, real or imagined. Picture yourself listening to it on sound radio. Would it hold you, and could you follow it? (Not a universal test, but sometimes a good one.)

If there is one golden rule for short stories, it is the rule of economy. The unkind advice to 'murder your darlings' is more apposite here than in any other form of writing. Whenever you feel specially pleased with a sentence, regard it with the deepest distrust. You are in danger of putting it in for its own sake and not the story's. If you see the slightest ground for thinking it unnecessary, discard it.

Chekhov gave another piece of ruthless advice. It was perhaps needed more often in his time than in ours, but it is still valuable. *When you have finished—or rather, when you think you have finished—cross out the beginning and the end.* Don't take this maxim too literally, but digest it as a fair statement of the spirit in which you ought to work.

Exercises

1. Read as many as you can of the following short stories: Guy de Maupassant, *The Necklace*; Anton Chekhov, *Gooseberries*; O. Henry, *The Gift of the Magi*; Rudyard Kipling, *At the End of the Passage*; Somerset Maugham, *The Alien Corn*; D. H. Lawrence, *The Rocking-Horse Winner*; Evelyn Waugh, *Mr. Loveday's Little Outing*; Ray Bradbury, *The Veldt*.

   (*a*) Decide which you like best. Write two pages saying why. Pick out things the author has done which supply useful hints to other short-story writers.
   (*b*) Decide which you like least. Write two pages saying why you don't like it. Pick out things the author has done which, in your opinion, warn other short-story writers what *not* to do. (Make allowances for changes in taste and reading habits.)

2. Write the first 150 words or so, and the last 150 words or so, of a short detective story. Then write a summary of what happens between, connecting your beginning and ending logically.

3. Write the first two paragraphs of a short story told by the chief character. Get the reader interested through this character's self-revelation, rather than through anything that actually happens (as in *Georgy Porgy*, page 145).

4. Re-tell the biblical parable of the Prodigal Son (*Luke* xv: 11–32), as a short story. Give it either an ancient or a modern setting, whichever you prefer. But tell it in a modern style, and from the point of view of either (*a*) the *elder* son, or (*b*) one of the Prodigal Son's girl-friends.

CHAPTER THIRTEEN

PLAYS

The Theatrical Medium

Many of the principles governing fiction apply to plays as well. Fiction is story-telling through narrative; drama is story-telling through directly presented action. While *avant-garde* productions may diverge from this norm, drama could not exist if the norm were not there.

We can make the parallel, and the contrast, more specific. A full-length play is longer than a short story (try some comparisons in print for yourself), yet writing one is more like writing a short story than a novel. In a play there is a similar need for unity, sharpness, and the right kind of clarity. Sub-plots and digressions, though somewhat more feasible, must be kept severely within bounds. Also, there is a similar need to economize and cut. Plays are closer to short stories because of the amount of ground they can cover and the way in which they must cover it. (Novels, of course, can be dramatized, but only by a highly selective treatment.)

As when we surveyed the short story after the novel, so now in surveying drama after fiction-in-general, we must ask chiefly: how is dramatic writing different? What are its special features?

Dr. Johnson expressed a view echoed by Maugham, who was successful himself in both media. Drama, they asserted, is the easier art, more suitable for beginners, because it is essentially talk, whereas fiction is essentially narrative. Johnson's exact words are: 'It is much more easy to form dialogues than to contrive adventures.' True, as far as it goes. Most people can mock up a conversation of sorts, and even invent it as they go along. That is why extemporized drama is used in therapy, management teaching, and other non-literary fields, to enable patients and trainees to enact their problems instead of merely discussing them.

But this ease of improvisation is treacherous. If you attempt a play, rather than a short story or novel, the dialogue may pour out so effortlessly as to put you in much greater danger of imagining you have achieved something when you haven't. Hence you may be slower in attaining self-criticism, and coming to grips with the issues that determine success or failure. The flaw in the Johnson–Maugham view, if adopted by anyone with less than their talents, is the implication that talk constitutes drama. It doesn't.

So again, how does story-telling in drama differ? To begin with, we are dealing with an artistic form which is vastly senior to the novel and short story. It is rooted in a different society, pre-literate, and without the rising middle class that made modern fiction what it is. Attempts to divorce drama from its origins, and turn it into something as much like contemporary fiction as possible, have had only a partial success.

Origins of Drama

Drama is thought to have begun, in the western world, with dances and choral singing at Greek religious festivals. Those of the god Dionysus, or Bacchus, are usually credited with the major role. At some stage, probably in the sixth century BC, soloists took to advancing out of the chorus and reciting myths of the god. Presently they progressed to miming, and outright acting. In due course performances were scripted, and contests were held, with plays based on mythological themes in general. But serious Greek drama (tragedy in the original sense) always remained intensely stylized, a ritual with very little illusion of reality. The chorus sang songs only marginally related to the story; the actors wore masks and spoke in verse; violent action never took place on the stage—it was described by messengers in long, rhetorical speeches; and sometimes gods intervened. The principal tragic dramatists—Aeschylus, Sophocles, Euripides—presented traditional stories and characters in different ways, but never radically changed them. The one major exception is Aeschylus's *The Persians*, commemorating a recent war in which the author himself had fought. But even this has the apparatus of chorus, verse, messenger-speech, and the rest, with a ghost taking the place of a god.

A Social Art

Drama (and here is the point of this historical retrospect) began as a social art. Far back, there was probably a phase when most of the community took part in the singing and dancing, and no sharp distinction existed between performers and audience. Gradually that distinction took shape, and hardened. Yet at its apex of development, Greek drama was still participatory. The onlookers, though quiescent in their seats, were deeply involved. They still joined in with their emotions. The representation of a story which they knew, charged with religious or patriotic passion, stirred them and was expected to do so. Aristotle, in the first major work of literary criticism, speaks of tragedy as a spiritual experience, purging the emotions through pity and terror.

The Greek theatre, and the Roman theatre which followed its lead, did finally produce plays with invented plots and no stylized machinery. These were comedies. Comedy too had a religious birth, but it evolved further towards realism. The Roman farces of Plautus, however, still take place in a make-believe world of stereotyped characters, with masked actors talking in verse and stepping aside to address the audience.

After the post-Roman cultural gap, the European theatre had its second birth during the Middle Ages. Much the same things happened again in the context of another religion. In the towns of western Europe, the craftsmen's guilds celebrated Church festivals by staging plays based on the Bible and on legends of saints. Here also it was humour that finally led the way towards realism. The religious plays had scenes of comic relief, and in the sixteenth century authors began writing comedies with secular plots made up by themselves.

The extent to which drama retains the semi-magical aura of its infancy, even in the modern theatre, is open to dispute. But the first thing to understand is that however completely it seems to shed that aura, it never ceases to be social. If a play comes to life at all, on a real stage or screen, it is not simply its author's creation. It is a result of the joint efforts of many people besides: the producer, the financial backers, the players, the technicians . . . and the audience. All of them contribute and interact, all of them have to be considered.

After two and a half millennia, a play still achieves its effect through a collective spell such as no book can evoke. The onlookers are together, usually in a darkened room, cut off from the outer world. Something is going on in front of them that has a direct impact through eye and ear. As a rule they do not take part physically; yet in the live theatre, their reactions (laughter of the right sort, laughter of the wrong sort, attentive silence, bored restlessness) have a crucial bearing on the atmosphere and the final product. An audience can alter the nature of a play. In 1934, a would-be serious drama entitled *Young England* turned out to be so full of unintended humour that the cast took to speaking their lines for laughs, with audience participation, and it became a popular success as a comedy.

The Author's Attitude

Hence, the author who tackles drama needs to get it into his head, as soon as he can, that he is not holding forth alone on a printed page. Merely getting his play as far as a theatre will raise numerous queries as to who-likes-what, who-will-finance-what, who-will-pay-to-see-what —queries apt to be far more complex and personal than the corresponding ones raised by books. Then, when the play goes into casting and rehearsal, the author will probably find that it slips out of his hands and he becomes curiously unimportant. The producer who transforms the play altogether, in the manner of Joan Littlewood, is an exception; but there is likely to be plenty of mauling and re-interpretation. When the players begin to speak the lines, and work out the action, the author will discover many things in his script (virtues, with any luck, as well as failings) which he never suspected.

As a dramatist, then—if that is your ambition—you must grasp from the outset that unless you are quite extraordinary, you will not so much be writing plays as writing rough drafts which plays can be made from.

You must learn special kinds of adaptation to context, going beyond those I recommended for writers in general; and you must study, more carefully than in other media, how to adapt without surrendering what is vital.

Obviously you will always aim to submit a script that is as nearly satisfactory as possible; as close as possible to a finished play. Hence you must think theatrically. You are not telling the story directly, but through characters who will be impersonated by actors. Hence you must make these characters tell their own tale, to an even greater extent than in fiction, and give the actors who will play them the fullest scope for creative interpretation. Draw a plan of your set, and, as you write, imagine the actors moving about on it.

You have several manifest advantages. The audience will see and hear your characters as if they were real, and the cast's abilities may lend them a stature and colour which you could never have supplied through your own words. Plays, in fact, are sometimes written for particular players, whom the author knows to be well qualified to make such-and-such a character live. Shaw wrote *St. Joan* for Sybil Thorndike.

You also have disadvantages. An audience can never be allowed more than a moment to pause and think, and it can't go back to re-read. Bad acoustics or coughing may impede communication. So you have to write with these hazards in mind, and also with an eye to various details which don't arise in print. (For example, have you given all your characters names which are easy to catch at some distance, easy to tell apart, easy to remember?) Furthermore, you can't supplement the dialogue and stage business by addressing the audience yourself. Nor can you describe anything, as you can on paper. Description in play-writing is confined to stage directions. The audience doesn't read these, and they may or may not emerge from the mill of production with the results you planned. The efforts of a few dramatists (A. A. Milne, for instance) to control performance closely through very copious directions are better not copied.

Once again: it is normally as a social thing, an outcome of co-operation by author and producer and actors and others, that a play comes to life. Rigid, line-by-line regulation through stage directions, if insisted upon, is likely to inhibit this natural growth.

How the Theatre Affects Story-telling

Drama moved farthest from its ritual origins, and closest to modern fiction, in the last quarter of the nineteenth century. Authors such as Henry Arthur Jones and A. W. Pinero (with counterparts in other countries) were writing 'well-made' plays with characters not wildly unlike actual people, and prose dialogue not wildly unlike actual talk. The set and costumes were realistic, the plots were entertaining. An illusion of reality, or of reality somewhat enhanced, was now at last the watchword. Despite much that has happened since—which will be noted in its place—the commercial and amateur theatres are still not immeasurably remote from Pinero's. Suppose, for the moment, that we take the conventional type of play, which is as near to ordinary fiction as drama ever is, and examine the differences in that setting (with sidelights from other sources, such as Shakespeare, where apposite).

We could go far towards summing up in one sentence. *Plays are like stories in books or magazines, only more so.* Because of the theatrical spell, the onlooker is more closely involved. He is more strongly drawn to identify with characters he can see. He is more intensely keyed-up than a reader, less equable, more liable to swing between tension and relaxation; he is readier to jump, readier to laugh. And the theme should be handled in that spirit. Everything we traced in fiction—situation, conflict, suspense, climax—must be built up similarly, but with a constant awareness that they seldom work in the theatre exactly as they do in print.

Openings

Let us begin at the beginning. The opening of a play, like that of a short story, should strike the prevailing note and suggest the mood. The first few minutes should convey the main features of the situation. But the author has to do these things through action, dialogue, scenery, without speaking in his own person; and the psychological hazards are different.

For example, you would be unwise to start on a high note, with an immediate dramatic scene or an intense atmosphere. You won't be able to keep it up. After the shock, the audience will relax too much and momentum will slacken when it shouldn't. John van Druten, a dramatist who achieved success rather slowly, used to recall a mistake he made in one of his apprentice efforts. When the curtain rose, a woman was standing with a gun over the body of a man she had shot. Nothing could come after that but a let-down from which the play never recovered. The opening should strike the keynote, but not with an instant *fortissimo*; the first minutes should enable the theatrical spell to take a firmer hold and grow more compelling. A favoured and good technique, used in *St. Joan*, is to start with a conversation that builds up to the entry of a major character.

Then there is the notorious problem of telling the audience what it has to know. In the Elizabethan theatre, as in the Greek, it was allowable to open with a character simply coming forward and talking. Shakespeare did this in *Richard III*, though he refined his methods later. As drama evolved towards the illusion of reality, exposition could no longer be so direct. It had to be disguised; and with the sharpened alertness which the theatre promotes, disguise grew ever more difficult. Sheridan, in *The Critic* (1779), is already making fun of informative pseudo-dialogue, with a satiric wit that is still a warning. A blank-verse play about the Armada is being rehearsed. Sir Walter Raleigh and Sir Christopher Hatton have entered.

Sir W You know, my friend, scarce two revolving suns,
    And three revolving moons, have closed their course
    Since haughty Philip, in despite of peace,
    With hostile hand hath struck at England's trade.
Sir C I know it well.
Sir W Philip, you know, is proud Iberia's king!
Sir C He is.

After several further exchanges in the same style, an onlooker murmurs: 'As he knows all this, why does Sir Walter go on telling him?'

Why indeed? Such lines might still get by so long as the theatre was accepted as a make-believe world governed by its own rules. But with the rise of realism, authors found themselves hemmed in ever more closely. Ibsen leads into *A Doll's House* (1879) by having Nora talk to a friend whom she hasn't seen for years. Such conversations, occurring (so to speak) under a microscope, can seldom be made to sound convincing. Some authors have taken the bull by the horns and made one of the characters actually say, 'Why are you telling me all this?'—which is honest, but no solution.

Within the limits of conventional drama as defined, there is no good alternative to feeding information in gradually, planting each item so that it sounds natural when it comes. Dialogue is of course the main method, but much can be done visually. You can convey plenty about the family that inhabits a living-room by your choice of furniture, colour scheme, pictures on the wall and books on the shelves. One practical consideration in favour of the gradual feed-in is that when the curtain goes up, and for a little while afterwards, the audience will still be settling down and late-comers will still be arriving. Hence, too much vital information should not be packed into the opening dialogue. But visual communication through scenery and props can begin at once. And this can happen again in each new scene. Act 2 of J. B. Priestley's *Time and the Conways* takes place in the same room as Act 1, but changes in the wallpaper and furnishings show that a long time has passed.

Holding It Together

When the action is fairly launched, it has different laws of motion from those of fiction. Drama, like the short story, needs to be concentrated and held together, but it has its own ways of cohering. Misguided attempts to bind it in with rules account for the artificiality of the classic French dramatists, such as Racine, in contrast with Shakespeare. Owing to a misunderstanding of Aristotle, the theory of the 'Three

Unities' took a grip on the French theatre which was hardly to relax till Victor Hugo's *Hernani* (1830). Besides the unity of interest and theme which any story requires, it was maintained that the whole action must be completed in a single day (unity of time), with no change of scene (unity of place).

'Regular' drama thus constricted produced a few masterpieces— Racine's *Phèdre* is the best known—but by the time realistic theatre arrived, the rigid frame had fallen apart. The reason for recalling the Unities here is that it is helpful to appreciate what they were intended to do, and understand why they are not necessary in order to get it done.

The true source of the concentration which drama needs is the theatrical spell itself. We know, in practice, that audiences can accept a play covering a long period, with many different scenes. Breaks in chronology and shifts of locale fit into the pattern of controlled tension and relaxation which all competent plays involve. Where the advocates of the Unities went astray was in thinking that any mental adjustment, any change of mood or focus, must snap the spell. For the same reason they disapproved of comic relief in tragedy. Actually, however, the spell should be potent enough to hold everything. If it is (and that, of course, is the great 'if'), a play can safely zigzag and jump about more than a short story, and handle more characters and motifs. That is why there is no artistic objection to intervals between acts, or to comic relief in tragedies.[1]

A famous instance of the latter, and a target for criticism even from some of Shakespeare's warmest admirers, is the Porter scene in *Macbeth* after the murder of Duncan. This is not very amusing; it is a series of topical jokes, now dead, with an underlying irony; but it has a proper function. It allows a release of held breath, not invalidating the mood of the play, but making it possible for another wave of tension to gather and lift.

The Logic of a Play

Waves, be it observed, have direction as well as altitude. When near a beach, they roll towards it. The strongest constituent of a *sustained* theatrical spell is a sense of logic, of inexorable movement towards a climax. This is even more important than it is in fiction. Other elements are often less so.

Thus, the same factors that work against the too-contrived informative opening also work against the too-contrived plot. When the theatre was still a fairy-realm, an author could bring his play to a close

---

[1] There may be practical objections, especially to intervals. At a revival of a certain ill-starred production, I heard an usher explaining that there would be no interval, 'because if the audience had a chance to go out we'd never get them back'.

by having X turn out to be Y's long-lost brother. With the advent of a modicum of realism, such devices quickly became a joke, and even skilful plotting grew more and more difficult to employ seriously. Old-style 'complications' hung on into the twentieth century chiefly in farce—*Arsenic and Old Lace*, for instance.

Apart from special cases such as crime thrillers, an inner logic going deeper than the plot-mechanism is usually the life of a play. It arises from a situation-with-characters, which is firmly established and conserved by the theatrical spell; which itself enhances the spell as it develops, with snowballing effect; and which is clearly *going somewhere*. Galsworthy's *Loyalties*, a tragedy of anti-Semitism in high society, begins with an upper-class house party. One of the guests is a rich, socially pushing young Jew, who jars on the others and can never quite manage to be a gentleman in their sense. A sum of money is stolen from his room in circumstances suggesting that one of the 'gentlemen' is the thief. Take it from there.

Logic applies to comedy, even farce, as it does to tragedy. A surprising amount of farce depends on making some crazy assumption and then tracing its logical consequences. Most of the Marx Brothers' films are touched off by the appointment of the Groucho character to a responsible job for which he is insanely unfitted and which he wouldn't, in real life, have got.

This point brings us back again, from another angle, to the problem of how a play should open. The essential situation and hence its logic (not, of course, all the details) should be established quickly. Even more often than in short stories, therefore, it is wise to start at a late phase in the developments. A late start, with the situation ripening towards a crisis, minimizes drift and uncertainty. Bernard Shaw drew attention to this practice as one of Ibsen's virtues. Ibsen ended, perhaps, by overdoing it; his final plays seem to happen when the story is over, and to consist largely of conversations about the past. But his main lesson, rubbed in by Shaw, has not been lost on later authors. Thus Herman Wouk's dramatization of his own novel *The Caine Mutiny* handles the substance of a long story by starting with the court-martial at which the alleged mutineers are tried. The story comes out in the hearings. Comparison with the original reveals that the play begins when the novel is three-parts over.

Once the logic is clear, it must develop decisively. The normal seesaw of tension and relaxation will allow the action to progress through a series of sub-climaxes, as a short story cannot always do. A natural place for one sub-climax is at the end of the first act, when the curtain falls for the interval. As the sub-climaxes cast their shadows before, and as the main climax looms cloudily in the distance, the audience may form fairly definite anticipations. These are apt to be more precise than in fiction, because the drama is more vivid and pointed. It has been said that if you have a gun on the stage, the audience will expect to see it fired, and feel cheated if it isn't.

Many plays, in fact, build up so as to foreshadow what has been called a *scène à faire* or obligatory scene. Their logic tends towards a well-defined climax which the dramatist can hardly avoid writing. The main suspense arises from waiting for this scene, and wondering how it will resolve the conflict or conflicts. It is difficult to cite examples, because any play that is familiar enough to cite is too familiar to evoke much suspense; one already knows how it ends. But try to picture yourself at the first performance of *Hamlet* or *A Doll's House*. Eventually Hamlet will kill the King, or try to—but under what circumstances and with what result? Eventually Nora will have a showdown with her husband—but will they come to a better understanding, or will the marriage break up? The shock of *A Doll's House*, when first staged in England, was due to the audience foreseeing the showdown but tacitly assuming that it must turn out in the husband's favour.

Dialogue and Action

As a dramatist, then, you have to present a situation and work it out to its end, using dialogue and action almost exclusively. To say this may suggest that writing a play is rather like writing a short story under tighter limitations. But the loss of the nuances of description and style can be made up in other ways. Action and dialogue on the stage are not the same as they are on paper. They have greater potentialities.

Actors can do things which it would be hopelessly tedious, and perhaps too confusing, to describe. The boundless possibilities of visual impact, expression, dexterity, and timing supply the dramatist with resources which the writer of fiction lacks. One of the obligatory scenes we just glanced at, the climax of *Hamlet*, can be staged in a variety of ways, any one of which has more in it than a narrator could keep pace with. Its complexity and tempo mark it as the product of a theatrical mind; it is not dramatized fiction.

The difference is even plainer in comic scenes. There could be no narrative version of Charlie Chaplin . . . or of the unassuming but funny stage farce associated with Brian Rix. More is involved than the star quality of a single comedian. Take any scene that depends on swift interlocking movements by several people, such as the coke-stealing episode in Arnold Wesker's *Chips with Everything*. Read the stage directions for this and turn them into a narrative. Could a reader follow it throughout in his mind's eye, and would it amuse or interest him if he could? The effect is peculiar to a medium that presents action directly.

Dialogue, too, is more than the dialogue of fiction. Not only can it gain weight from the actors' voices and intonations, it can be made more forceful, more studied in itself, without sounding improbable.

It needs to be, partly because it will soon drag if it isn't, partly because the audience can't go back to re-read; and in practice, it can be.

However realistic the play, the theatrical heightening remains. Even quite pedestrian sentences mean more, and the audience expects them to mean more, and will be disposed to infer the maximum meaning from them. A few words will suggest a character, with what has been called 'theatrical shorthand'. Show a man refusing a drink twice and he has labelled himself a total abstainer.

Because of this atmospheric impression of charged lines and sharpened words, stage brilliance is acceptable, even in drama that does appear more or less realistic. Oscar Wilde was a master of witty speech, and he put it in fiction as well as plays; but it has a much happier ring in *The Importance of Being Earnest* than it has on the lips of Lord Henry Wotton in *The Picture of Dorian Gray*. Shaw following on from Wilde, and Noël Coward after his own fashion, demonstrate the same truth—that under the theatrical spell, we can listen to people talking as people manifestly don't talk, yet without feeling that it makes them unreal.

A further proof of the capacity of stage dialogue is its power of assimilating epigrams, jokes, and other matter which would sound unnatural in fiction. With epigrams, Wilde is the classic case. As for jokes, here is one that may serve as a test.

A pious Catholic, making a retreat at a monastery, confessed to the abbot that his besetting sin was pride.

'Can you recommend a good book on humility?' he asked.

'Oh, yes,' replied the abbot. 'I know the very best book on humility. As a matter of fact, I wrote it myself.'

Observe how pleasantly that exchange would go into a play, and how artificial it would look in a novel.

Exhaustion and Renewal: the Rebirth of Ideas

So much for the conventional theatre, as it flourished till about the middle of the twentieth century. It flourishes still, but not unchallenged. At the very least, the challenges are a reminder that drama raises profounder issues. The rest of this chapter must be taken up with talking-points and thinking-points rather than advice.

In Greek tragedy, let us recall, there was scarcely any pretence of realism. Song and dance, a chorus partly aloof, explanatory prologues and messenger-speeches, poetry—all these composed an art-form that never ceased to be a ritual. Since the plays were based on well-known, richly significant themes, the actors' lines had reverberations going beyond what they said. Serious ideas could be aired freely, as in Sophocles's *Antigone*, which asserts the rights of the individual against the state. A mysterious awe brooded over the action.

The Christian play-cycles of the Middle Ages were homelier and less polished, yet they had many of the same qualities. In the secular theatre which Elizabethan England evolved, it is worth noticing what altered and what did not. Verse remained; there was still no triumph of realism in that respect. Nor was there much of an approach to it in the stage sets, which were simple all-purpose structures. What did happen was a partial de-mystification. Sacred, beloved legends gave way to invented plots with crude human motivations, such as revenge and ambition.

Shakespeare followed the fashion; yet one of his distinctive features is a very interesting conservation of mystery. Repeatedly he takes over an existing story with a shallow, quasi-realistic motive, and cuts out the motive. The pre-Shakespearean *Hamlet* was a simple revenge-play, in which Hamlet was slow and circuitous about killing the King because the King had a bodyguard and was hard to get at. Shakespeare removes the bodyguard, making the task physically easy, and Hamlet's delay and self-reproach thereby acquire new dimensions. The play opens into psychological depths, and means more than it says.

Through the civilized prose and plot-construction of Congreve and Sheridan (with kindred developments in other countries), the drama moved into the age of realism; or rather, the illusion-of-reality age, in which the Joneses and Pineros laid the foundations of the theatre we have been analysing. Late-Victorian producers staged Shakespeare himself with elaborate scenery. The audiences of the time were allured by spectacular effects—waterfalls with real water, sieges with real cannon, chariot-races. David Belasco, author of *Madam Butterfly* in its pre-operatic form, carried this sort of realism to a high pitch. Plays, generally speaking, meant just what they said and had no sub-surface implications. Religion, if introduced, was respectable and without mystery. Ideas were avoided as being controversial, liable to offend, and poor box-office.

From Realism to Seriousness

The successive revolutions which transformed that state of affairs were due to a number of pressures. But in assessing what happened, and is still happening, we must draw a distinction. Some of the new movements were absorbed—and have stayed absorbed—with no break in the essential scheme. Others have disrupted it. Generalizations that span the lifetime from Pinero to Wesker do not fit Samuel Beckett.

The ponderous appeal of mere spectacle succumbed to two adverse factors. First, Ibsen proved that a hint can outdo a mock-up. The riot in *An Enemy of the People* takes shape more menacingly as a stone crashing through a window than it would if enacted by a mob of extras. Secondly, when the cinema showed that it could do spectacle better than the live theatre, the live theatre practically gave up competing. Meanwhile a new wave of Shakespearean producers, led by Poel and Granville-Barker, learned to scrap the scenery and restore

Elizabethan simplicity; while Gordon Craig broke with photographic realism in stage design.

More and more, the illusion of reality focused on human relationships. Inside that field there was a rebirth of ideas. Ibsen had already assailed middle-class values, and revived symbolism in *The Wild Duck*. Now Shaw expounded Socialism and other doctrines. Galsworthy wrote plays showing the collision of rival ideals—*The Skin Game*, for example —with the curtain falling on an unaswerable question. Sherriff took a sad look at war in *Journey's End*.

One outstanding result, which now seems permanent, was a shift in the relationship between the theatre and actual society. Formerly content to lag behind current *mores*, the theatre, from Shaw onward, gradually began showing signs of an aspiration to lead. Here is a piece of dialogue from Shaw's *You Never Can Tell* (1897).

M'Comas.   There is only one place in all England where your opinions would still pass as advanced.

Mrs. Clandon. The Church, perhaps?

M'Comas.   No; the theatre.

In the same spirit Maugham estimated that the theatre was always thirty years behind the times.

The reversal which Shaw pioneered, and Maugham did not, was belated; but finally it came, partly through the rise of successful dramatists from class levels previously silent. In England, after John Osborne's *Look Back in Anger* (1956), John Arden's *Serjeant Musgrave's Dance* (1960), and the left-wing plays of Wesker, an influential part of the theatre was no longer behind the times. It was in a state of persistent and strenuous effort to be ahead of them. This of course raised questions as to what you could get away with in a public performance. Any apostolate of progress or revolution demanded the flouting of every suburban inhibition, and for a while this was impracticable. With the waning of censorship in the later 1960s the battle was won, or appeared to be. Anything went. The only remaining enemy was saturation.

Modern Challenges

All these developments proved most amply that experiment and adventure could occur within the familiar dramatic frame. However, the twentieth-century upheaval has also imperilled the frame itself. It has restored—tentatively at least—the unrealistic language, the mystery, even the ritual quality, of the theatre of Greece. It has sacrificed the illusion itself in various ways, and undermined logic.

Realistic dialogue was a victim of its own success. Shaw raised it to such perfection that it had nowhere to go until the language altered. Moreover, because his characters said so precisely what they meant, they could never mean more than they said; and the hunger for lost mystery and subtlety took its revenge. While Shaw drifted towards a temporary eclipse, verse drama was revived by T. S. Eliot, Ronald Duncan, Christopher Fry. Long, unrealistic speeches became acceptable again, and actors ceased to feel uneasy delivering them. Also, thanks partly to Agnes de Mille's transformation of the musical show from *Oklahoma!* onward, plays could again become a mélange of song and dance as well as speech.

Once these changes were under way, the illusion of reality was expendable. Verse in itself tended to stress the gulf between a play and the actual world, and remind audiences that they were *not* watching reality. Bertold Brecht pursued this 'alienation effect', as he called it, much further. Once again people on the stage detached themselves like the Greek chorus (or unlike it) and commented on events. Plays with dialogue and action in the traditional form acquired characters who switched roles openly on the stage (like the Common Man in Robert Bolt's *A Man for all Seasons*) or moved from locale to locale and period to period with no change of set (as in Arthur Miller's *After the Fall*).

Experiments of the 1960s
The theatre of the 1960s also produced experiments in the opposite direction. Instead of emphasizing a play's separateness as a work of art, divided from the actual world by a barrier, some productions tried to abolish the barrier and bring actors and audience together in a single mêlée. 'Theatre in the round' favoured such attempts. There was a deliberate reversion here to primitive festival, and also to a more recent type of naïveté which has been made the subject of jokes, as in the story of the woman who called out from the gallery to Othello, 'But you great black fool, don't you see?' Some of the experimental companies would have been delighted to hear her. At a New York show entitled *Dionysius '69*, the actors invited the audience to come up and make love to them.[1]

[1] New ground is still waiting to be broken by anyone who will pursue this line further, more seriously, and fathom the social psychology of theatrical illusion. Recognition that a play is not life, that you don't shout advice to Othello, does not come instinctively. People are conditioned, and might be re-conditioned.

Chateaubriand records that as a child, in the 1770s, he knew puppet plays but not live ones. When he saw a performance with live actors, he watched the actors and thought they were the puppet-masters preparing. He waited and waited, increasingly surprised that they should discuss their private affairs so freely before an audience, and was bewildered in the end when no puppets appeared.

A producer once told me that when he took his players on a country tour, and they met local people after the performance, some of the villagers found it hard to adjust to the fact that the actors' relationships in real life were different from what they were on the stage.

Under such unsettled conditions the dramatic representation of experience has taken strange forms, sometimes brilliantly, sometimes dubiously. The 'Theatre of the Absurd', for instance, consciously defies normal coherence. Beckett's *Waiting for Godot* is an almost monomaniac build-up to an obligatory scene which doesn't come: Godot never arrives and the play is a riddle. *Oh, What a Lovely War* is an instance of a successful hybrid, a revue-documentary.

It would be futile to generalize in detail, or deduce rules from a situation that has fluctuated so restlessly. Each wave of experiment has brought gains to the drama. On the other hand, some of the alleged 'trends' and theatres-of-this-and-that have had far too much pretentiousness and sensationalism about them.

Perhaps the most useful moral to draw is one that can be drawn from a much-publicized 'trend' that began about 1968 and went on for some years—the trend towards nudity. As soon as the censors let this pass, it began to happen rather often. Clearly dramatists should be free to have their characters naked when they genuinely need to; this liberty is an unqualified advantage; and the rush of mere exploitation was an occupational hazard which the theatre could easily survive. As a trend, however, nudity contained its own piquant *reductio ad absurdum*. When people have taken all their clothes off, they can't take off any more. Therefore the process must have a limit, and cease to be radical or exciting. Though the limits of other 'trends' may be less obvious, they always exist. The best maxim for a writer is: 'Learn from them all, but keep your head.'

Earlier I suggested that if you want to write fiction, you should try to explain the secret of Sherlock Holmes. Now for a theatrical equivalent. Why do you think *Charley's Aunt* has gone on and on?

Exercises

1. Read three plays with 'messages'; Shaw's *Major Barbara*, Galsworthy's *The Skin Game*, Wesker's *Chips with Everything*. Which author do you think is the most successful in making his points dramatically? Do you feel that these plays are dated, or less effective, because today's issues are not the same?

2. Read three 'poetic' plays: W. B. Yeats's *The Countess Cathleen*, T. S. Eliot's *The Family Reunion*, Christopher Fry's *The Lady's Not For Burning*. These plays are very unlike each other. Do you think the poetic treatment—the use of verse, the sometimes non-realistic language—is justified in all three? If so, can you see anything which the plays have in common that justifies it?

3. Write one of the following scenes.

   (a) A husband tells his wife that he has lost his job through his own fault. (You can make him either admit responsibility or try to blame someone else.)

(*b*) A daughter tells her father that she is unwilling to take up a university place which is open to her. (Give her any motive you like, but make it clear to the audience.)

(*c*) A journalist, of either sex, tries to blackmail a dress designer, of either sex.

4. Choose one of the short stories in Exercise 1 at the end of Chapter Twelve, and outline a dramatization of it for the stage. Write the first two pages.

5. John Osborne's *Look Back in Anger* (1956) is often said to have given the English theatre a new direction. Read it, and see if you can understand why it had such an impact. Could you form any notion of a play which—if it were good enough—might mark a similar turning-point today?

CHAPTER FOURTEEN

POETRY

Attempting the Impossible

No advice can make you a poet if you aren't. Here the myth of the Muse rings truest. Homer's prayer to her prefaces what is still one of the greatest poems, the *Iliad*. But we do not know why she came when Homer prayed. The *Iliad* says nothing about her. We can read it through without being able to explain why it is poetry. Conversely, many alleged poems are optical illusions: they are only verse, competent or otherwise; and with these too, there may be nothing to show the reason.

As with authorship in general, so, supremely, with this form of it. Handbooks and discussions cannot give you a special vocation you haven't got. They can, however, help you to judge whether you have it, and cultivate the gift if you do.

Poetic Spontaneity

We may not be able to define poetry, yet we feel various things about it. As so often, while the feelings are sound, the way they express themselves is apt to be wrong.

Thus poetry is always felt to be a spontaneous art, and highly personal; not laboured, not like a scientific report. A computer can be programmed to put together verses that rhyme and scan. It couldn't— surely!—compose a genuine original poem.

Yet in fact, why not? Acquaintance with poets' rough copies and literary confessions will soon show that the romantic notion of poetry as a careless, undisciplined warble, or an inspired outpouring that goes straight on to the paper untinkered-with, is utterly false. Poems don't just happen. They are worked at like any other form of writing. Ben Jonson, indeed, quotes somebody's assertion that Shakespeare 'never blotted out a line'. But Jonson's comment is, 'Would he had blotted a thousand'; and the only bit of writing that looks like a Shakespeare manuscript (a scene in a play on which he may have collaborated) does show traces of second thoughts.

The rough copies of Alexander Pope are a shambles. Those of Keats are sometimes no better. Poe's cold-blooded account of how he constructed one of his best poems, *The Raven*, may be over-simplified and over-cynical yet is well worth reading. There is no doubt of the main fact. At the stage of actual composition, poetry can be as much a business of drafting and re-drafting, thinking and re-thinking, and sheer uninspired-looking assembly work, as the most laborious, plodding prose. If you try writing poetry and it does pour out easily, mistrust it. You may be under the same sort of delusion as the musician who takes drugs and thinks he is playing better than ever, when those who hear him know he is playing worse.

The mysterious, uncalculated effusion does occur, but not necessarily, perhaps not normally, in the writing. It is farther back, so to speak. It happens in the poet's mind. He feels a need or impulsion, and wrestles with his vocabulary till he has a pattern of words that satisfies the need, or carries the impulsion through to its term. Wordsworth brought spontaneity in at the right point in a famous sentence about poetry being a 'spontaneous overflow of powerful feelings,' taking its origin from 'emotion recollected in tranquillity.'

The Poetic Experience

'Emotion', though, is not quite specific enough. Great poetry can be written about (say) love-in-general—as by Shakespeare and Mrs Browning in their sonnets—but even so, the poet's insight comes from a particular love. What the poet 'recollects in tranquillity' is more than an emotion, it is an event or train of events that aroused it. The source of a poem, as of any piece of 'inspired' writing in our sense (page 111), is an *experience*: either personally undergone, or, as in *The Raven*, strongly imagined. The experience takes hold of the poet's mind and clamours to be communicated. This unforced welling-up of experience is the true spontaneity, in which, if ever, the Muse makes her visitation. As to the actual language, she may drop hints, but she seldom dictates in detail.

Almost any experience might create a poem, although an odd, very unfamiliar one would present problems. Browning conveys a simple experience in the song of naïve well-being which he gives to the Italian girl Pippa ('The year's at the spring, And day's at the morn . . .'). Keats is more thoughtful, but still quite simple, in his account of a personal literary revelation, *On First Looking into Chapman's Homer*. Milton's experience in *Paradise Lost* is long, complex, multiple, a living-through of the Christian explanation of the human condition. T. S. Eliot's in *The Waste Land* is a sombre meditation on modern society; he does not convey it in plain terms at all, but in a series of scenes, images, and symbols, 'objective correlatives' in his own phrase, which prompt the reader to reflect along the same line with the same emotions.

While almost any experience might create a poem, it does not follow that every successful communication of experience is poetry. Nor does communication become poetry merely by being personal or emotional. Millions of letters and telephone conversations prove the contrary daily. When a poet's experience makes its pressing demand on him, his special psychology casts it into a form which is unlike everyday communication in prose. Inspiration, as we defined it in Chapter Ten, clearly plays a major part. So does imagination. The two may be hard to distinguish. But the question now is: what happens? what makes the result special, and poetic?

Why Poetry Goes Beyond Verse

To begin with, can we define the difference between poetry and verse?

Verse alone does not make a poem, and we shall have to ask why not. But before doing so, we should appreciate that the ordinary person's ideas on this matter are more right than wrong. When most people think of poetry, they do think of verse—meaning conventional metre, rhyme, and so forth. Now admittedly poets can dispense with these; but they cannot dispense with what underlies them. At the basis of all poetry is *rhythm*—an audible pulsation, simple or complicated; a musical effect through words.

Rhythm

In the literature of most nations, verse comes earlier than prose. It is the rhythmic language that goes with song and dance. Also, for a people with no system of writing (or none that is widely used), it has the advantage of being easier to memorize.

The more polished verse of literate societies codifies rhythm, so to speak, giving it various forms, and subjecting it to rules. Classical Greek and Roman poets built up elaborate metres from prescribed arrangements of long and short syllables, like the bars of music. They added other, subtler rhythms—repetition of sounds, especially alliteration; refrains that brought the same line back at fixed intervals, like the chorus of a song. In English, most metres are different from the classical ones, and the rhythm comes mainly from the beat or stress, but the principles are much the same. English, in common with most modern languages, adds a further species of repetition which the Greeks and Romans never developed—the recurrence of sounds at the ends of lines. In other words, rhyme.[1]

Poetry cannot break away from verse altogether. A poet can do without rhyme; Shakespeare and Milton did. He can abandon fixed metre, in favour of what is called free verse; Walt Whitman did, T. S. Eliot did, and so, in various ways, have most twentieth-century poets from Auden and Spender onward. But even the freest verse still requires a feeling of rhythm in the background. Even if the beat of conventional metre goes entirely, a beat of phrasing and meaning must remain—a succession of impacts coming faster than those of prose, more insistently, with a more urgent pulse, and very likely some sort of pattern.

---

[1] For detailed information on verse-forms, see books by R. J. Brewer and E. Hamer in the reading list on page 254.

Without that, any writing which purports to be poetry is only prose chopped up.

Consider three specimens. Byron's *She Walks in Beauty* is a traditional anthology piece, in regular metre, rhymed throughout.

> She walks in beauty, like the night
>   Of cloudless climes and starry skies;
> And all that's best of dark and bright
>   Meets in her aspect and her eyes:
> Thus mellow'd to that tender light
>   Which heaven to gaudy day denies.
>
> One shade the more, one ray the less,
>   Had half impair'd the nameless grace
> Which waves in every raven tress,
>   Or softly lightens o'er her face;
> Where thoughts serenely sweet express
>   How pure, how dear their dwelling-place.
>
> And on that cheek, and o'er that brow,
>   So soft, so calm, yet eloquent,
> The smiles that win, the tints that glow,
>   But tell of days in goodness spent,
> A mind at peace with all below,
>   A heart whose love is innocent.

Hilaire Belloc's *Tarantella* has varying lines and irregular rhyme arrangements. But rhythm remains—is, in fact, the main secret of the poem. Some of the oddly placed capital letters may be meant as guides to the emphasis.

> Do you remember an Inn, Miranda?
> Do you remember an Inn?
> And the tedding and the spreading
> Of the straw for a bedding,
> And the fleas that tease in the High Pyrenees,
> And the wine that tasted of the tar?
> And the cheers and the jeers of the young muleteers
> (Under the vine of the dark verandah)?
> Do you remember an Inn, Miranda,
> Do you remember an Inn?
> And the cheers and the jeers of the young muleteers
> Who hadn't got a penny,
> And who weren't paying any,
> And the hammer at the doors and the Din?
> And the Hip! Hop! Hap!

Of the clap
Of the hands to the twirl and the swirl
Of the girl gone chancing,
Glancing,
Dancing,
Backing and advancing,
Snapping of a clapper to the spin
Out and in—
And the Ting, Tong, Tang of the Guitar!
Do you remember an Inn, Miranda?
Do you remember an Inn?

Never more;
Miranda,
Never more.
Only the high peaks hoar:
And Aragon a torrent at the door.
No sound
In the walls of the Halls where falls
The tread
Of the feet of the dead to the ground
No sound:
But the boom
Of the far Waterfall like Doom.

Finally, Dylan Thomas: the first and last stanzas of *Fern Hill*.

Now as I was young and easy under the apple boughs
About the lilting house and happy as the grass was green,
*   The night above the dingle starry,*
*   Time let me hail and climb*
*   Golden in the heydays of his eyes,*
And honoured among the wagons I was prince of the apple towns
And once below a time I lordly had the trees and leaves
*   Trail with daisies and barley*
*   Down the rivers of the windfall light.*

Nothing I cared, in the lamb white days, that time would take me
Up to the swallow thronged loft by the shadow of my hand,
*   In the moon that is always rising,*
*   Nor that riding to sleep*
*   I should hear him fly with the high fields*
And wake to the farm forever fled from the childless land.
Oh as I was young and easy in the mercy of his means,
*   Time held me green and dying*
*   Though I sang in my chains like the sea.*

Regular metre has gone. Rhyme has virtually gone; it survives only in faint echoes, at the ends of lines so far apart that we scarcely notice. The rhythm of the nine-line stanzas is complex and hard to schematize. Yet it is there. You could never run the lines together and pass the poem off as prose, to anyone with the slightest musical ear.

The Poetic Incantation

Why this prevalence of rhythm? To answer the question is to identify the first word which we can apply to poetic language in general. It is *incantatory*. If that term conveys a hint of primitive magic, I cannot help it. The hint is justified. In fact the great themes of ancient poetry, the myths, may well have arisen out of earlier magical rituals. But however that may be, the incantatory quality is present in all true poems. Byron's, above, is a kind of hymn; Belloc's (as the title implies) is a dance; Thomas's is a conjuring-up through images and a harmony of sound.

Poems are evocative. Some of the purest, most echo-arousing are songs and nursery rhymes. 'Oranges and lemons' accompanies a children's game and is almost nonsensical without it. Yet its list of old London churches, with the parallel phrasing and the recurrent 'bells', has a poignancy for the exile which is seldom surpassed. Rhythmic sound, incantatory magic stirring the depths of human nature, is inseparably bound up with poetic expression. This fact has received special emphasis in recent times through the revival of spoken poetry, notably by Alan Ginsberg and Christopher Logue.

Indeed there is great poetry which comes near to being incantation alone. Coleridge's *Kubla Khan* is the surviving remnant of a much longer poem which came to him in a dream or trance, but most of which he forgot. Though the existing fragment is full of reminiscences of his reading and his waking thoughts, these do not come through to us in any explicit message. What does come is a weird and haunting music, soaring, in the last eighteen lines, into a stratosphere of its own:

> *A damsel with a dulcimer*
> *In a vision once I saw:*
> *It was an Abyssinian maid,*
> *And on her dulcimer she play'd,*
> *Singing of Mount Abora.*
> *Could I revive within me*
> *Her symphony and song,*
> *To such a deep delight 'twould win me,*
> *That with music loud and long,*
> *I would build that dome in air,*
> *That sunny dome! Those caves of ice!*
> *And all who heard should see them there,*
> *And all should cry, Beware! Beware!*

His flashing eyes, his floating hair!
Weave a circle round him thrice,
And close your eyes with holy dread:
For he on honey-dew hath fed,
And drunk the milk of Paradise.

Clearly no poet should despise conventional verse. An ability to compose in it is almost a precondition of safely dispensing with it, if one chooses to do so. Moreover the essential need goes deeper than mastery of scansion and rhyming, valuable though that can be as a discipline. Rather, it is the necessity of learning to *think in rhythm.*

There is experimental evidence that this actually is a vital point. It has been found that practice in 'thinking in rhythm' is a quick and sure method of drawing out the poetic gifts of children. A primary school teacher once explained to me how she asked all the members of her class to write an original paragraph in prose, on some easy, familiar topic. Then they wrote it out again, broken into short lines. By this rearrangement she could induce a poetry-conscious mood. Next she asked them to write another original piece, but in lines immediately, without leading up through the prose stage. The result—sometimes— was a poem. Certainly the exercise could not be reversed, the lines could not be run together into natural prose. Once accustomed to composing in lines, but with no inhibiting fuss over formal metre, some of the children had begun to acquire a sense of rhythm and the poetic deployment of language. They handled words in different units, in a different atmosphere.

Christopher Searle's collection of children's poems *Stepney Words* (1971) arose out of his similar experiments teaching classes in the east of London. He used the beat of pop music to set the children's minds moving along the path he wanted. They worked in a free, sociable atmosphere, sometimes on a set theme, sometimes on themes of their own choosing, but always spontaneously and with no feeling that they were writing exercises.

Two of the resulting poems give contrasted views of the district. The first is by Diane Conlan.

I come from Stepney, lived there all me life
Loads of cheap markets
Bargains at half price
Jumpers and skirts, trousers cheap
All muddled up in any old heap.

Dirty old women, shouting out their wares
Everybody stinks, nobody cares
All dirty, greasy things bunged into bins
Stinkin' rotten hole is Stepney.

The second is by Rosemarie Dale.

> *I think Stepney is a very smokey place*
> *But I like it*
> *People in Stepney do things wrong*
> *But I like them*
> *Everything in Stepney has its disadvantages*
> *But I like it*
>
> *It does not have clean air like the country*
> *But I like it*
> *The buildings are old and cold*
> *But I like them*
> *The summer is not very hot*
> *But I like it.*

And with these came many hints of deeper and graver experience, as in this poem by Intiaz Malek.

> *Time and distance*
> *They both travel equally*
> *Waiting for no one*
> *Time is sometimes wasted*
> *Time is sometimes fastened*
> *The green grass is taken by time*
> *as time goes into the future*
> *and makes it present and the grass*
> *is polluted.*
> *Sometimes people are left behind by*
> *time, when people are old the time*
> *leaves them.*
> *The world and people get old*
> *but time goes on and on.*

Language that Transcends Itself

After all, however, a computer can compose verses, it can master at least a simple rhythm. Surely then it could write poems?

Evidently we haven't yet gone the whole way. And there must be a 'whole way' to go, because we do know that poetry is more than verse, however rhythmically adroit. Lines may scan and rhyme, yet be quite unpoetic, as Dr. Johnson demonstrated:

> *I put my hat upon my head,*
> *I walked into the Strand,*
> *And there I met another man*
> *Whose hat was in his hand.*

Furthermore, lines may scan and rhyme and also be felicitous or amusing or rousing, yet still be unpoetic. Thus W. S. Gilbert, Rudyard Kipling and John Betjeman are expert, memorable versifiers, far better than some recognized poets, without being poets themselves—except in snatches. One of the finest flights of imagination in miniature that I know is a limerick:

> *There was an old man of Peru*
> *Who dreamed he was eating his shoe;*
> *He woke in the night*
> *In a terrible fright,*
> *And found it was perfectly true.*

I remember this while I may forget Donne, Masefield, Ezra Pound. Yet somehow the imagination is not poetic imagination; the limerick is not poetry.

So, what quality do poems possess besides rhythm? We have already hit on the word: they are evocative. But this is a term which needs closer attention, and finer definition.

I would like to inject two more ideas. A literary critic once put forward the startling claim that 'poetry is the shortest way of saying something'. This is inexact, but far more perceptive than most such utterances. We will keep it in reserve for a moment, and turn to a comment of Chesterton's on Bernard Shaw, which follows closely on something we noted in the last chapter. Shaw, Chesterton said, is the one man of whom you could be certain that he had never written a poem. No verse by Shaw had then been published; eventually, some was, and its prosaic feebleness confirmed Chesterton's judgment. (So, in another way, does Shaw's failure to make the poet Marchbanks in *Candida* sound like one.) I propose a negative definition: *Poetry is what Bernard Shaw—one of the most dazzling, most eloquent, most versatile masters of modern English—couldn't write.*

With that in mind, recall the characteristic of Shaw's dialogue which we picked out as self-defeating, a spur to the revival of poetic drama: its perfect explicitness. People in his plays say precisely what they mean, therefore they can never mean more than they say. The same is true of his non-dramatic writings. His English is a closed system. It is exquisitely focused, it is witty or passionate or whatever he wants to make it . . . but closed. There is never anything beyond.

Now poetry should be just as exquisitely focused, just as precise, but the language of poetry is different. It is *self-transcending*. There is always something beyond. It is not closed and functionally explicit. When an experience is communicated through a poetic temperament, it stamps this quality on the language that expresses it.

What a Poem Can Convey
Take a specimen, Blake's *London*.

> *I wander thro' each charter'd street,*
> *Near where the charter'd Thames does flow,*
> *And mark in every face I meet*
> *Marks of weakness, marks of woe.*
>
> *In every cry of every man,*
> *In every infant's cry of fear,*
> *In every voice, in every ban,*
> *The mind-forg'd manacles I hear.*
>
> *How the chimney-sweeper's cry*
> *Every black'ning church appals;*
> *And the hapless soldier's sigh*
> *Runs in blood down palace walls.*
>
> *But most thro' midnight streets I hear*
> *How the youthful harlot's curse*
> *Blasts the new born infant's tear,*
> *And blights with plagues the marriage hearse.*

It would be easy to make a prose statement of the experience. Like this, more or less: 'The poet has walked through London reflecting on the evils with which a commercial society afflicts itself: on the insecurity and bondage; on the irony of squalor and war alongside an allegedly Christian establishment; and on the hollowness of "respectable" birth, marriage, and death, where sex itself is commercialized and debased by the pressure of need.' That is what is called 'paraphrasing'. It can be a useful exercise, so long as you never slip into thinking that the paraphrase is equivalent to the poem.

In literal terms, the poetic statement says no more than the prose one. Nor is it simply the prose statement dressed up in flowery phrases, or made less definite. Wordsworth's preface to the *Lyrical Ballads* (where he coined his phrase about emotion recollected in tranquillity) attacks the eighteenth-century concept of 'poetic diction', which embodied just that error—that a poem is in essence a prose statement translated into a special jargon, with metre and rhyme. In reality it is more. It must be. Poetry is so different from literal statement that according to many puritans, from ancient Greece onward, it is a kind of elegant lying. That is unfair; it has its own truth. Nevertheless, if you can take what appears to be a poem, and paraphrase it in prose so that nothing is lost, then it isn't a poem.

With *London* you cannot do this. The dictum that 'poetry is the shortest way of saying something' is right in spirit, but misleading in form. It implies that the 'something' is the experience which the poet consciously starts with, and poetry is a shorthand for summing it up. The fact is rather that when a poem is complete, the poet has created a greater 'something' than he consciously started with, and this is what is expressed in the shortest possible way.

London is more than the meditations of Blake during a stroll. It is a haunting, elaborate image of a society fallen and self-enslaved. The more you examine it, even without a knowledge of Blake's ideas, the more you see. By the repeated 'mark', for instance, he hints at the brand of Cain. In his first draft of the poem he used the word 'dirty' instead of 'charter'd'. That alteration alone—from a literal word which anyone could have thought of, to a word of branching implications which only Blake could have thought of—is a lecture on the poetic process in itself.

And this greater 'something' which a poet arrives at could not be conveyed so briefly in any other way. He may feel unsatisfied because the strength of his feelings hinted at something greater still, which eluded him; Shelley thought this disappointment was unavoidable. What the poet has, however, can be infinitely precious.

For him the experience is a trigger. More than with other kinds of author, it sets off an eruption from subconscious levels. The final pattern of words still expresses the original experience, but with an evocative power that reaches depths and awakens echoes in others. The poetic drama of Greece, as we saw, did this partly by appealing to deep-rooted collective passions through ready-made myths. The Christian plays of the Middle Ages spoke of birth and death and suffering through their enactment of the Nativity and the Crucifixion. While most poetic language has a less definable universality, the source of its self-transcending magic is much the same. The reader takes in the experience, responds to it with a degree of recognition, but feels that the poet has given it new dimensions: 'I never saw it like that before.' His own depths are stirred, his own subconscious reverberates.

Richness and Strangeness

It follows that poetry must usually deal with subjects which are more or less familiar, or at any rate not so utterly remote and bizarre that the reader cannot relate them to himself or have feelings about them. Yet however familiar the subject is, poetry must treat it so as to surprise, and jolt into wakefulness. It is the least predictable kind of writing. You cannot compose it in a style dominated by clichés or stock rhymes. Pope ridiculed stock rhymes in his *Essay on Criticism*:

> *Where'er you find the 'cooling western breeze.'*
> *In the next line it 'whispers thro' the trees';*
> *If 'crystal streams with pleasing murmurs creep.'*
> *The reader's threatened (not in vain) with 'sleep'.*

Yet when Pope's own techniques passed into inferior hands, the result was machine-made 'poetic diction', and an exhaustion of English poetry not to be overcome till the advent of Blake, Wordsworth, Coleridge.

It should now be apparent why a computer could not compose poems. It could match rhymes and string together prefabricated phrases. But any computer programme, however sophisticated, however vast the memory banks, is a closed system handling a finite number of counters. It can never transcend itself. With enough ingenuity, technicians might build a computer which you could instruct to write a poem about a nightingale. The trouble is that this is exactly what you would get—a poem, or rather a set of verses, about a nightingale. Unaided, the computer would never think of Keats's

> *Magic casements opening on the foam*
> *Of perilous seas, in faery lands forlorn.*

Nightingales, after all, don't perch on the window-sills of hotels overlooking the Marine Parade. Even if the computer, by a fluke, did combine its phrases so as to make an authentic poem, it could never know it had done so, nor could any other computer. The fluke would be that and nothing more, and you couldn't programme the computer to do the trick again.

This quality of self-transcendence and evocation is the key to most of the features of poetic language: its use of metaphors and symbols, for instance, which link the literal sense to other realms of experience; and its allusions and multiple meanings. When Macbeth has murdered the sleeping Duncan, he has an aural hallucination:

> *Methought I heard a voice cry, 'Sleep no more!*
> *Macbeth does murder sleep,'—the innocent sleep,*
> *Sleep that knits up the ravell'd sleave of care . . .*
> *Still it cried 'Sleep no more!' to all the house:*
> *'Glamis hath murdered sleep, and therefore Cawdor*
> *Shall sleep no more, Macbeth shall sleep no more!'*

Such matters are personal, yet for me the first line, when encountered at the age of fifteen, was one of the most terrifying things I ever read. So far as I can recall, the double meaning of the passage did not sink in till much later. The horror struck at once. Literally, I suppose, Shakespeare's message is that Macbeth has murdered a sleeping man and will lose sleep himself worrying about it. The poetic statement says no more, yet says infinitely more.

The nature of poetry accounts even for its obscurity, when the obscurity is of the right sort. This is not the mere verbal entanglement of second-rate Browning, which makes the going tough without any adequate prize for solving the puzzle. The right sort is the obscurity of a rich complexity, of loaded ideas or images, which make the reader think but reward him when he has thought, out of his own newly-tapped resources. That is why cerebral verse, such as Donne's, and verse based on startling acrobatics with language, such as Hopkins's, can still be poetry of the highest order.

And to revert—this explains why poetry seems inseparable from rhythm. Poetic speech is *self-transcending* and it is also *incantatory*: to be the first in full measure, it must also be the second, weaving a spell that transfigures the literal meaning through patterns of sounds and images and ideas. When we have applied those two adjectives and understood them, I think we have said most of what can be said.

Self-training

What can you do yourself, besides simply reading poetry and trying to write it?

First, keep a notebook, and jot down phrases and lines that occur to you. They will come unexpectedly, and perhaps with no obvious connection. But presently you should find that various experiences link them together, and they are on hand to help you say something you want to say. The main point is not to let them escape.

You may be able to adapt the children's exercises already mentioned, re-aligning your own mental habits so as to think and combine words in a new style. Use your notebook to record the results, and look them over from time to time.

Then, as a measure of progress, you may find it useful to follow a suggestion of Matthew Arnold. Store your memory with a private anthology of short passages—a line here, a stanza there—which you respond to strongly as poetry. When you think you have written some yourself, test it against whichever of your extracts may be relevant, lyric against lyric, epic against epic. Compare yours with them. This, if done honestly, is a ruthless self-discipline. It can quickly convince an aspiring poet that he isn't—not so far, anyway; and if persisted in with the same daunting outcome, it can divert him into channels more suited to his gifts. (I have always found excerpts from Milton specially humbling.)

An adolescent in a novel by Sinclair Lewis, his head echoing with magnificent lines by other people, exclaims: 'Oh God, if I could only *do* it!' The point is not that you should be able to write, instantly, as well as your test-poets. Almost certainly you won't. But if you can reach a stage where, in absolute honesty, your own work stands up at all in the others' presence, then press on. Sooner or later you may 'do it' indeed.

Exercises

1. Read Shakespeare's sonnet beginning 'Full many a glorious morning' (No. 33), and Wordsworth's *Westminster Bridge* sonnet 'Earth has not anything to show more fair'. Both have fourteen lines; but compare the rhyme-

schemes and arrangement of ideas. Write two sonnets yourself, one in Shakespeare's form, one in Wordsworth's. Which form is easier? Why? Which of your own two sonnets do you like better?

2. Compose Miranda's reply to Belloc (pages 171–2. Your poem should rhyme, and have between 20 and 40 lines. Choose your own metre.

3. Reconsider Johnson's 'hat' verse (page 175). Could this incident be described in a way that would make it poetic? Or is there something about it that excludes poetry?

4. An elegy is a poem of lamentation, often for someone dead. Read three great elegies: Milton's *Lycidas*, for Edward King; Shelley's *Adonais*, for Keats; Whitman's *When lilacs last in the dooryard bloom'd*, for Lincoln. All three deal with other themes besides the person whom the poet is mourning. Do you think this makes them better or worse as poems?

CHAPTER FIFTEEN

NON-FICTION

Defining Your Subject

An author may be incited, by the same impulsions as the story-teller or poet, to write what is neither a story nor a poem. 'Non-fiction' is a negative term with a wide range. It embraces, for example, history and biography; religious and literary studies; surveys of current affairs; travel books and philosophic discussions.

It is in this field that the suggestions on pages 29–35 and 63–8 apply pre-eminently. If you are following one of the many paths which the term 'non-fiction' opens up, reflect on those suggestions again, and relate them to your own plans. This chapter is offered chiefly as an aid to reflection and to the application of the results.

Any work of non-fiction has its source in an idea. The initial obstacle which you, as the author, must surmount is the obstacle of definition. Almost certainly, your idea will turn out on scrutiny to be less clear-cut than you suppose. If you try it on a publisher, even after days of thought, he may still distress you by asking: 'But what is this book going to be about?' An answer like 'Why, *dogs* – I told you in my letter,' is insufficient. The publisher may not put it so bluntly, but he is likely to ask the question in some form, from some specific point of view. What ground, *precisely*, do you propose to cover? What sort of presentation do you intend—for what public? An idea, as such, is hardly ever exact or complete enough. Before it can get a book under way, it must be carved and sandpapered into shape—by discussion, by exploratory research, by the drafting of an outline and one or two specimen chapters; probably by all of these.

When approached by an author with an attractive idea but no script, a distinguished publisher told how a friend of his in Aden asked some Arabs to build him a boat. After several weeks he went to see how they were progressing, and found them sitting near the beach with no sign of activity. 'We will get busy soon,' their spokesman explained, 'but first we must be sure that we are all thinking of the same boat.'

How, then, do you define the boat which a publisher would be willing to think of in terms of launching it with you?

The starting-point is that your projected book must have a single theme, so that the question 'What is it about?' could be answered in one descriptive sentence or phrase (a potential title perhaps). You should be able to word the sentence, or phrase, so that it would apply to this book alone and not to any other already existing. That is, *you*

182

must be original. The requirement is less alarming than it sounds. If the same topic has been treated before, but only (say) in German, or in a work that is highly academic and hard to come by, you can still consider tackling it. Your brief description would then include the words 'in English' or 'in popular form'.

Originality need not mean total uniqueness, which is rare and often suspect. Nor is mere novelty, strained after for its own sake, a merit. (When achieved—as it seldom is—it soon loses its gloss.) At the opposite extreme, however, pure trend-following is unlikely to produce work of much value, even in a financial sense. Thus the late 1960s and early 70s saw a flood of sex books; some were published, the majority were not. In spite of the apparent success of trend-following and cashing-in, the fact is that most of the sex books that did succeed showed originality or some kind.

As a rule, the best kind of originality is not the most way-out. If an author packs a book from end to end with material that is fundamentally strange to most readers, it is apt to be too hard to take, and too eccentric to last. Marshall McLuhan's *Understanding Media* (1964), a widely read classic in the field of communications study, has been cited as an instance of such a book having a powerful impact. So it had, at the time; but too much of it proved to be indigestible. It seems likely that McLuhan would have achieved more solid results by confining himself to a few of his more promising theories, and working those out in a clearer relationship with the ordinary reader's experience.

With rare exceptions, the most effectively original author is not the one who soars off into a world of his own, but the one who takes hold of a theme of established interest, and handles it in a fresh, stimulating, perhaps revolutionary way. This is what the best of the sex writers did. And before they came on the scene, there was C. Northcote Parkinson. To a public long familiar with bureaucratic ineptitude, office time-wasting, and kindred woes, his pseudo-scientific survey *Parkinson's Law* appealed instantly as a wittily novel summing-up of what millions felt but could not express.

What Competition?

When you have an idea of your own, begin by getting it just so clear in your own mind that you can visit a library (the bigger the better) and form some notion of what has already been published on your topic. Reference libraries will help, as well as the circulating sort; and when you have a topic that can be looked up in standard works, such as encyclopaedias, the articles on it may supply reading lists.

If you find that there is no book which adequately covers your ground at all, your idea may be very promising. Alternatively it may be an already proved non-starter. Conversely, if you find that somebody else has done *exactly* what you propose, and done it well, you had probably better think again. But don't be put off simply because there are books along the same general line. Look them up and assess them. With each one, ask these questions:

1. *Does it cover the topic in the same way as you intend, from the same aspects?*
2. *Does it cover it on the level you have in mind (specialized, popular, juvenile)?*
3. *Is it up to date? Has more material become available since it appeared? Does the topic look different now in the light of later experience, re-thinking, scientific discovery?*
4. *Does the existing book fail or fall short in interpretation? Do you think the author is wrong, or feel strongly that he has left questions unanswered which you could answer?*
5. *Is the existing book a good one?*

Question 3 is most important. One reason why authors do keep bringing out new lives of famous people, new accounts of famous events, is that fresh material has become available since the last ones were published. Many official papers are released to the public only after a thirty-year interval, and some are held back for longer than that, so new histories are constantly being written as various bans are lifted. Again, the reputations of eminent figures alter with the passage of time. There are apt to be biographies fairly soon after their death, and then more biographies, which read rather differently, twenty or thirty years later.

The answer to question 4 must be as objective as you can make it. A fresh view of a familiar thing or person can often inspire an effective book, but you must be quite certain you do have a clear-cut argument for a new approach. Henry Adams's *Mont-Saint-Michel and Chartres*, ostensibly a study of medieval architecture, manages to say what no previous architectural study ever said. A fresh solution to a familiar problem, or—more ambitious—a theory shedding light on a whole range of problems, which the author fits together and elucidates, can be equally potent. Sir James Frazer's anthropological masterpiece *The Golden Bough* is a supreme instance. Frazer collected thousands of myths, fables, and customs from many countries, and showed how they might all be explained in terms of ancient magical practices concerned with the seasons and the fertility of the earth. A more recent, less monumental instance is the series of books exploring the riddle of the 'real King Arthur' which appeared during the 1960s. Works of non-fiction devoted wholly or partly to this theme were written by R. W. Barber, Beram Saklatvala, and myself; and Rosemary Sutcliff applied some of the investigators' findings in a novel, *Sword at Sunset*, plausibly reconstructing a history barely hinted at in school textbooks.

The same problem-solving principle (sometimes applied to what may be non-problems) accounts for the steady flow of 'fringe' literature on such topics as flying saucers and the authorship of Shakespeare. Most of these crankish books are too poorly reasoned and poorly written to have much impact, but the occasional eccentric with a certain knowledge and style is apt to be startlingly successful: Immanuel Velikovsky, for instance, the author of *Worlds in Collision*, who tried to prove that many obscure passages in legend and scripture preserve traditions about upheavals in the Solar System not so enormously long ago. Though dismissed by astronomers, Velikovsky acquired a huge public.

Question 5 may lead you into subjective byways of judgment, but if you are sure you are capable of doing the same thing much better than any previous writer has, that alone may be enough justification for pressing on. You will still have to persuade a publisher that you are right.

In any case, ask all these questions about your predecessors, tailor your own idea in the light of the answers, and with any luck you will be able to formulate a potential book which is worth writing and which nobody has yet written.

Do you Like Your Subject Enough?

A second process of definition should run concurrently with the first. To revert to the advice on page 29, be sure that the subject-matter to which your inquiries dispose you is something you really know and care for—something with enough life in it, for you, to sustain you through the labour of producing a book, which may take a year or more. And if not, then go on re-thinking and re-defining the basic idea till it does take fire. Where your knowledge and concern are perfunctory, you won't write very well or carry much weight. Also you will be bored, and run the risk of boring your readers.

Imagine an author who is fascinated by the motor industry, and contemplates a book on its pioneer days. He decides that no one has written an adequate account of the growth of mass-production techniques. Here is a theme to stress. But factory mechanism in itself has too little inspiration for him. While he can understand it and deal with it competently, it doesn't excite him. His interests are more on the human and social side. He can bring mass-production to life if he concentrates on the inventors and operators—on Henry Ford and the problems he set out to solve; on the workers, and the effects of the techniques on their skills, wages, and conditions. This, then, is how he should approach the theme: he can handle mass-production well and enthusiastically by placing it in the social context. (As Upton Sinclair actually did in the documentary parts of *The Jungle*.)

To know about a subject doesn't mean to know everything. As you develop your idea further, and pursue your researches, you are likely to learn far more than you knew at the outset. Moreover, to deal with every relevant aspect, you may have to branch out into related fields where you are less at home. Harold Nicolson, writing the life of the French critic Sainte-Beuve, was forced into an uncongenial study of French religious disputes in the seventeenth century, because Sainte-Beuve himself had written a major work on them, which any biographer was bound to discuss. You may realize that your own idea, however you align it, has inbuilt hazards of this kind. As long as you can plan the prospective book so that the heart of it *is* 'what you know and care for', you can face such necessary forays with equanimity.

But if the essential topic, the topic that is truly yours, is so slight that you cannot make it support a whole book, reconsider. Could you combine it with other topics that interest you also, or shift the perspective so that it fits into a larger scheme? At any rate, don't start writing with a limited concept that will force you to build the book up by padding, or by wandering into digressions which you can't get stirred about yourself, but hope will appeal to readers. An archaeologist (for example) who had dug up a small Roman temple, dating from the reign of the Emperor Elagabalus, would be unwise to inflate his description of it into a book by adding an account of that Emperor's vices. Unless, of course, he could write of these too with originality and authority. In that event, however, his book ought probably to be a life of Elagabalus, with the temple put in to exemplify architecture during the reign.

Keeping to the Point

So to the third process of definition. It comes in as a restraint rather than a positive factor. While important at the thinking and planning stage, like the others, it needs to be held in mind more especially after composition has begun, so as to keep the idea developing along correct lines. This third rule is complementary to the second. Knowledge and concern are vital, yes; but never let yourself be seduced into including irrelevant matters merely *because* of your knowledge and concern, merely *because* they happen to interest you. The reader may not sympathize, and they will not be what he is looking for when he buys or borrows this particular book.

An insidious temptation is the temptation to talk indiscriminately about yourself, or enlarge on views of your own which are beside the point. People in our mass-media age of stars and celebrities are prone to this. Interviewers encourage actors, athletes, TV personalities, to lay bare their home lives and express themselves on all sorts of topics. In the minds of readers of papers and magazines, and TV viewers, there is a resultant impression that if a person is important enough for public attention, everything about him has the same importance. Hence, the inexperienced writer is apt to feel vaguely that if he can catch the public's eye at all, he can perform whatever antics he chooses in front of it; and any publisher who approves his idea for a book, reads an outline and specimen chapters, and tells him to go ahead, fortifies him in that belief. In due course his completed script arrives. Let us say the writer is Mr. N., a diver who salvaged the treasure from a sunken galleon. Mixed up with Mr. N.'s expert and engrossing story are dozens of pages dealing with his holiday in Austria, his divorce, his two children, and the iniquities of the educational system they are exposed to.

You protest that you know better than Mr. N. and would never do such a thing. Doubtless you wouldn't. Still, be careful. You may not hold forth undisguisedly about yourself, you may keep your prejudices in check . . . but are you quite sure about your obsessions? Do you have pet subjects, pet notions, which you work in on the slightest pretext? This is an occupational hazard of authors who have been converted to a religion or ideology—or have abandoned one. The old term for such a preoccupation is 'hobby-horse'. A slightly more recent phrase is 'King Charles's head', which derives from *David Copperfield*. One of the characters, Mr. Dick, is mildly insane; he is perpetually working on a piece of writing which he never completes, because he can't restrain himself from digressing to bring in King Charles's head. Watch out for your own counterpart of it. An editor once told me that whenever he received an article from a certain author, now of considerable repute, he had to blue-pencil the anti-American tirade which invariably seemed to creep in.

Researching the Facts

When you know what book you are thinking about, and are satisfied (through consultation with a publisher or otherwise) that you should proceed, you can launch out on a research programme. There is no need to do the whole of it before you start writing. Even when you think you have finished your research, the progress of composition will almost certainly raise new issues necessitating further inquiry. At the outset the only part of the book needing immediate and thorough research is the part you want to write first. This may or may not be the first chapter. Sometimes an author will go straight through from the beginning to the end; sometimes he will prefer to start by writing certain key passages which establish the structure, and then write others that lead up to them and connect them. Do whatever comes naturally, bearing in mind that you will be able to reconsider and revise everything you put down: the point is to get in motion, to put *something* down.

Library catalogues list books by subject as well as author. You can very likely get research openings by consulting a subject-index. If research in books, periodicals, and manuscripts is going to be the main basis of your work—if, for instance, you are writing history—a few initial openings will be enough, because many books contain bibliographies referring to other books, with notes on the sources for various pieces of information; so that each book leads you to several more.

Read them. And, in general, trace your facts and quotations to the original sources. It is amazing how many matters get twisted in the course of copying from one book to another, and how many responsible-sounding writers misquote or suppress or misinterpret. Check what you read.

How should you organize the facts you collect? It is up to you. As you read a book, take notes on the items in it that are relevant to your own work. Some authors put each note on an individual file card and build up a card-index, classified in any way that is handy for reference. Others use ring-binders with a sheet or sheets for each source consulted, and put all the notes on these. When writing a section of his own book, the author will go through his notes (in whatever form he keeps them) and assemble every item which is of use for that section. The particular method that suits you can only come by experiment.

A further point on research. Don't ignore what your predecessors have done, just because you 'want to be original'. Miss X., a would-be writer formerly known to me, had a theory about some ancient inscriptions. She refused to look up any books that dealt with the subject, for fear of finding that someone else had hit on the same notion already . . . in which case, she explained, it wouldn't be original. Obviously, if someone else had indeed hit on it, Miss X. would only have been showing ignorance or discourtesy by putting it forward as her own; and if the theory had been published *and disproved*, her position would have been worse still.

Or course it is excellent to have ideas of your own, as Miss X. had. But in such fields as history, biography, and literary studies, you must be careful not to get too enamoured of them. Verify your theories as far as you can, and be strictly honest. Don't quote facts that support them while omitting facts that fail to support them. Quite apart from ethics, an astute publisher's reader who knows the subject will probably catch you out, and that's that. If it's a point that gets past the publisher, a reviewer is sure to see it, and then your whole book may be discredited, even if the lapse is exceptional.

Respect for the Facts

Don't twist the facts, either, or try to bolster a doubtful case with special pleading. A few pages back I glanced at the people who propound theories on the authorship of Shakespeare's plays. Among them there was once a teacher who worked out an ingenious proof, backed by interesting evidence, that the real author was the Earl of Oxford. Unfortunately Oxford died in 1604 and *The Tempest* cannot have been written till around 1610. Rather than give up his beautiful theory, this literary detective went through weird contortions to prove that *The Tempest* wasn't a genuine 'Shakespeare' play.

Be warned. Facts are stubborn and sacred. Approach your theme with ardour, commitment, imagination by all means—but face the facts. If they do compel you to modify your ideas, you may well find that the modified ideas are more interesting and fruitful than the original ones. Above all, if you run up against a fact that proves you wrong and can't be argued away, never pretend that it is not there. Recast the entire book, or drop it, rather than try to publish what would amount to a deception. An author of the same cast of mind as the Oxfordian teacher might compose three hundred pages on the theory that Jack the Ripper was Lord Curzon in disguise, and then discover letters or photographs demonstrating that Curzon was in Lancashire at the precise time when two of the murders were committed. Sad as the conclusion might be, he should forget his theory rather than suppress the documents, or try to make out that they were forged.

In some fields, books must be the chief source; yet they are seldom the only source. There are many avenues of approach to truth. You can usually increase your knowledge and understanding by talking to people, visiting places, getting the feel of things The research worker who relies wholly on written or printed evidence is apt to be swamped by it, and to make mistakes because he has fallen into the delusion that no other evidence exists. It is easy to cite examples of learned investigators who have gone wrong because they could not see farther than the library shelves, and were refuted by men of broader insight who could. A famous case is that of Heinrich Schliemann. Fascinated by the legendary city of Troy, he wanted to prove that it was real. Professional scholars, who had dissected the evidence in approved scholarly fashion, said it was a fairy-tale. But Schliemann was more than a dreamer, he was an astute business man. Having made a fortune, he spent it on excavating a hill in Turkey which he believed to be the right spot; and there, sure enough, was Troy. His sensitivity to tradition, his practical insight into human beliefs, his assessment of the actual ground, and, at last, his use of archaeology—digging instead of merely reading and arguing—defeated critics who knew more than he did, in their own fields, but who relied on books alone.

When you come across gaps in the evidence, how far should you indulge in speculation to fill them? Use it within reason, so long as you make it clear that you are speculating, and don't allow guesses to harden into pseudo-facts propping up your favourite notions—the defect we noted in Lytton Strachey (page 66).

Biography—Its Importance for Non-fiction Writers

You may be attracted, as Strachey was, to biography, and biography illustrates most of this chapter with peculiar clarity.

Thus, it raises the issue of 'defining the topic' in its most exacting form. How far should a biography be somebody's 'life', how far a 'life-and-times'? How elaborate a setting, how much background explanation, does an historical figure need? Again, is enough known about the person to support a whole book without padding? One model 'life' on a big scale is Robert Blake's *Disraeli*. Study it, and observe how skilfully the author has handled masses of essential political data without ever losing sight of the hero.

As with theories, so with persons. A biographer should start with a conception of his subject, but not a rigid conception. It should be allowed to change as he goes along and learns more. Here sympathy is required, and it is better to write about a person you can like and admire than one you feel cold towards. Always, however, the rule of honesty applies. If you try biography yourself, you may have to leave out certain facts because of friends and relatives who are still alive; you must be careful of the laws of libel. But whatever you do put in must be true, and where human beings are concerned, the duty of truthfulness is all the more manifest.

Biography involves considerations that come with fiction and, as we shall see in a moment, have their relevance to other non-fiction. A figure whom the reader can be led to identify with, in some degree, is usually more promising material than one who is remote or unpleasant. (Lives of Hitler have sold, but chiefly because he affected so many readers through the war.) If the biographer can show his subject developing and growing and learning, like a character in a novel, the result will be all the more effective. In my own case, when writing a life of Mahatma Gandhi, I found that Gandhi had left a full account of the reading and contacts which had influenced him as a young man. By looking up the books, and finding out more about the people, I was able to trace the progress of Gandhi's mind and shed light on his career as a national leader.

Because the biographer, like the novelist, has the task of presenting human beings through touches that bring them to life vividly and significantly, his art focuses attention on a paramount problem of non-fiction in general. When you are not inventing a story, *how can you communicate facts with feeling, excitement, style, yet never sacrifice or distort the truth? How can you convey the fulness and colour of experience when your raw material is dry information?*

This is not just a question of 'fine writing' or literary cosmetics. Take a classic historical theme, the French Revolution. Its most notable early historian in English was Thomas Carlyle, who inspired Dickens's *A Tale of Two Cities*. Carlyle's prose style is personal, wayward, and to modern readers, off-putting. As a recorder of events he has been superseded by more academic writers, whose knowledge of the facts is far greater. The trouble is, though, that the French Revolution didn't happen in an academic atmosphere. To write about it in the scholar's 'factual' terms, tamely and statistically, is to lose the excitement *which is itself a fact of history*. Carlyle, whatever his faults, conveys the excitement. It carries over into Dickens where Dickens writes under his influence, and a deep sense of the occasion comes with it. Having read *A Tale of Two Cities* at the age of sixteen, I still feel that the chapter on 'Monseigneur in Town' told me why the Revolution happened, better than anything I have read since.

History, science, and other objective studies can possess fire and passion and high literary quality without being misleading. When this occurs, it is because of a temper of mind on the author's part: he allows himself to feel, and to have ideas. The danger with brilliant or committed authors is that they tend to rig the facts in the interest of their beliefs, or for the sake of literary sparkle . . . and it won't do.

Can you have it both ways? Can you deal with serious subjects objectively, impartially, yet with life and colour as well? The answer is *Yes, you can and must.*

I have stressed biography because if offers a clue. Recall another of our rules (page 32)—to tell *through people.* The historian must of course study such abstractions as economic trends and so forth, just as other non-fiction writers must study the equivalents in their own fields. However, to show these abstractions in relation to actual human beings and their lives, is to bring them on to a level where they are more comprehensible, and where the quality of life can be more amply conveyed, the energies of style can be more amply deployed, without the objectivity getting lost. Bertrand Russell shows in his *History of Western Philosophy* how superbly this humanization can be done, even with abstruse topics.

To the prospective writer of non-fiction, an obvious piece of advice is: 'Read good books of the sort that you hope to write, and see how the authors handle their themes.' A less obvious piece of advice, which admittedly does not apply to all non-fiction, but does apply to a surprising amount, is this: 'Whatever you hope to write yourself, read good biographies. See how the authors communicate matters of history or philosophy, economics, or politics, through the careers and actions of particular human beings.'

Exercises

1. Choose a topic which you know something about, and which is already the theme of at least one book—e.g. a hobby, a game, a country where you spend holidays. Any public library will help you in thinking of a subject and finding what has appeared on it. After looking at this material, write a paragraph suggesting a different approach to your subject, which might be the basis of a new book.

2. You have made a genuine discovery which is so far-fetched that it sounds like a crank theory or a hoax. Write the first two pages—or more, if you feel inclined—of a book about it, so as to convince a publisher's reader that you must be taken seriously. (Suggestions: you have visited a colony of Martians living on a Scottish island; you have dug up remains of 6,000-year-old

computers and aircraft near a ruined temple in Burma; you have found documents in an antique chest proving that Francis Bacon wrote the works of Shakespeare.)

3. Buy or borrow a fairly recent biography of some person whom you find interesting. Read it carefully. Then:

(a) Write a short assessment. Does the book make the person come to life for you? Does it give you definite feelings, for or against? Does the author keep to the point and tell you what you want to know? Has he gone wrong anywhere?

(b) Make a one-page summary of the main facts in the biography, as if you were writing an article on the person for an encyclopaedia, giving just the essentials (date and place of birth; education; major landmarks in career; and so forth). Does the book give you all these facts readily, or do you have to dig for them? How useful is the index?

A DEFINITION OF TERMS

We must now deal with writing in situations where it becomes more like a job. This book is not about jobs in the full-time occupational sense. Other books can give you advice on journalism as a profession,[1] and on the technicalities of producing a television show. They can also supply you with detailed treatments of those forms of writing that belong so entirely to a specialized occupational world—or at any rate, are so entirely an affair of assignments and commissions—as to lie outside our scope; for examples, composing advertising copy, or cinematic scripts for film studios.

The theme of Part Four is, in essence, writing which has a different *bias* from the activities discussed in Part Three: writing which may not be frankly the writer's full-time job, but is not purely his individual creation either—writing which has to fit closely into an organizational context, as a commodity itself or as a means to the organization's ends, or both.

Thus, a newspaper company publishes a paper. This is not the work of a single writer, but it uses the work of a large number. Many of them may not be on the full-time staff. Yet they must all conform, more or less, to the paper's requirements. They are paid to do so. Even the freelance whose work is only bought once is no exception. Furthermore, the paper goes on (if it does go on) whether or not Contributor A, B, or C is writing for it. Its existence is governed by commercial, non-literary factors. Much the same is true, with a shift of emphasis, in television. As for the reports and other communications which travel to and fro in industrial concerns, or which go out from them to interested parties, their influence on the business may be great, but always it is the business that counts.

Except perhaps in the last category, we have a wide overlap here with all that has gone before. Within the given framework, the scope for an author's talents can still be immense. In Chapter Fifteen we examined non-fiction in terms of books. Non-fiction on a smaller scale, usually meaning articles, raises similar issues in the journalistic setting. It is subject to editorial policies, and to the nature of the medium. Yet the writer remains a writer. He can compose his articles well or badly by standards that apply to books.

Journalists, whether freelance or salaried, and script-writers for television and sound radio, do not belong to a wholly separate class

[1] See especially David Wainwright's *Journalism Made Simple.*

from the 'born authors' described in Chapter Ten. The 'born author', as we noted, may figure among the writers for papers or magazines or television, either occasionally or regularly. He may do it by choice, or simply to earn money. He is still employing the same abilities that he uses in novels, biographies, or whatever. The difference lies chiefly in a mental adjustment. The author who does a piece of writing for an organization must relate himself to it, and act accordingly.

Hence, though we are now making a transition, we are not crossing a frontier between distinct territories. The feature article, the television script, even the management consultant's report, is still *writing*—only adapted to the demands of a corporate entity which is bigger than the writer, has aims of its own, and pays him to further them. Think of the process, if you like, as a special case of the adaptation-to-context discussed in Chapter Three.

It is in this spirit, by the way, that you should regard various kinds of composition which are not literary forms with a status of their own, to be analysed as such, yet which take up the energies of many writers— by choice or otherwise. They may have an important role in the educational system or in branches of government. What shall we say, for example, about a school textbook in a series, which the publisher commissions a teacher to produce? Or the manuals and rule-books for trainees in specialist fields? Where does the Highway Code figure in the Art of Writing? What about the essays which unwilling students have to churn out, and the theses which they have to submit for higher degrees?

When approaching such an assignment, a writer's prime need may well be to treat it as a job, in the broad and challenging sense defined here. It is not a piece of functional word-carpentry, unrelated to literature or to writing-in-general. It belongs to that class of work in which writing-in-general is tailored to the requirements of institutions. In this case the institution may be a university, an examining body, a government department. Yet the same principle holds.

Admittedly there is a great deal in this book which does not apply to a Highway Code, or to a thesis expounding some minute point in botany. But there has already been a great deal that does, in Chapters Four to Eight for instance; and while a chemistry manual is not journalism, any science teacher who contracted to write one could profit from a little attention to some of the guidelines which a journalist follows . . . as we shall see.

CHAPTER SIXTEEN

JOURNALISTIC WRITING

The Instant Impact

Journalism has been called 'literature in a hurry'. While the phrase applies more pointedly to a news story than to an article in a popular weekly, it always has a degree of truth. Writing for papers and magazines is, above all, *ephemeral*. That is not the same as being scrappy or insignificant. Most readers probably will be hasty and careless, but by no means all. Some will go over an item most attentively if it happens to interest them. They may reflect on it, and be stirred up by it to act or think or protest. But only a minority of people with personal reasons will keep a periodical and return to it later for pleasure or instruction as they would to a book. It is the current issue alone that matters. As each comes out, it pushes its predecessor into obscurity.

Journalistic writing requires an awareness of this fact. It is not easy to do well. It makes heavy demands on anybody who tries—heavier, often, than the composition of stories or essays. But the skills which it calls for arise from a readership situation where things will happen swiftly or not at all. Towards that situation the press is oriented. Even with its fiction there is a difference. In most papers and magazines a story cannot be very subtle. Most readers won't go over it carefully, or read it through twice, or come back another day.

Exceptions do exist. The *Times Literary Supplement*, for instance, carries articles and book reviews which are a permanent source of reference for scholars. A file of the *T.L.S.* is a vital adjunct to literary research. So also with various 'quality' and specialist publications, such as the *Cornhill Magazine* and the *British Medical Journal*. These, however, hardly belong to what we normally think of as journalism. Within the field of journalism, a writer's task is not to labour over exquisitely-sculptured prose, or to develop step-by-step arguments requiring concentrated logic and background reading. His task is to convey essentials to readers who will be face to face with him for a moment only, and will then go away, almost certainly for ever. What he has to communicate must be presented so as to catch these readers' not very enthusiastic attention, and hold it at least long enough to make the main points.

Editors have different policies and purposes, but the quick impact is a requirement which they must all observe; and it implies a standard by which a vast amount of material—even material they could use, if it were suitably written—must be rejected.

195

Adapting to the Press

If you take up journalism as your full-time profession, you will learn more from the job itself (at any rate under a good editor) than you can possibly learn from a few pages of hints. Advice will be of more value if your efforts are confined to approaching the journalistic world from outside: submitting articles on gardening, for example; or sending in news items about a football club which you are secretary of; or making up press releases about a rural anti-pollution drive. To do all such things with the best hope of publication, you must attune yourself to the medium. Consider the particular journal you are aiming at, and what it prints. Consider what its readers are likely to find interesting. Consider how the news editor or features editor is likely to react to your material, in the light of his knowledge. And remember, remember always, that your material will be only a single item in a deluge of competing ones in the editor's office.

Incomprehension of journalistic requirements is amazingly common. I have heard people on an archaeological dig, which was getting frequent and generous coverage in a Sunday paper, grumbling at the paper for focusing on a few popular aspects and not giving a 'weekly list of finds'. As if the ordinary public wanted lists of finds! The diggers should have been delighted at being mentioned at all.

This lack of attunement is not confined to the uninitiated. Public relations officers live by their alleged expertise in wrapping up information and getting items into the press. Yet in some quarters it is almost a platitude that if you want publishable facts about, say, a commercial company, the PRO is precisely not the man to go to.

I once helped in the publicity campaign for a research project, and showed a draft press release to the PRO of a famous establishment.

'This would be all right for a professional journal,' he said, 'but no news editor would look at it.'

As, however, he didn't offer to re-write the draft, I sent it out anyway. It brought telephone inquiries from nearly every national newspaper, and most of them printed stories on the project. Somebody's judgment had seemingly been sound, but not the PR expert's.

How, then, *do* you adapt writing-in-general to journalistic conditions and concerns?

Length

The first point to watch is absurdly elementary—length. Editors know that an item of such-and-such a kind can seldom exceed such-and-such a wordage. It would look too forbidding as a mass of type, or it would trickle on wearily through too many columns, crowding out other matter. When writing an article, or any item intended for publication as it stands (such as a short story if aimed at a journalistic medium), look at the periodical you hope to get into. Find a comparable feature or story, and estimate the number of words. You can come close enough without undue drudgery by counting the words in a ten-line sample, taking an average per line, and then counting the total number of lines and multiplying. Having settled what is a proper length for that kind of item in that paper, if necessary by trying more than one specimen, don't submit anything appreciably longer.

Over-long articles can of course be accepted, and cut to fit the paper; but it only happens if the editor is interested enough to spend an appreciable amount of time on the process, and you can't rely on that. You are competing against many other would-be contributors, some of whom will have got the length right, and can therefore be accepted with less trouble. A too-long piece of fiction, being difficult to cut at all, is almost certainly a lost cause.

Hooking the Reader

The kind of prose that suits journalism has an arresting quality. While the press seeks broadly to inform and entertain, it has to do both in ways that will hook readers during their few minutes of appraisal, and sell the paper. Any writer who is trying to get into a paper (and the same applies to magazines, if not so intensively) needs to absorb at least some of the methods by which this quick capture is attempted.

Newspapers seek a high concentration of personal allusions and 'human interest' . . . the cliché is valid. They often give people's ages. It makes them easier to imagine, and enables readers to identify with them, or compare them to friends and relatives ('a 42-year-old man', like Uncle George).

Newspapers also describe people—colour of hair, colour of eyes, height and so on—and say what they are wearing. This adds even more to the reader's visual image and helps him to identify.

As newspapers are predominantly black-and-white, descriptions can often be livened up and heightened by the mention of colour. For instance, instead of saying 'a woman in a trouser-suit crossed the road,' you would say, 'a woman in a red trouser-suit crossed the road.' This may seem a small detail but it can make all the difference and is worth remembering.

Northcliffe of the *Daily Mail* claimed to have created the first paper which dealt with matters that people actually talked about—personalities, gossip, out-of-the-ordinary events; also, that he did this with an eye to women. Beaverbrook's *Express* carried the recipe a stage further, and with eventual success in terms of circulation, by presenting this familiar world livened and speeded up and made more exciting.

Papers have a great deal in them besides reportage, and the writer who submits work from outside does not thereby become a freelance reporter. Yet there is no substitute for news, and reportage, which is the heart of journalism, affects it throughout. Any would-be contributor

should try to pick up a touch of the reporter's attitude. As Defoe, himself a brilliant pioneer journalist, put it two and a half centuries ago:

> If any man was to ask me what I would suppose to be a perfect
> style of language, I would answer, that in which a man speaking to
> five hundred people of all common and various capacities, idiots or
> lunatics excepted, should be understood by them all.

The good reporter has this capacity for speaking to everybody . . .
sometimes including the idiots and lunatics. He can be all things to all
men. He has a flair for making a subject interesting. No student of
style should undervalue the skill that goes into the best sports writing,
which consists largely in treating repetitive events so as to make them
sound fresh, and transmit an echo of the spectators' excitement to the
reader who wasn't there. The good reporter, for the sports pages or any
part of the paper, has a prehensile mind and an excellent memory. He
has a knack for finding the unexpected angle, the non-routine fact. It
has been said that while a competent reporter gets the story he was sent
out to get, an outstanding reporter gets the story he wasn't sent out to
get.

A cautionary tale. The editor of a student paper, confronted with a
girl seeking a news assignment, told her to cover a political meeting.
Hours afterwards she drifted back to the office empty-handed, and made
no attempt to write a story.

'What about the meeting?' the editor asked.

'Oh,' she said, 'there's no story. The meeting never happened. They
banned it.'

News Style

As the gathering of news supplies a key to the journalistic attitude,
so its writing-up shows how press requirements impose a structure and
logic. A good newspaper is created not only by good reporters, but also
by good sub-editors, make-up men and technicians. One reason for
Arthur Christiansen's sustained triumph as editor of the *Express* was
that he thoroughly understood these jobs, having learnt to do them
himself superlatively well.

With partial exceptions such as *The Times*, papers generally favour a
'news style' peculiar to themselves. On page 71, I urged that any
writer should be careful to answer the basic questions. A reader, consciously or unconsciously, is asking: *what? where? when? who? how?
why?* The same questions have to be asked and answered all the time in
a wide range of pursuits (work study and crime detection, to look no
further), and the news writer's obligation to deal with them is of course
absolute. He must make it clear what happened, where and when it
happened, who was involved; with details and explanations. In Christiansen's words:

What is a bad story? It is a story that cannot be absorbed on the first time of reading. It is a story that leaves questions unanswered. It is a story that has to be read two or three times to be comprehended. And a good story can be turned into a bad story by just one obscure sentence.

But the news writer handles his basic questions in a special way which the medium dictates. He tells all the essentials as rapidly and precisely as possible. The main facts must be stated, the basic questions must be answered, in the first few lines. A major news story may go on for many lines more, but everything after the first few, the 'lead', should only enlarge on the main facts without adding further facts of equal importance. Moreover, the main facts themselves, grouped at the top, should be worded so as to highlight whichever aspect of the story has the strongest impact.

An American authority on journalism, Professor Irving Rosenthal, offers the following theoretical model lead:

> George Nelson, 37, a *Time Magazine* writer, was injured while driving along the New Jersey Turnpike early this morning when a bee flew into his car and caused him to lose control of the wheel.

This opening paragraph gives a plain summary of the facts and answers all the basic questions, whatever elaboration may come afterwards. But which is the most newsworthy aspect? Rosenthal points out the possible variations on the theme. The reporter might word the lead so as to start from any of the basic questions.

Who? A *Time Magazine* writer fractured two ribs when . . .

What? An accident caused by a bee sent a *Time Magazine* writer home here today with two fractured ribs and a repair bill of $300 for his car . . .

Where? While driving along the New Jersey Turnpike near Teterboro Airport . . .

When? Early this morning, while driving along . . .

Why? Because he couldn't keep his eye on a road and on a bee at the same time . . .

How? Losing control of his car when he slapped at a bee buzzing around his head . . .

All these openings remain coolly objective. The reporter might also try a surprise: 'A bee put a motorist into hospital today.' Or a colourful description: 'Holding his side in pain, George Nelson, a *Time Magazine* writer, pulled himself out of his overturned automobile,' etc. Or a question: 'If you had to keep your eyes glued on the road ahead of you as you drove along, and a bee came buzzing at your head, what would you do?' Or a quotation from the victim: '"I never knew a bee had such a sting." George Nelson, a *Time Magazine* writer, was putting it mildly as he lay in bed at home with two fractured ribs—the result of an encounter with a bee.' Other devices are employed, but these will do for illustration. Obviously a reporter must use his judgment, and he will not try to answer all the questions in the first paragraph if the result is an overstuffed effect. But he will not postpone any of them far, and he will certainly put his crucial 'news' fact, in this case the bee, near the beginning.

There are two reasons for this arrangement of lead-followed-by-development. One of them should be manifest. Most readers will look at the story casually and without much detailed going-over, so they must be able to take in the essentials at a glance, without having to work right through to the end. The second reason is technical. No news story stands alone. The making up of the page is a mosaic operation. It means fitting together all the items, composing headlines, and arranging them in relation to pictures. It also means accommodating the whole pattern to the advertising matter on the same page. The advertisement space has been sold under fixed conditions, and cannot be interfered with. Therefore, it is the news that must yield.

Here the sub-editor comes in, crossing out, re-writing, compressing. When a story is written as prescribed, with all the essentials near the beginning, the sub-editor can shorten it by cutting off a piece at the end: he knows he will not be snipping away any vital data. If vital data were liable to be scattered all through, and to appear anywhere, sub-editing would be far slower and more hazardous. Under the pressures of a newspaper office, in fact, it would sometimes be almost impracticable.

When submitting an item to the news editor of a paper—a press release, a report on some activity, or anything else—you must accept the likelihood that if he uses your item, he will have it rehandled anyhow. But observe how news is written up, and try, without undue cleverness, to present your information in a workmanlike 'news style'. Write it so that the essentials can be grasped quickly, and write it so that the most arresting aspect, for that newspaper's public, comes at the top.

The Nature of News

What makes information 'news', and likely to be put in a paper? To begin with, a certain hardness, a *factual* quality. Intentions and expectations are not news if they lack substance. People are too apt to fancy that they can get press publicity for ideas, speculations, hopes, and events that *may* happen. In general, these cloudy figments have at most only marginal news value—unless they emanate from a person who is already known, and therefore rates attention.

Suppose a man told a news editor that he had a scheme to invent a language for talking to elephants. The editor might hand him over to a reporter. But no serious story would be likely to emerge unless at least one of two conditions were met. If the man were a zoologist of high standing, he would be treated with respect. Or if he took the reporter to the Zoo, and proved that he could already exchange a few words with elephants, he would also be treated with respect. The mere notion of talking to elephants, however, is not news.

Timeliness is also important. Information on matters no longer recent only has value if it puts them in a fresh light. Even then, the news is the contemporary announcement rather than the past occurrence. A rehash of an unsolved murder in 1970 would not be news, even if it were far better written and more informative than any account published at the time. The belated discovery of a fresh clue, however, might be. To apply this rule to non-professional reportage: if a society were launched to compile the early history of pop music, and the secretary wanted to get it mentioned in the papers, any press release should begin with news of the formation of the society—date, inaugural meeting, founder-members, objects, funds—and not with half a page on the origins of rock-'n-roll in the mid-fifties.

Angle of Story

Once again, what does give an item the attention-arousing character that makes it news? To stand a good chance with your intended message, you must find an angle that will appeal to a large number of people, not to a few specialists. The closer you come to home, in every sense, the better. Local information is more effective than foreign information. Matter that appeals to mass human emotions—sympathy, indignation, the desire for escape or entertainment, anxiety over health, anxiety over income, sex, fondness for animals—has more impact than matter that appeals on a purely intellectual or impersonal level.

With this knowledge in mind, stress any aspect of your information that will enhance its impressiveness. Remember, however, that the facts are sacred and that without them you have nothing to offer. Get them clear yourself, think about them, and state them accurately. Never distort or exaggerate them. Don't try to colour them with overdone language, superfluous comment, or facetiousness. Don't intrude your own personality beyond what is necessary; and when referring to other people, be fair. An editor who decides to use your material will cut out any libel you may have put in, but he will not be at all favourably disposed by your putting it in.

Features

As with short stories, so with articles: the freelance formerly had a wide field which has now contracted. Dozens of periodicals have died. In those that survive, feature material is largely commissioned, or written by the permanent staff.

The hopeful feature-writer can usually find a market of some sort in local papers, and magazines catering to special interests. Articles are 'non-fiction' and governed by the principles we have already noted for non-fiction on the larger scale (page 182–91). In the journalistic setting, the proper style for them is a relaxed version of news style. They should be factual, with the same kind of appeal. But they can wander a little more, explore ideas and arguments, and hold part of their message in reserve for an effective close; and they need not always be as rigidly timely as news—even history can be worked in, especially if you have occasions like centenaries to write about.

However, to aim at national media with any chance of success demands more than literary skill. It demands *the ability to offer what nobody else offers.*

Before experience disenchants them, writers often suppose that they can sell 'think-pieces'—dissertations on current affairs, for example, which contain nothing beyond their own ideas. They also fancy that they can sell general chat. As a sardonic observer put it, such an aspirant is liable to send off, by the same post, two articles entitled 'Literature Today' and 'The Pigeons at my Window'. Both will assuredly be rejected. One of the primary lessons to be learnt is that your own ideas, as such, are of no national interest. Indeed you yourself are of no national interest, unless you have some special qualification.

Rare expertise, rare knowledge, an unparalleled achievement—all these can still bring a freelance into favour at the highest levels. Our hypothetical talker to elephants could sell an account of how he did it, if he could prove that he did, and explain lucidly; and if he couldn't manage the second part of the job, the paper would help. A scientist with a journalistic knack, and the popular touch, can sell occasional articles on his science. Increasingly, however, even the genuine expert has to face some such editorial question as this (asked or implied): 'We don't doubt that you could do a fine article on agrarian reform in Iraq, if we sent you there to collect some more material. But why couldn't our Middle East representative do it equally well, and cheaper?' To which the only retort is—once again—the ability to offer what others can't: such as experience of work on an Iraqi experimental farm. Anything is saleable, even the think-piece or the chat, *if* you can give it a unique twist.

The twist may be wildly original, or blindingly obvious once revealed; and it need not depend on outright personal achievement. Countless literary amateurs could dash off a string of generalities about the Surrey commuter country. Few could match these relentlessly eloquent paragraphs by John Pilger (*Daily Mirror*, March 16th, 1971):

> The villages are joined by the main Leatherhead to Guildford road, and by their commuter residents' common aspirations among which are:
>
> To send their children to the best schools the mortgage will allow; to entice roses from a garden within sight of a common; to walk a

collie or a labrador to the village and to buy Radox bath salts, South African sherry and fish fingers in bulk.

To play a little golf, cricket or bridge; to acquire a second car and a second mower (one for the difficult patches), and also an oak door, a deep freeze, a double sink, two coloured telephones, a wine rack, an outside Christmas tree and perhaps even a bidet.

To hold parties of repute for the children, preferably with gas cylinders to blow up the balloons; to employ a twice-weekly woman or even an *au pair* (Portuguese rather than French; more efficient and cheaper).

And to assist a good cause, preferably Multiple Sclerosis or Guide Dogs for the Blind; to drink real coffee with sugar crystals and Earl Grey tea, and to receive deliveries from Bentalls of Kingston (Motto: To strive and not to yield).

People in and about Effingham achieve all of these things, some of them or none of them. They are civil servants, accountants, surveyors, bank people; people in oil, advertising and computers.

Pilger is a professional journalist, and a freelance who submitted the same sort of material from outside might not be published. But any freelance who showed Pilger's flair for significant scrutiny and bringing generalities down to earth, and who applied this to a topic which no staff writer had got around to, would stand a better-than-even chance of acceptance *somewhere*—in a magazine if not in a newspaper. For practical purposes, amateurs just don't show this flair, and the rare one who does would catch an editor's eye.

There are other kinds of exceptional offering which can still be potent. The ability, for instance, to present a hard or abstract topic by working up to it from a simple anecdote or easily-pictured experience. The ability to reach, and interview, a celebrity who doesn't co-operate with reporters. The ability to make a colour-supplement feature idea viable by producing illustrations which a staff research assistant would never have found.

Unhappily, however, the note of warning must remain dominant. The scope for the freelance is far smaller today than it was. The main advice must be: unless you have that distinctive 'something' to offer, recognize that there *is* no formula for writing articles for the national press. At less ambitious levels, fair possibilities still exist.

Book Reviewing

A minor but notable exception is the opportunity to get into print by reviewing books. Apart from writers under contract, few do this often enough to make much impact or earn much money. Nevertheless the scope is appreciable. To start a reviewing connection, you must persuade a literary editor that you have special knowledge in a certain area. But the knowledge does not have to be unique or extraordinary, and if the editor likes your reviews, he may extend the range beyond what you originally proposed as your subject.

In this branch of journalism, some of the general rules still hold, some do not. Care about length remains important, The editor will probably say how many words he wants when he sends you a book, and you should respect his wishes.

While 'news style' does not apply as stringently as in news, don't forget the news-writer's aims. A review should begin forcefully, and give the facts, and give the main ones quickly. A critic once cited, as the most unappetizing opening he ever struck, the first sentence of a book article: 'Oswald Spengler was formerly much read in Germany.' Surely you can do better than that. As for giving the facts, it is surprising how many reviewers don't. Tell the reader what a book is about; discuss it, evaluate it; add ideas of your own by all means, if you have room; but in any case *discuss the book*.

Quote from it. Give the author a chance to speak for himself a little. Be fair to him, whether you think he is good or not. Draw attention to faults, but never try to score, in the sense of picking out a few minor flaws and exploiting these to discredit the entire work; or, worse, misrepresenting the book as an excuse to vent your own prejudices.

The paper or magazine which prints your review is not your private platform. When you have built up a reputation, the editor may allow you a few vagaries. But your job as a reviewer is to review, in a manner not too frantically at odds with the context. The same applies to all journalism. The press informs and entertains; it protests; it is a check on the abuses of power. It provides a voice. And that voice is, or should be, collective. Even a paper's owner can wreck it, if, like the first Lord Rothermere, he makes the paper exclusively his personal mouthpiece. A contributor is far less than the owner. To write under journalistic conditions has something in common with playing in an orchestra. Players come and go. The orchestra continues, and even the most honoured and talented guest-artist is not performing by himself.

Exercises

1. Imagine you are a reporter for a popular daily. Write a 200-word news story on each of the following subjects. (Assume, of course, that you have visited the scene and interviewed at least one person.)

   (a) A fairly successful demonstration of talking to elephants, by the man mentioned on pages 200–1.
   (b) An international chess tournament for women.
   (c) The discovery of a headless corpse in a wood.

2. Study some newspaper colour-supplements (*Observer, Sunday Times, Telegraph*). Think of an idea for a feature article suitable for one of them.

Outline your proposed treatment of it, with detailed suggestions for the pictures. How many pages would the feature take up?

3. Buy or borrow a recent book—either a novel, or non-fiction—on a subject you know something about. Write a 150-word review of the book for a 'middle-brow' paper or magazine.

CHAPTER SEVENTEEN

RADIO

Introduction: Words for the Ear

With the broadcast media, sound radio and television, we enter a field of vast size and importance. From the writer's point of view it is different from the rest in several ways, but supremely because it is not concerned with words on a page, and the consumer is not primarily a reader.

A species of writing so sharply distinguished from other kinds is a study in itself. This chapter and the next cannot take the place of specialized handbooks, any more than the last chapter could take the place of practical training on a newspaper. Nor can they offer the detailed technical advice which handbooks can give. But they can show the way. Following the same course as before, we can define what is special, what is distinctive about writing for radio and television. We can try to conjure up the 'feel' of the media; to understand (as in previous cases) what *won't* do; and to form a picture of the needs, and the nature of the market.

We are dealing here with things that are collective, changeable, often difficult to pin down. There is no obvious authority. It would be hard to name a great practical exponent of script-writing as one names Christiansen in journalism. Yet if you listen to professional workers in the media, you will observe a certain consensus on major points. The consensus has remained fairly constant for some years through various shifts of outlook and policy. I shall try, in these chapters, to sum it up, and give it practical application.

Radio as a Medium

In sound radio the audience's hearing-without-reading is the dominant fact. It does not, of course, transmute every literary form beyond recognition. A play is still a play, and many broadcast dramas are adapted from stage ones. A talk is a sort of article. But in writing for sound, you must always think of your script as *something that will be heard only*.

Hence, *reading aloud* whatever you write is essential. But to do this by itself, in the ordinary manner of reading aloud, will not fully show you either the advantages or the disadvantages. It will not fully reproduce the conditions, either of the studio, or of the receiving end in listeners' homes.

Awareness of the need to adjust to radio, as a different medium from others, dawned early in its career; and the first conspicuous instance has an odd interest, precisely because it occurred so long ago, yet can still supply a hint fifty years later.

In the British General Election of 1924 each party leader was allowed one broadcast. Ramsay MacDonald for Labour, and Asquith for the Liberals, simply had a fixed microphone on the platform at a public meeting, and proceeded with the speeches they would have given anyway. Since MacDonald orated walking up and down, his speech only came through the microphone intermittently, and his platform manner, without his handsome visible presence, failed to impress. Asquith did little better. Baldwin, however, the Conservative leader, realized that the radio audience would consist mainly of people sitting at home, many of them women—people to be chatted to, rather than harangued. So he wrote out a talk specially aimed at these, read it to his wife as she knitted, asked her advice, and broadcast the final text from a studio. He won the election easily.

Broadcasting has travelled far since Baldwin, yet not so far that his point has become too obvious to need underlining. When writing for the printed page, you must picture your readers; and when writing for radio, you must picture your listeners. You have to catch their attention and hold it, just as strongly as the writer of a short story or article, if not more so.

Furthermore, however, there are special obstacles which Baldwin-style reading aloud does not reveal. Listeners will not all be attentive. They may switch on late, they may wander in and out of the room, they may be interrupted. Above all, they can never ask the person who is broadcasting to go over a sentence again.

These are disadvantages, or at any rate they seem so. On the other hand, as pioneer broadcasting progressed during the 1920s, a fact gradually became apparent which should be apparent still—that a radio programme can do many things which no reader can; even with a straightforward-looking text. It can employ sound effects and music. It can use several voices instead of one. It can suggest space, movement, and transitions of time and place. To appreciate how refined an art this can be, try playing Blind Man's Buff in a large room. Listen to the other players, more analytically than children do. Which voice is coming from where? How far off is the person? What can you infer from non-vocal sounds—the rustling of clothes, the creaking of boards, the street noises signalling how near the window you are? Which clues are really informative, and how could a producer make use of them to convey a sound-picture of a room with people in motion?

The Creative Magic of Sound

Especially in its amplest development with drama and documentary, radio is *evocative* . . . not quite in the same sense as poetry, but in the sense that the listener fills in the scene out of his imagination, and forms his own idea of it.

All the warnings (page 46) about the impossibility of using a tone of voice in print become void in radio. On the air, with no visual accompaniment at all, the voice alone can work marvels—or cause disasters. Leaders have always known its power; modern ones, since the 1920s, have known that the spell of oratory persists on radio though in a different way. An actor can make a mediocre script sound like an effusion of genius. Indeed, even a good script, skilfully composed with the voice in mind, may appear flat in print; writing for the voice has a character of its own.

Conversely, the same good script can be ruined by a poor voice, an inept delivery, an accent that is wrong for the purpose. So can any broadcast words. Celebrities in the studio can emasculate a strong message if they are not also effective broadcasters. A writer can be his own worst enemy, if he reads his work aloud. Even an experienced actor can almost destroy his lines if he misinterprets them. The ear, when it does the main job without the eye, becomes acute and intolerant. Radio can show a speaker up with deadly immediacy. Long-windedness is felt as such very soon. Boredom and insincerity are hard to disguise.

Since sound performs the entire creative act, radio is flexible. In a play you can change scenes almost without limit, so long as the nature of the change is made clear, because a change of scene doesn't involve the upheaval and expense of a change of set. You can manage an immense range of sound effects. And there are larger and subtler freedoms. Where the audience has no visual image to go with the words, and little time for reflection, a script can be bold. You can get away with a great deal that would be risky in other media.

The reader of a book can pause, and think, and ask himself questions. Just *how* is such-and-such an event supposed to have happened? Radio can gloss over difficulties without necessarily cheating. Again, the audience in a theatre can see, and is therefore liable to be puzzled, or amused, or otherwise awkward. Fantasy is the notorious instance. Creatures of fable, from elves and dragons to hobbits and science-fiction monsters, are almost impossible to make visually impressive. A radio listener accepts them. The medium has a mystery of its own.

One acid test would be Algernon Blackwood's story *The Wendigo*. Look up this masterpiece of horror, if you don't know it already, and ponder the hazards of adaptation. It is concerned with the shattering experience of 'seeing the Wendigo', a huge, undescribed, more-than-Medusa-like being that haunts Canadian forests. The story could be dramatized for radio. But could it be filmed? Either the spectators would never see the Wendigo, and feel swindled, or they would see some plastic absurdity and laugh.

Organization

Radio is differently organized in different countries, with profound implications for the writer. It may be a department of state, as in Russia. It may be operated by privately-owned companies, as in America. Under the American system the money comes from advertisers, who buy time on the air and sponsor the programmes. Some countries, such as Canada, have a state corporation and a commercial network as well. State-run radio and commercially-sponsored radio are both subject to a degree of control from the sources of funds. A writer aiming at an American programme must be sure that his script will not offend the prospective sponsor. Thus (as a trivial example) a drama programme sponsored by a razor-blade firm would be the wrong market for a play in which the characters kept using electric shavers.

In the United Kingdom, the British Broadcasting Corporation has held a monopoly until very lately. Commercial radio is still too tentative to discuss. The BBC is a public body, operating under government charter. It carries no advertising, and is financed by licence fees which the owners of sets (both sound and television) are required by law to pay. The licensing is administered through the Post Office. Thanks, however, to its first head, Sir John Reith, the BBC has avoided direct government control. Hence the writer does not have to worry about either commercial sponsors or political paymasters. But he does have to take account of the policies prevailing in the Corporation at the time when he works. He can only do so by a careful study of programmes, plus, if possible, consultations with BBC staff.

The BBC runs four main domestic services. Radio 1 is for pop music. Radio 2 broadcasts miscellaneous 'light' programmes. Radio 3 is chiefly for serious music, talks, and drama. Radio 4 is middle-brow. There are regional variations, and separate short-wave broadcasts from local stations, a recent addition to the system. The BBC also maintains extensive services for listeners overseas, some in English, some in other languages.

Types of Programme

Most programmes, on the BBC and on radio in general, can be roughly classified under twelve headings.

(1) *News, news magazines, news features*
This classification includes actual newscasting, and programmes of background information, current-affairs interviews, parliamentary reporting, and so forth; also special extended coverage of such events as moon shots.

(2) *Music (including opera)*
The transmission of music was originally the BBC's main function,

and it is still a major one. Some is recorded, some comes live from recitals and concerts.

(3) *Sport*
Outside broadcasts from races, football matches, and other sporting events, by staff commentators.

(4) (*a*) *Drama: plays not written for radio*
Adaptations of stage plays.
  (*b*) *Drama: plays written for radio*
Single plays of various lengths; series; serials (the 'soap opera' type of programme); adaptations of fiction.

(5) *Light entertainment*
Variety shows, comedy shows, quiz programmes, panel games.

(6) *Documentaries*
Programmes on interesting topics of the present and past: about current issues (e.g. the quality of life in a new town, the revival of the airship); and about historical figures and events, often on an anniversary which recalls them. May use 'actuality' material such as on-the-spot recordings and interviews.

(7) *Discussion programmes*
Discussion of current affairs, books, the arts.

(8) *Talks*
Reminiscences, lectures, general chat.

(9) *Readings*
Of existing books and poems; and of short stories written specially for radio. Either read by one person, or semi-dramatized by having different voices for the different speakers in the dialogue.

(10) *Education*
Schools broadcasts, and study programmes on Radio 3.

(11) *Children's programmes*
Chiefly story-telling, as in the BBC's *Listen with Mother*.

(12) *Religion*
Church services, and programmes under other headings with a religious theme.

The examples given under each heading are precisely that. No such list is likely to be exhaustive. Some programmes could be classed under at least two headings—for instance, a comic play series might count as light entertainment rather than drama—and a magazine programme like *Today* or *Woman's Hour* combines items of several kinds. It must be said at once that few of these fields offer any appreciable scope for the uninvited contributor from outside. A freelance writer can submit odds and ends, such as news items, or snippets of information for a religious programme. But even when such an item is used, it will not be used as submitted. The producer will simply pick it up with thanks, and present it in his own way with his own team.

As with newspaper colour-supplements, some doors at least are open to the freelance with unique and interesting matter to offer. An ethnologist who had found an unknown tribe of pygmies in the Amazon jungle, compiled tape-recordings of them singing and talking, and interwoven these with a lively account of his adventures, might sell the result as a documentary . . . or as the nucleus of a documentary. For practical purposes, however, the only kinds of programme we need consider here—since this chapter cannot provide a complete manual for the professional on the inside—are talks, original short stories, and plays.

Talks

Most radio talks are given by invitation. However, you may succeed in placing one with a magazine programme that uses them. Or an invitation may come your way, if your writing in other media has attracted notice, so you should at least be prepared. To compose a talk just as an exercise, even if it is not likely to be used, is a good introduction to some of the fundamentals of broadcasting.

Scripted prose is like any fairly easy prose on the printed page. Being ephemeral, and addressed to a large audience who must take it in instantly, it is closer to journalism than to books. In England a fraction of it does reach print in *The Listener*, but even this is usually the most erudite kind. Far less ever gets into hard covers.

Broadcast sentences should be short, conversational, or at any rate uncomplicated. Their meaning should be lucid, and proof against misunderstanding. Their language should be concrete rather than abstract.

Suppose (whether by invitation or as an exercise simply) you are drafting a talk of a prescribed length—say five minutes—on some quite unassuming topic such as 'My Favourite Game'. The basic requirements are *unity, clarity, emphasis*. Your talk should hold together and keep to its theme, without digressions. Every sentence must have a plain meaning, and lead to the next, so that the ear will take in the sequence which the eye cannot. The impression must be firm; your listeners should be interested enough to remember the gist of your message afterwards. (Ideally, you would hope to hear that some of them had taken up your 'favourite game'.)

To achieve these ends, since the listeners cannot pause to think as you go along or ask for repeats, you must aim at a fairly well-defined structure, and discipline yourself sternly. First try to sum up the point you intend to make, in one sentence of reasonable length. If you can't do this, your ideas may be too complicated to fit into a five-minute period; simplify them. Then decide how to begin. Think of an arresting question or incident that will seize the audience's attention. Follow this up with a direction-pointer, a sentence or two foreshadowing what you plan to say in the first section of the main talk. When you have got this down on paper, and the first section itself, write a second direction-pointer introducing the next batch of material. The second batch will probably bring you close to the end. Add a quick, forceful conclusion.

Re-write the draft till you feel provisionally happy with it. Then try reading it aloud, in several ways. This is a step towards 'foolproofification' (page 41) that is peculiar to radio. Read your script as if to a friend beside you, conversationally. Read it as if to a group of strangers, seeing if you can sound friendly and pleasant throughout, speaking the words you have written. Read it as if to a big audience, with energy and feeling. Read it very slowly and carefully, testing it for sound and stress. In the light of all this evaluation and any flaws it has uncovered, make further adjustments.

Then ask yourself a few searching questions and answer them honestly. Would your talk genuinely interest many listeners? Is it simple enough for them to follow without seeing the text, as you do? Does it say anything which they would feel to be important *to them*? Would the opening catch their attention if they were busy with some other activity when it came on the air? Is the main point stressed enough, and repeated? Is the end effective, or anti-climactic? And *is the talk exactly the right length*?

This checklist may seem elementary. Yet a full practical appreciation of all it implies can teach you plenty about writing for radio, whether your talk ever reaches the studio or not.

Short Stories

For original fiction by freelance authors, a solid demand does exist. The BBC has regular programme slots for them, such as *Morning Story*. Aim at such a programme, study the type of story it uses, write a story *of the correct length*, and send it to the producer (with a stamped self-addressed envelope for return if rejected).

There is little else to say beyond what we have already said in Chapter Twelve. A story is a story in whatever medium. But write with the qualities of broadcast prose in mind. Try the self-discipline and evaluation suggested for talks, and query your script in the same spirit.

Does your story begin at a point where the audience will soon grasp the situation and know what the central conflict is? Does the story *move*, progressing from event to event, and approaching a climax? Is there enough suspense; or is there a risk that listeners will either foresee the end or stop caring what it is? Do you finish quickly after the climax, without tailing off?

In production, the main difference from a talk is that you are not likely to read the story yourself on the air. Somebody will read it for you. That reader may be more practised than you, but, not having originated the script himself, he may also be more liable to get the tone or emphasis wrong at crucial points. Hence, prior 'foolproofification' is all the more vital.

Plays

Drama, in one form or another, offers easily the best opportunities for the freelance.

Look at Chapter Thirteen again, and then reflect on the differences which radio makes. To write a play for it is to forgo the theatrical spell, and everything visual which the theatre provides, but to gain in other respects. We have glanced at some of radio's advantages—the flexibility, the adaptability, the evocation and mystery. Notice, now, what exactly your ingredients are. They are *words, sounds* . . . and *silence*. Don't overlook the last.

Dialogue

But first, words. Discussing drama in general, I said that dialogue on the stage carries a heavier charge than it does in real life, and is expected to. Though radio loses the theatrical spell, it offers dialogue without visual competition; and on balance, the lines are apt to acquire a heavier charge still. Even an ordinary conversation can sound more significant in a dark room. A script that looks feeble, when read to yourself in cold blood, can come alive with a mysterious magic on the air. Drama scripts usually need to be under-written by theatrical standards, and stage actors have to learn a quieter, less demonstrative style, or the play will sound over-emphatic and exaggerated.

Exploit these facts. Use words that will take advantage of the magic. Give the actors lines which they can enrich and weight to the full. Poetic language is more acceptable on the air than on the stage, precisely because radio unleashes its multiplicity of meaning more naturally. A line, a phrase will arouse echoes if you give it a chance.

A radio play by Robert Bolt, *The Drunken Sailor*, contrasted the landsman's and seaman's attitude to ships in the days of sail. A character on the shore looked at a ship and said dreamily that the sails looked 'like feathers'; a sailor actually working on them said they were 'like bloody iron'. Many writers could have gone on for ten minutes and said less.

Orchestrate your voices. Contrast your characters sharply, not only in personality but in mode of speech. Make it easy for the producer to assemble a cast in which all the speakers will be distinguishable, yet build up a harmony like the harmony of several musical instruments.

Because the listeners' imagination does so much, you must be careful to supply it with the proper materials. They must know what is happening and where, and imagine along the right lines, yet never feel that they are being dictated to or manipulated. You may be able to use a narrator, as you seldom can in the theatre, but there are limits to the amount of outright narration which even a radio play can carry. As a rule, dialogue must still be the chief source of information, and here radio raises issues of its own. The problem is like the general exposition problem in drama, but more pervasive.

If two characters, Charles and Helga, are both watching a third person in the distance, how does the dialogue convey what the third is doing? Charles wouldn't really say to Helga, 'Oh look, he's crossing the road.' Every such contrived remark weakens the illusion and checks the imaginative process. Your writing needs to be intensely, convincingly functional. Sleight-of-hand—or rather sleight-of-voice—may occur, but it should have the conjuror's deftness. Charles's speech might run: 'I wonder why he's crossing the road. Perhaps he's going to buy a paper?'

Effects and Music

After words, sound. This falls into two categories, effects and music. Both should be as functional as the dialogue. A radio play should not attempt to include every background noise which would be heard in real life. The result would be a hubbub, and a very expensive one at that. Every sound—a car starting, a door slamming, a bell ringing—must have its role in the action. Of course there is no need for every sound to be specially made. The masses of recordings in BBC sound archives and libraries (and their equivalents in all countries where broadcasting is well established) are equal to most occasions. Also, the marvels of jugglery with tape and electronic gadgetry—speeding-up, slowing-down, mixing, reversing, and many other techniques—are limitless.

As for music, the main point is that you should not use it merely for background, or to mark intervals. It should add to the script, commenting on the dialogue, emphasizing changes of mood. It can also provide a unity which a miscellaneous, episodic story may lack. A few bars of a peasant dance for a play set in the Balkans, a few bars of the Charleston for a play set in the Twenties, weaving in and out between scenes: these may sound like naïve devices, and perhaps they are, yet they can define time and place, remind the listener of the atmosphere, hold the action together.

Silence

Lastly, silence. Never forget its power. Silence on radio, unlike silence in a film, is (or can be) the real thing. There is not even a picture to watch; only a vacancy. That vacancy can fill with suspense, anguish, surprise, at a terrific pace, and then give way to an explosion of emotion or laughter. Or it can drive home a mood, say of emptiness or hopelessness, as music does. Samuel Beckett is one of the masters of silence.

Evaluating and Selling a Script

As with a talk or short story, so with a play when you have drafted it, you can use a checklist of questions. Is your plot exciting enough to make people want to find out how it develops? Does every scene advance it towards the climax? Is the nature of the main conflict made clear fairly soon? Does each character speak distinctively? Will the audience always know which ones are present and which are not? Is any scene overcrowded with characters, so that listeners will find it hard to sort them out? Is it always clear where the scene is happening? If you use narration, have you kept it to a bare minimum?

Plays, like stories, are usually fitted into fixed programme slots, such as the BBC's *Afternoon Theatre*. Read the *Radio Times*, or an equivalent paper, to find out what these are and how long a play must be to fit into one. Then try. At the BBC's regional centres, or at broadcasting offices in other countries, your script will reach the right hands if you address it to the 'Drama Producer'. At Broadcasting House, however, the BBC's London headquarters, there is a special 'Script Editor, Drama'.

Lastly, if you achieve your goal and your play is accepted—don't treat your script as sacred. The producer may ask you to re-write, and may go on making changes till the last moment. As with an editor, recognize that he probably knows best, and don't make rigid stands except on essentials.

Remembering the Switch

In broadcasts of any type, always remember the difference that is caused by the switch on the set at the receiving end. Your listener can stop with the utmost ease. If he elects to stay with you for a while, he is still not a captive audience. You compete with all the distractions around him—talk, meals, comings and goings. Drama in the theatre is conditioned by the theatre itself and the spell it casts; drama on radio is not. Nor is any other broadcast material. The word and the voice must weave their own spell.

As the listener may switch off at any time, so he may switch on at any time, or come over to your programme because he is bored with someone else's. You can't assume that all your hearers will be with you from the beginning. Hence, if you can avoid making the whole script depend on some crucial point which is heard only at the start, it is best to avoid it. Otherwise you may cause confusion, misunderstanding, even alarm: as in the classic instance of Orson Welles's dramatization of *The War of the Worlds*, when millions of Americans missed the opening and thought they were listening to reports of a real Martian invasion.

Exercises

1. Write the five-minute talk on 'My Favourite Game' (page 211).
2. Write a two-minute talk on the same subject.
3. Which of the short stories listed in Exercise 1 at the end of Chapter Twelve would be suitable for reading aloud on radio? Would any be definitely wrong? If so, why? (Ignore considerations of length in this case; the longer stories might be abridged if necessary.)
4. Write the opening of a radio play, using one of the following situations. Do not use a narrator.

(*a*) Four students, all aged around 19, have walked several miles and climbed a hill. One of them resents the whole trip, owing to a personal grievance.

(*b*) English Civil War, 1642. A middle-aged Cavalier and his sister are waiting in their home for a messenger from a royalist general. A man comes to the door, but he isn't the messenger; he is a local Roundhead sympathizer who might pass information to the enemy.

(*c*) A disgraced official in a Communist country is alone in his office, contemplating suicide. The telephone rings. (You may *not* make him talk to himself. But if you wish, you can make him start recording a farewell message on tape, and you can let the audience hear both ends of the telephone conversation.)

CHAPTER EIGHTEEN

TELEVISION

The TV Public and its Response

We have paused, once or twice, to contemplate television already (pages 19–20 and 34). It is a medium with a colossal public. Britain has a set for every three human beings, approximately. In the United States the proportion is higher. World-wide, the number of sets is well past 150,000,000 and may be nearing 200,000,000.

Television has inspired—and still does inspire—a regrettable amount of loose talk about its nature and impact. A short-sighted contempt among the intelligentsia has waned, but not vanished. Organized protesters, from various angles, continue to make assertions about the medium's baneful influence, without proving them. Its output is so multiple and diverse that all such general dogmas are suspect. Moreover, much of the criticism has come from a false notion, which the television writer needs to expel firmly from his own mind—that the viewer is passive, a mere recipient of what the box dictates to him.

As I indicated in Chapter Three, that belief is a hangover from older modes of communication. Even the most inert-looking viewer is often very active indeed if he is attending at all. It takes more internal activity to make that little picture-show intelligible than it does to absorb articles in popular papers. The viewer's sense-organs and nervous system have to do more; and in a programme of any complexity (and that includes even quite simple-seeming entertainment), his mind has to relate unlinked images, infer what isn't on the screen from what is, retain memories, supply much of the continuity, pick up hints, and put the message together from them.

All this activity will often be profoundly affected by his own interests and convictions, which it brings potently into play. Tests have shown that two people who have watched a controversial programme, on politics for example, are apt afterwards to give wildly discrepant accounts of it. They go through an inner process of selection and reconstitution. The programme, for each, rapidly becomes not so much 'what he is seeing' as 'what he is putting together himself from the materials provided'. Sometimes, in fact, from materials which are not provided, but which his own preconceptions read into the programme. Viewers are quite capable of quoting speeches that no one made and mentioning scenes that were never shown.

This process is clearly not the same as the imaginative response of the radio listener. It is still imperfectly understood. Because it is inseparable from viewing, and because so much of it is complex and below the threshold of consciousness, the glib generalizations about television's 'effects' are mostly ill-founded. The alleged influence on behaviour—for example, in encouraging violence—is far too uncertain to debate here. On the purely communicative side, a little can be said. Thus there is no solid evidence that television competes with serious reading, or is adverse to it. There is no solid evidence that it stultifies. On average, children from homes with a set are better informed than children from homes without one. (Though not always in the traditional sense of being informed. They may know the names of public figures, yet not have the slightest notion of how to spell them.)

As we might expect from the internal activity of the viewer, we can be surer that television stirs people up than that it teaches them any particular lessons, or makes them think in any particular way. This stirring-up is especially marked in poorer parts of the world. The peasants of southern Italy have never settled back into their old routines since they began to catch glimpses of how northern Italians lived (not to mention Americans), and to draw inferences and comparisons.

The changed character of the writer's task in a TV-conditioned age becomes most manifest, naturally enough, in television itself. The technique consists not so much in handing out packages of material which is 'right' by abstract standards, as in getting the audience responding as you would wish. Since the nature of audience response is still so obscure, there is still plenty of playing by ear and navigating by hunch, and plenty of room for the unexpected.

In the late 1960s the BBC added a new figure to English folklore with Johnny Speight's play series *Till Death Us Do Part* (afterwards adapted for the American market). His character Alf Garnett was a comic monster meant to embody every disagreeable prejudice—nationalistic, racial, social, political. The show was a triumphant hit. Yet it subsequently transpired that many viewers agreed with Alf, and saw him in all sincerity as the hero.

Different Kinds of Viewer and their Attitudes

How is this immense, wayward public made up? Despite market research, generalizations are risky here also. Most of the audience in Britain, most of the time, is working-class, but the tastes of other social groups are by no means ineffectual or irrelevant. The age-group between 16 and 24 watches less than others. However, the distinctions which would be really valuable are much harder to draw. Research can show that about four million sets were switched on at such and such a time; it cannot determine how many people were in front of each set, or why.

There are viewers—mostly with full-time jobs—whose habit is to switch on early in the evening and watch, or not watch, more or less indiscriminately for hours. There are others, such as invalids and pensioners, who likewise have the set on for a large part of the time, but watch closely and critically. There are others who switch on for a chosen programme only, watch that with full attention, and switch off when it is over. There are gradations in between.

All these groups doubtless have different reactions; but how large is each, and what are the differences? No one can tell with certainty. Surveys suggest that well over half the British population has its television sets functioning on five or more days a week. Assessments of the average time per day vary widely: it may be three or four hours. But what do the figures mean? The only proved fact is that choices of some sort do occur at all levels. Estimated audiences can range from less than two million for a programme of minority interest, such as an opera, to the 25 million for Churchill's funeral, and the 30 million or more for World Cup football. Totally indiscriminate and indifferent switching-on-for-nothing-in-particular, if it were the norm, would scarcely produce so wide a spread.

Organization

Television in Britain, unlike sound radio, ceased to be a public monopoly some time ago. An Act of Parliament in 1954 allowed the formation of a private-enterprise network, Independent Television (ITV), alongside the BBC.

The BBC itself has two channels, BBC1 and BBC2, with separate programmes, though a programme shown on one may be repeated on the other BBC2 does not extend everywhere, and many sets are still in use which do not receive it.

The independent companies are financed by the sale of advertising time, like their American counterparts. However, the law forbids sponsored programmes. In Britain the advertisements are brief commercials, inserted in natural breaks during programmes, and unrelated to them. The writer is only affected by advertisers' demands in the sense that he should provide the natural breaks, and allow for the few minutes which commercials will take up.

At the apex of the system stands the Independent Television Authority (ITA), which operates the transmitting stations, supervises the companies, and is maintained by rentals from them for the use of its facilities. It decides which companies shall be authorized to broadcast, and exercises a degree of control over programmes and advertising, so that everything on ITV shall meet certain standards prescribed by law—standards of truth, impartiality, balance, and taste. (These of course are tricky words, and the actual results are open to debate.)

At present there are fifteen companies supplying programmes under contract with ITA, plus a special news company jointly owned by six of them. The companies are associated with regions—for instance, Thames with the London area, Harlech with Wales and the West of

England, Granada with Lancashire, Grampian with northern Scotland. Programmes are often angled towards the region of origin, but they are not confined to it. In principle anything may be seen anywhere. A normal day in Kent can include programmes supplied by Southern Independent, Thames, Granada, and Yorkshire.

Since ITV was set up, the effects of competition have been, in some respects, the reverse of what was anticipated. It was argued in 1954 (with some justice) that BBC programmes were conformist, dull, often trivial. Independent Television would supply a spice of adventure and irreverence. What actually happened was that the BBC received a jolt, and, under Sir Hugh Carleton Greene, moved towards a fresh boldness and maturity; whereas ITV, being dependent on advertising, had to aim at a mass audience and therefore tended to stick to material that was more 'popular' than the BBC's and, as the 1960s advanced, less experimental.

Today ITV has the regular programmes with the largest faithful public, but neither network is consistently ahead in its share of the viewers. The difference is a difference of bias rather than kind. Many BBC programmes, especially comedy series, have competed successfully for the millions. ITV has a higher proportion of working-class viewers, but, again, the contrast is not extreme.

Types of Programme

Most programmes can be classified under much the same headings as those of sound radio (pages 209–10), though vision gives many of them an utterly different character. Television offers wider scope to programmes of mixed type, such as Ken Russell's dramatized documentaries on composers and authors, in the BBC's *Omnibus*. Children's programmes are more diverse, and so are educational programmes. In Britain both networks do substantial amounts of adult education as well as schools broadcasts, and the BBC runs an Open University that gives degree courses. Television has one major function with no radio counterpart, the showing of feature films which are no longer current in the cinema. The commercials, also without parallel on radio in Britain, are made by agencies, not by the programme companies; but they are mini-programmes in their own right, often expertly filmed with well-known professional actors.

With most of these types of programme, as in radio, the uninvited freelance has little chance. Outside the few areas that do hold out prospects for him—of which, more in a moment—there is one minor potentiality not to be entirely scorned: the sale of jokes. Television has transformed the comedian's position. In music-hall days he could use the same material for months, meeting a new audience every night. Television enables him to reach millions in a single performance, making more money, but also exhausting his repertoire very quickly.

He can't repeat himself. Hence, he has two choices. Either he must try to get a show of his own in which he acts, exploiting his special talents (Eric Sykes, Charlie Drake); or he must have a team of gag-men. In any show where jokes are much used, the producer may well be in the market for them, and it is worth sending them in.

But the scope for a writer's larger endeavours is narrow. I shall discuss only two types of television presentation: documentaries (with a sidelight from commercials), and drama. Even with these, most writers find that only drama is worth attempting. But a full appreciation calls for the wider view.

Documentaries and What they Bring Out

It is in documentary that the nature of the medium, and some of the rules of writing for it, emerge most vividly. Hence, this type of pro-gramme deserves a careful scrutiny. If you are a freelance, you are per-haps not very likely to find yourself commissioned to write a script, unless (again, as with newspaper colour-supplements) you can offer unique experience or unique expertise. But documentary is a powerful object-lesson, helping to lead up to drama, which you are more likely to be doing. It reveals priorities, guidelines, and the right modes of thinking about them. By grasping what a script involves, watching documentaries with this in mind, and planning imaginary ones yourself, you can learn to *think televisually* in more depth than you can learn it from drama alone.

Furthermore, from about 1964 onward, some of the techniques of documentary began invading drama itself. The modern drift away from universal theatre-style naturalism; the freer use of film, actuality shots and stills, and narration and interior monologue related to images—this trend produced such successes as *Up the Junction* and *Cathy Come Home*. The intending television dramatist needs to understand documentary techniques, and this in turn means understanding the framework in which they are employed.

'*Don't say it, show it*'—and the Problems

A would-be writer's first business is to take in a fact which, for some, seems too obvious to see: that the medium is visual. The first rule is: *as far as possible, don't say it, show it.* If you have a programme idea which you can't 'show', stop there. Don't attempt to work it up into a script of any kind. It won't come to life.

With documentary, this is so far the case that the form is dominated by the producer rather than the writer. Sometimes a producer compiles a film first and then commissions a writer to supply the commentary . . . or supplies it himself. Alternatively, producer and writer may work in partnership. But the writer, as such, doesn't start things off. No professional with a documentary idea that looked promising would begin by roughing out a verbal script.

The process of preliminary reflection is more like this. What visual material on the theme is available, or could be obtained? How informative and close to the point would it be? How much could be done with still pictures from a photo agency, or with film from existing film libraries? (The BBC has the biggest of these, and the independent companies have their own.) What are the gaps, and could a camera team fill them effectively at moderate cost?

Past and Present on Television

You can see the problems best of all in a sub-species of programme which is rather uncommon, partly because of them: historical documentary. The further you move away from here-and-now, the more sharply the special difficulties and challenges stand out.

Thus it is all very well to say (and people writing to the BBC have said it), 'Why not do a programme about the Princes in the Tower and the argument over whether Richard III killed them?' The story is famous and interesting—no producer would dispute that. But what could be shown to viewers that would blend with text into an adequate statement, and fill enough screen time for the statement to be made? There are no fifteenth-century newsreels, and few portraits. Though the Tower is still standing, the few relevant locations could all be shown in a minute or two. What would the audience be looking at the rest of the time, while the commentator was explaining the argument?

Three kinds of historical documentary, dealing with a more or less distant past, have succeeded. Each one shows, in its own way, why writing cannot do the television job by itself.

A few historians with an agreeable television presence (Sir Brian Horrocks, for instance) have managed to explain a clear-cut event, such as a battle, with only limited visual aids—plans, models, and so forth. Then there have been a few memorable programmes in which events were partly or wholly dramatized, as in the BBC's reconstructions of the Gunpowder Plot and the Battle of Culloden. Also there have been a few expensive prestige programmes, with special filming of places and buildings and art works, and a commentary by a major authority. Sir Kenneth Clark's *Civilisation* series, first broadcast in 1969, belongs to that select company.

With all three types, the demands of the medium impinge on the writing. Even a low-budget 'Horrocks' programme, which is as close to a straight lecture as television normally gets, depends on the personality who can carry it, and must be written for him.

If the producer and writer are to dramatize events in the full sense of the word, they must bring in actors and get them to the spot or to a spot that looks like it, or use sets. These proceedings are apt to be complicated and costly, and the writer will almost certainly find that he still can't tell the tale through the actors just as he would wish. When material exists, he can exploit the camera to make dramatic use of still pictures—zooming in, panning across, cutting rapidly from one to another so as to build up a cumulative effect. This has been done brilliantly in documentaries on the American West, where photographs could be found. But it is a specifically television technique, which must, to some extent, dictate the text that goes with the pictures.

As for the expensive history programme entailing numerous shots in art galleries, and films of far-off countries—here again, even if the funds are forthcoming, the text must fit in with the possibilities; and the programme will fall flat anyhow in the absence of the famous commentator with a suitable appearance and manner (unless of course the writer is famous and suitable himself).

Suppose, now, that we move our thoughts on documentary towards modern times. What happens? Do the problems vanish? No, they remain. It is purely a question of degree. You might expect that it would all be much easier as we come into the age of film and newspaper photographs. Surely the producer and writer who deal with the twentieth century can keep on top and say whatever they want, because they can always find the picture? Only with qualifications. Their task certainly is easier. The result can be superb, as in Tony Essex's marathon production *The Great War*, written by Correlli Barnett and John Terraine, which traced the 1914 conflict through twenty-six instalments without flagging. Yet when the authors began a sequel, *The Lost Peace*, they soon discovered that a crucial item was missing. The lost peace was the one imposed by the Treaty of Versailles in 1919, and there was no film of the signing. The occasion had to be conveyed through glimpses of the Peace Conference, with politicians coming and going, and a commentary to interpret.

Finally, come right down to the present. A documentary on a subject that is current now—pollution or automation, hunger overseas or a new political movement at home—allows filming for the programme's needs. But the issues which history throws into relief apply here as well. What photos can be got, from agencies or newspapers . . . and at what price? Who will be willing to co-operate on interviews, and how will they look on the small screen if interviewed? Where the programme involves something the audience ought to see, such as a new method of teaching children to draw, can it be filmed live—or failing that, can it be dramatized by persuading the people concerned (who aren't actors) to mime it or mock it up for the camera? And if not, how is it going to be conveyed at all?

How Television Handles an Argument
Then what about the presentation of ideas, arguments, discussion?

It is no use trying to concoct a programme simply by having two alleged experts debate (or pretend to debate) in a studio, or by having one expert draw diagrams on a blackboard. The visual matter mustn't just *illustrate* or *accompany* the words, often it must largely *determine* the words; and it does make a difference who appears on the screen, whether talking or acting.

Moreover, with television as with sound radio, the text itself can seldom be exactly like the text of a book. Viewers can't stop the programme while they reflect, or go back for a repeat. This is not a medium for interwoven reasoning and developed arguments. When a script does set out to reason and argue, it has a different logic from printed prose, even the prose of the television age. It proceeds, or rather leaps, from Point 1 to Point 2 to Point 3—visual stepping-stones with associated words.

The BBC series *Chronicle* once made a film on a topic which, as I mentioned earlier in this book, began attracting public attention during the 1960s: King Arthur. The *Chronicle* programme was a mixture of the historical and the contemporary, because one of the chief reasons for public interest was an archaeological dig going on at the time at Cadbury Castle in Somerset, believed by some to be the original Camelot.

The documentary began with a school in Birmingham where a class was doing an Arthurian project. It gave no account of the project. Viewers simply saw the children enacting scenes from the legends. Next came a clip out of a Hollywood medieval epic; then, on-site interviews with archaeologists who were working, or had recently worked, at places connected with Arthur; and shots of a rocky western coast, accompanying the reading of an ancient poem; and close-ups of medieval books illustrating the stories; and so on.

After the unexplained, eye-catching opening, a commentary introduced each part of the film, and strung it loosely together. But nothing like a lecture ever took shape, and there was no formal conclusion. The film ended with people lighting a beacon on a hill, to test a theory about signalling in early Britain. The corresponding sound was a recording of snatches of conversation among them. To the extent that the documentary tried to solve basic problems of history (did King Arthur exist? if so, when and where?), most of the problem-solving took place in the mind of the interested viewer. His reasoning was mainly his own and came afterwards. It was not thrust at him from the screen in academic detail.

This is the norm for documentary; and while television drama—even drama of detection!—may not have the same sort of intellectual content, the same principles apply to its logic. A writer should let the viewer do much of the mental linking-up for himself. Verbal discussion, the weighing of pros and cons, rarely makes good television. You can suggest opposing theories, or contrasted aspects of a subject, by showing related pictures; or (within limitations) by allowing exponents of rival views to state them. Even this can distort rather than enlighten. Appearance and manner can tip an argument to one side when it ought, rationally, to go to the other.[1] At any rate, the speaker on television— whether seen or unseen—who merely gives a discourse with phrases like 'X thinks . . . on the other hand Y maintains . . .', while nothing connected with it appears on the screen, will probably lose touch with viewers. He will fail to integrate.

Relating Text to Pictures

So when drafting a script of any sort, keep the image always in mind. On radio, your flow of words has to be almost constant, except when interrupted by music or sound effects. On television it need not be. In fact it should not be. The second rule is: *realize that the text is only one factor in the programme. You don't have to have talk going on continuously.* Learn the virtue of keeping quiet. Understand that a good television writer will often abstain from writing, and give the picture a chance to speak for itself, with sound effects or musical accompaniment.

Whatever you do write should be very precise. Television calls for a more painstaking exactitude on concrete detail than radio. You won't get away with things so easily. You can't gloss over difficulties with a phrase, or evoke unseen mysteries with well-chosen words. As you work, you must picture that image on the screen; picture it at every moment; relate your text to it; write *for television*, all the time. Without getting entangled in studio technicalities, always make it clear *what* the audience is to see, and *how*: how close, for how long. Learn the uses of fading-in and fading-out, of cutting and zooming and panning, of switching from camera to camera. Learn them by watching them in action, critically and analytically, on your own set.

An Illustration from Commercials

The last paragraph raises the question of how you actually put a script down on paper. The television commercial comes in handy here, as the script that can be given in full in the shortest space. Let us imagine somebody making up a commercial for nail-varnish. His first draft might come through something like this:

	FEMALE VOICE
Close-up of typewriter with typist's fingers darting over keyboard. Office noises in background.	Fingers . . .

---

[1] Some say that this happened in the historic Kennedy–Nixon debates during the presidential election of 1960, which influenced all subsequent political campaigning.

Tennis racket coming round to strike ball; fingers grasping handle rush into centre of screen. Tennis-court noises in background.

... fingers ...

Piano keyboard, fingers playing. Music heard, not loud.

... fingers!

Close-up of two spread hands, held up. Piano music up for an instant, then sharply down; but it goes on tinkling in the background.

There they are, a whole set of them to take care of. And remember, people *do notice them* ...

Girl carrying file-folders through office. Camera zooms in on hand, with nails showing, and holds picture for a moment.

... at work ...

Same girl at table, playing cards; similar shot.

... at play ...

Same girl at party taking glass of champagne; similar shot.

... wherever you go.

The close-up of the spread hands again.

Remember those fingers! To give them the elegance they deserve, use WALDORF nail-varnish. In three shades to suit your colouring ...

Bottle appears at bottom left of screen. Second bottle appears at bottom centre. Third bottle appears at bottom right. Picture held.

... peach ...
... orange ...
... gold.

Bottles disappear. Camera tracks backwards. We see that the hands belong to the girl we were looking at, who is smiling over them. She lowers her hands, gets smaller in the distance, and is finally seen stationary (the hands still just in the picture) in an oval space in a card bearing the name WALDORF and any other necessary printed matter. Piano music up to a final flourish.

WALDORF nail-varnish. Finger-tip flattery at all times!

On reflection the writer might decide that this draft is too elaborate and ought to be simplified. But the parallel-column method is the general method of approach. I say 'approach'. The eventual shooting script, for the briefest commercial or the longest documentary, will add many technical directions not indicated here. These, however, belong to a later stage. It is not the writer's job to anticipate them when he is making his draft.

Plays

While documentaries (and commercials too) can help immensely in understanding television, the freelance writer's most hopeful field is drama. The medium has a ravenous appetite for it, demanding not only single plays, but episode after episode for the various series and serials. And here the writer does come first, though he must bear all the requirements of television in mind as he works.

It is the series or serial—such as *Doomwatch, Paul Temple, The Avengers, Coronation Street*—that generally makes the most lasting impression on the public, partly because of the sheer power of repetition, partly for a deeper reason which we shall look at in a moment. To write episodes for one of these programmes (they are not usually by the same author throughout) is a most desirable goal.

But an outside writer will seldom succeed by approaching the producer of a series directly. Your best strategy remains the obvious, conventional one: to write a single play from an idea of your own. To get this produced at all will of course be a success, even if it is forgotten within a week. However, there are ampler potentialities beyond that. Occasionally a single play makes a lasting mark by itself; perhaps by an intense timeliness, or a strong dramatization of some issue affecting many people. The supreme instance in Britain is the now proverbial *Cathy Come Home*, on the housing problem. Then again, a single good drama in a particular programme slot (*The Wednesday Play, Comedy Playhouse*, and their equivalents) may lead to a proposal for a follow-up, or a whole series based on the same characters. Finally, if a producer likes the single play, he may take an interest in its author even if he doesn't use it, and invite him to try his hand at an episode in an established series—so that the author finds his way in by the back door.

The 'Intimacy' of Television

Dramatic writing must be done for the medium, like any other kind. It must use images and sound televisually, and adapt itself to the atmosphere. It must stick, as far as possible, to what can be 'shown', not losing coherence in mere talk unrelated to pictures and visible action. As in documentary, indeed more so, the script must make it clear what the audience is to see at every point, parallel with the dialogue.

Television drama has to capture its audience by other means than the theatrical spell. Some of the principles of radio still apply, such as the need to make an early, interest-arousing statement, yet also help late arrivals to pick up the thread. But television has its own quality. Its images focus attention cinematically. On the other hand their appearance in the living-room, and their smallness, create an intimacy—often a rather relaxed intimacy—which is non-cinematic.

Keep this always in mind. A serial such as *Coronation Street*, portraying 'ordinary people', works partly because of a feeling that characters on the small screen are close. The cinema is the traditional medium for stars whom fans adore at a distance. A television star is less remote. He can talk familiarly to the viewers through the camera. One comedian, Frankie Howerd, hit on his characteristic style by doing this often even when he purported to be acting. He revived the 'aside' which the realistic theatre dropped long ago, and showed how television could give it a fresh liveliness.

Several stock anecdotes, even outside the drama field, reflect this half-belief or sub-belief that the person on the screen is in some sense present. Newscasters are said to receive letters from women, asking how they like the curtains. Such a viewer seems to think that the newscaster sees her in her home as she sees him in the studio. Then there is the joke about the Red Indian who had never encountered television. At last he visited a town-dwelling friend who owned a set. Left in the room with it alone, he rushed out almost immediately.

'What's the matter?' his friend asked.

The Indian was alarmed. 'I turn on heater and little men fight.'

Television drama really is a case of 'little men fighting' in the viewer's home . . . well, more or less. It is easy of access and close to everyday life—you don't have to go out to watch. It mingles with domestic surroundings and events, and, for this reason, can rarely transport the viewer with tension or horror.[1] It is intimate (the word bears repeating), not spectacular. Because of the range and size of the picture, it relies on close-ups more than the cinema. Actors are often nearer together than they would be on the stage or in real life. A sense of proximity is seldom absent for long.

The closeness, the matching of words to images, the ability (and the need) to show as well as say—all these give a dramatist opportunities for swift, sharp exposition. Necessary knowledge doesn't have to be rammed home. Viewers respond readily to hints and phrases. The picture may well say more than the dialogue does. A play begins, let us suppose, with a honeymoon couple sitting outside a French café with empty glasses in front of them. Suddenly the husband leaps up, hails a taxi, and almost pushes the wife in. 'Did you pay?' she asks. 'Yes,' he replies, 'don't you remember?' But as the taxi drives off, she turns and sees the proprietor hurry out of the café, glance at their table, and look up and down the street. She turns back towards the camera with a pensive expression. We now know that her husband is less than honest, and that she is capable of seeing through him; and the picture has conveyed nearly all of it, in a few seconds.

Appreciate, in fact, the effect of the image without any words at all.

---

1. Off-hand I can recall only one spell of sustained horror on television in recent years, and this was in a film, *Psycho*, which survived transmission on the small screen without losing its nightmarish power.

Some have lost their edge and become visual clichés—the sudden glare of headlights, the neon sign flashing outside a window, the man dying in a room while cheerful and irrelevant noises go on in the distance. Still, realize the impact of even the most threadbare once the audience is drawn in, and devise new ones yourself. Dialogue is important in television plays as in any plays, but remember once again, you don't have to have talk going on continuously.

The Key to Success with TV Drama

The intimacy and sense of contact supply the deeper reason for the frequent success of a series of short or middle-length plays with the same characters. Here is a major difference between television and live theatre. The theatre has no real counterpart of 'situation comedy' (*Steptoe and Son*, the Lucy cycles), or serious costume productions like *The Six Wives of Henry VIII*. Akin to these are the serials, among which *The Forsyte Saga*, compressing Galsworthy's novels into interlocking stories of acceptable length, retains high prestige.

All such marathon efforts—however brilliant, however funny— depend for their *sustained* strength on the viewer's readiness to get to know the main characters, develop attitudes to them, and renew his acquaintance with them each week, where he wouldn't go each week to see them in a theatre. In this kind of television the principle of the radio soap opera is taken further—sometimes with results that oddly underline the intimacy. Imaginary places acquire substance: when one of the houses in Coronation Street became vacant, the television company received several applications from would-be tenants. Imaginary persons become more real than the actors who play them: Bill Simpson, 'Dr. Finlay', used to find that strangers would strike up an acquaintance and start talking to him about their symptoms.

A general sense of reality and nearness is not precisely the secret. Important as it often is, it seems not to be an absolutely vital factor. What is essential for a series or serial is (I repeat) *the viewer's relation with the main characters.* And characters can occasionally work the magic alone. The stories in *The Avengers* were absurd, and meant to be so. It was easy to enjoy the incredible world of John Steed; it was impossible to feel close to it. But Steed himself—rich, well-connected, mysterious, versatile, unflappable—and his ambiguous girl partners, could hold a huge audience through one grotesque comedy-thriller after another, week after week, year after year.

The best moral for you to draw, therefore, is this. *Write so as to exploit the sense of intimacy, of closeness, of getting-to-know.* Invent characters and a situation and a style of dialogue that are likely to achieve a rapport, even if you are writing a single play, with no ambition for a series. The rapport can come in various ways. It can come through sympathy, or through love–hate; through familiarity, or through wish-fulfilling fantasy. It can often come through a sort of likeness-in-unlikeness. Successful programmes have been built on everyday work situations which were not shown realistically, but guyed or glamorized. The prototypes here are *The Rag Trade*, a series of half-hour farces set in a garment workshop, and *Compact*, a romantic serial set in the office of a women's magazine. There have been others since.

The rapport may be more complex. Part of the curious strength of *Steptoe and Son* was that it made contact with its millions of viewers on several levels—through humour, through work, through frustration, through the father–son relationship. Episodes could range from broad farce to near-tragedy without the programme disintegrating. *Doomwatch*, a series of the late 1960s and early 70s which would have been unthinkable ten years before, succeeded through its appeal to misgivings aroused by so-called progress. Its hero, Dr. Quist, seemed to be fighting the worried viewer's own battle against encroaching technological terrors.

It is easy enough to list types of television drama—war, police, spy, Western, domestic, and so on and so forth. But don't be spellbound by categories. And don't feel inhibited. Stimulate and provoke, so long as you keep the audience with you. Most taboos on subject-matter have gone, and—partly through dramatists' study of documentary—technique has shaken off theatrical naturalism as an unbreakable rule.

Be cautious of 'messages' in the manner of Bernard Shaw or John Osborne. As we have seen, television is a dubious medium for putting ideas over. Yet if you can wrap one up in a convincing play, it may slip through. Viewers of *Cathy Come Home* may have learnt a little about homelessness (even if the play was rather unfair); and viewers of *Dr. Finlay's Casebook*, and other doctor programmes, may have learnt a more humane attitude to various afflictions.

Some Notes on Technique

As ever, of course, a play is a play. Whether original or adapted, whether complete in one episode or running through several, it must observe dramatic principles and must prove itself as drama, however unpretentious or farcical.

Recall the relevant parts of our survey of plays in general (Chapter Thirteen), and study the special patterns of television. Structurally, television plays tend to lie somewhere between live theatre and cinema. They cut from scene to scene more widely and frequently than the former, but they are not as fluid as the latter. One of the main reasons is economic: there is a limit to what can be spent on sets and location shots.

Plan your master scenes first—the scenes that will carry the essential plot—but recognize that you will link them up by means of other material, which has no complete theatrical equivalent. In the finished product, scenes should often lead physically to other scenes as they cannot on the stage. The nearer you can get to showing concisely how it happens—how a character gets from A to B, what the layout of a house is—the more convincing, usually, the result will look.

Remember that you don't have to worry about some of the limitations of live performance. You can have a character in London one minute, in Manchester the next, and indicate his journey with an interposed film of him driving along a road with signposts. The actor can be filmed in the car before or after his 'London' and 'Manchester' scenes are shot in the studio. The producer puts the scenes in order.

You can combine acting in the same scene with film, as when characters meet in what appears to be Rome, but is in fact a studio with a film of Rome back-projected behind them. You can sometimes use still shots. For example, you might portray signatures being collected for a petition with a rapid series of stills of the organizer handing the petition to various signatories.

Decide what, if anything, can be done with music. And learn the resources of film libraries. Don't be deterred from showing an aircraft landing by the obvious expense of sending a cameraman to Heathrow to take one. He won't have to. Plenty of shots of aircraft landing are already on file.

Developing Your Ideas

When you have an idea for a play—perhaps with an eye to a series growing out of it—develop it in detail before trying it on anyone. A trap for the non-professional, and a cause of wasted time, is the delusion that because television does so often succeed with a series, the success is due to the basic idea . . . so that ideas are marketable. Not so. Even such an unfailing topic of interest as illness (the subject-matter of *Dr. Finlay* and *Dr. Kildare* and all the other medical sagas) cannot produce good television in itself.

Some years ago a producer remarked that he got letters from time to time saying, 'What about a comedy series set in a holiday camp?' His reaction was, 'Well, what about it?' The idea is nothing. The working-out is all. Nobody could have got anywhere by saying, 'What about a comedy series with two men in a junk yard?' *Steptoe* originated, as so many comedy series have, in a single half-hour which revealed the possibilities. Its offbeat, Chekhovian quality made it unique. This, however, had to be shown. The bare notion of 'two men in a junk yard' could never even have hinted at it.

Write your whole play—thirty minutes, fifty minutes, or whatever (the longer ones stand a better chance). Or at any rate, write a very big sample of it, big enough to display all the main characters and show your ability with dialogue, scene, and plot. The BBC has a Television

Script Unit to submit it to. The British independent companies have Drama Departments.

Before trying, get a thorough insight into the techniques by studying them in action, not just reading descriptions. Catch the flavour of television dialogue. This is pre-eminently a medium which the writer must, so to speak, get into. To write for it you must become television-conscious. You can only achieve this by watching a wide range of programmes yourself, perceptively, analytically, but appreciatively; both from your own point of view, and (so far as you can manage it) from that of the ordinary viewer who may have different tastes, but is often acute and never to be despised.

Teamwork

One word more. Television, like the theatre, is a collective medium. When you reach the point of production, your work must come to life through a producer, actors, and technicians as well—a team. The producer may want to alter your script radically. Actors can have constructive ideas . . . or make difficulties. Even the technicians can inject unforeseen hazards. (I recall a programme which was threatened with catastrophe at a vital moment because the camera crew wanted extra pay for taking location shots on a holiday, and the budget wouldn't stand it.)

Be prepared for all things, and—within reason—co-operate.

Exercises

1. Make up a commercial, not exceeding a minute in length, for (a) a drink or (b) a floor polish or (c) a new magazine.

2. Re-read the sketch of the 'King Arthur' documentary (page 224). Now suppose that an archaeologist has found traces of an outlaws' hideout in Sherwood Forest, and a producer is thinking of a documentary on 'Robin Hood'. Suggest how it might be handled.

3. Watch a television series currently running. Make a scene-by-scene synopsis for another episode in it, with the usual characters and the usual type of story. Include specimen dialogue if you like; but in any case, outline the complete half-hour (or whatever the duration is), so that the script could be written from your synopsis.

4. On page 231 a producer was quoted as saying he received letters suggesting 'a comedy series set in a holiday camp' but the idea wasn't developed. Develop it a little yourself. Invent three characters in the camp, and describe them. (If you don't know enough about camps, use some other holiday setting, such as a hotel.)

5. Think of an idea for a serial: either purely televisual like *Coronation Street*, or an adaptation like *The Forsyte Saga*. Write the opening scene.

CHAPTER NINETEEN

REPORT WRITING

General Procedure

A report, in business or industry, means a fairly substantial document that examines a given problem in detail, usually with a view to offering practical suggestions. Reports don't just happen, they have to be written. Most of the basic advice for writing them is the same as the basic advice for writing anything. The first question, therefore, is: 'Have you read Parts One and Two of this book?' If not, the first step towards report-writing is to read them, with special attention to what is said about clear thinking (pages 39–44, 62–8). The rest of the technique is largely a matter of 'drill' and procedure.

This breaks down into four stages: the preparation, the arrangement, the actual writing, and the revision. To draw up a report you must go through the stages in that order, but not rigidly one after another. There will be a certain amount of overlap and back-tracking.

Preparation

Reports are not voluntary products like sonnets. If you have to write one, the reason, almost certainly, is that somebody else has asked you to. You may find yourself diagnosing a factory bottleneck for the works manager, or studying retail outlets in Suffolk for a market research consultant. But nearly always the starting-point is an order or assignment. Therefore, you must begin by getting your briefing perfectly clear. You must know, with exactness, what you have been asked to do. Any misunderstanding can result in weeks of wasted effort, and a disaster when the report is read and found wanting.

Generally, the person who requests the report will expect to be provided with *information*, *analysis of information*, *conclusions*, and *recommendations*. Suppose a manufacturer with a new refrigerating system wants to explore the prospects of selling his apparatus to the frozen food industry. He goes to an industrial consultant, who tells a member of the staff to compile a report on the present position with frozen foods. Questions arise at once. Does this mean in the United Kingdom only, or does the client hope to export? In which parts of the industry might the new equipment be used: the initial processing of the food, the transportation, the storage and display in shops, or throughout? The scope of the data to be collected, and the placing of emphasis in the final text and proposals, will depend on the answers to such queries as these.

233

In planning a report, you should not only be clear what its prospective reader will want, you should try to imagine him personally. 'Picture your reader', as we have frequently seen, is one of the rules for all writing, and it applies to reports just as it does to fiction or journalism, but in a different way. The reader is more precisely defined. You may actually know him. He's probably your boss. At any rate he is someone in a particular position, with a particular interest. Define him further still in your own thoughts. How much will he know already? What will be the right kind of terminology to use with him, the right aspects of the subject to stress? Is his outlook executive or administrative or technical? In industry you find widely differing mentalities at different levels. The executive is concerned (theoretically, anyhow) with the broader issues of policy, and the firm's plans for several years to come. The administrative or technical specialist does not look so far ahead but is probably concerned with more immediate problems. Also, he is apt to see everything in terms of his own speciality (accounting or work study or whatever), and to understand better when approached on that ground.

One thing more about your reader, whoever he is. *Assume that he is busy*, and keep that assumption in mind constantly. He won't spend days studying your report exclusively, in a quiet room.

When gathering and sifting the material, the main requirement is a correct, conscientious logic. Your programme should follow the routine of scientific method in general. Having defined the problem and the mode of approach, collect the facts and take detailed notes on them. 'The facts' means *all* the facts. The most usual failure is stopping short, and not recognizing every fact that can have a bearing. After that, you should scrutinize and analyse; draw provisional conclusions; test them open-mindedly by experiment and further inquiry; and adjust them till you are satisfied. Your final task will be to devise recommendations. If you plan in advance to do all these things, and then do them, you will lay a firm basis for the report in which you write them up.

Arrangement

While the preparation should follow this pattern, the actual report, probably, should not. Your job is not to tell the story of your researches, but to present the results. Managerial tastes vary, but it is often a wise course, if not an official requirement, to summarize your findings and recommendations at the beginning. This counterpart of 'news style' (see page 199) enables your reader to grasp the essentials rapidly. Consultants, when drawing up a report for wide circulation in a company, sometimes produce it in two editions—a short 'popular' one giving the main points alone for general consumption, and a full 'technical' one for the personnel most closely involved.

Choose a title that sums up the theme accurately without being too long. Have a place at the beginning for a date, and perhaps a note on the circumstances, such as a reference to the memo in which the report was asked for. Begin—if you do work to the scheme suggested—with the summary, stating your recommendations as clearly and briefly as you can. Follow on with the body of the report. When planning this, consider how best to divide up the subject, and make a list of headings and sub-headings under which all the material can be grouped.

The 'frozen food' report, for example, if meant to cover the whole of the industry in Britain, might be broken up into seven sections:

(1) a short account of all the frozen food companies—their size, their resources, the type of plant they use;

(2) a survey of the distributive network and retail outlets;

(3) a description of the methods of transport—types of van, types of container, methods of keeping the products cold during transport;

(4) the varieties of food that are frozen and a study of trends in eating habits;

(5) a note on promotion and advertising;

(6) a review of recent technical developments, current problems, and the industry's likely progress in the foreseeable future. There should also be

(7) a list of sources of information, such as trade magazines, to substantiate the findings, and help the client to follow up specially interesting leads.

Where, as in this example, a report deals with a big and complex subject, it is apt to swamp the reader with vast quantities of supporting data. All the facts and figures may be necessary to prove the case, yet they get in the way of comprehension. Simplify them as far as possible by making the fullest use of tables, graphs, diagrams, and similar visual aids. In general, put these on sheets by themselves, not embedded in the text. If the mass of material of this kind is still too forbidding, consign it to appendices, and leave the text uncluttered.

The best way of building up a report is to have a ring-binder and put the draft pages in as they accumulate. Then you can switch them back and forth easily, and try out alternative presentations. When the report is really bulky, some managers are happy if the final text itself comes to them in a ring-binder, with dividers between sections, and coloured plastic tags sticking out to show where each section comes. Others are not so happy. I recall an executive in a motor company berating a subordinate who had handed him a binder most carefully embellished with what the great man called 'Christmas-tree lights'.

You will have to draw up a table of contents, and put it in the front. But since you won't know what the page numbers will be till the typescript is complete, and since you may have second thoughts on arrangement as you go along, the safest course at the preliminary stage is to insert a sheet simply headed 'Contents' at the front of the binder, and fill it in last.

Writing

Under this heading we have covered the ground already. The chief special guideline in reports is to be direct and specific, avoiding both misplaced cleverness and jargon. (See especially pages 89–95.) Write it in draft first so that you can work out the line of logic of your material and see how it fits together.

Revision

When you have composed the rough draft, lay it aside, take it up again after an interval, and assail it with ruthless impartiality. First impressions are important—so, what about them? What does your draft report *look* like? Now that you have deployed all the material, is your title still apt and informative? Does one see at a glance what the report is dealing with, and what it is meant to communicate? (The initial glance is apt to be crucial in practice. It can create a false impression which causes all the rest of the report to be wasted.)

Consider the effect of a single run-through on the busy reader whom you must always assume. Would he take in all the main points at a single quick reading, without becoming confused? Have you included too much argumentation pro and con, which he would have to pause over and sort out for himself? Have you given too little prominence to some vital fact, so that he could easily overlook it?

Evaluate the structure which you have ended up with. This may not be quite what you envisaged at the planning stage. Unexpected data may have changed the proportions of the original scheme, or compelled you to add new sections. Does the report still have a manifest and complete design, shown in the table of contents? If it doesn't, rearrange the sections again and re-write lead-ins and linking passages accordingly.

Criticize your language and manner, in the light of the advice in earlier chapters. Apply the Gunning Fog Index (pages 56–8). Have you used too many long sentences? too many long, abstract, or difficult words? too many verbs in the passive? too many clumsy, deadening stock phrases? Are you vague where you ought to be definite? Have you slipped into pointless clichés? Have you allowed managerial or specialist jargon to do your writing and thinking for you? (Of course scientists writing for other scientists use a specialized language of their own, but the same need for clarity of communication applies.)

Is everything lucid and unequivocal? Have you written any sentences that could be taken in a wrong sense? Some ambiguities can be comic, like the specimens quoted on page 42. Some can be downright dangerous, because a reader may misconstrue them in all seriousness. A report on traffic regulations in a city might say: 'X Street is a pedestrian precinct closed to traffic, except goods vehicles, between 5 p.m. and 11 a.m.' Does this mean that X Street is closed to traffic between those times, except for goods vehicles, but open at other times; or does it mean that it is closed to traffic at all times, except that goods vehicles may enter it during that period?

More elusive, but important, is rightness of tone. Pretend mentally that you asked for the report yourself, and that somebody else has now submitted the draft to you. Would you like it? Would it arouse your interest? Does it address you as you would wish to be addressed, or do you get a feeling of being talked down to, or dictated to, or conned? Get an outside opinion, if you can find a qualified, constructive critic.

Go over the draft in detail. Is every statement accurate, and relevant? Do any of them conflict with each other? Could any be falsified by quotation out of context? Rivals and opponents are liable to do this, and you are very lucky indeed if you haven't got any. What about repetitions? These may be justified, if a fact needs emphasizing in several contexts. But beware of repeating yourself through sheer forgetfulness, or through a desire to pad out a skimpy passage. What about gaps? Have you omitted things that ought to be treated? Is any of your text really camouflage—vague words covering up deficiencies? And what about the reasoning? When you state your conclusions, and offer your proposals, are they warranted by the facts you have given? Might those facts be interpreted in some other way? Even if you are satisfied that your proposals are good, can you think of better ones?

Assess your draft in the light of all these points, and revise unsparingly. When the text is in its final form, number the sections and paragraphs for easy reference. Last of all, see to the date that goes in the front. The report which you submit on that day should conform to what might be called the Five C's of report-writing: it should be *clear, complete, concrete, consistent, correct*. If it is, take heart. Writing may not be your vocation, but the proved ability to do it with flair is so valuable to an alert employer that the possessor's prospects are bright.

Exercises

1. A factory has three fork-lift trucks for transporting crates across a large yard from one building to another. Delays cause the manager to suspect that the trucks are not being used as well as they might be. He asks you to investigate and report. Plan your investigation, and draw up tentative headings for the report. (*Hints*: you will need to find—among other things—how much of the time the trucks are running loaded, how much of the time they are running empty, or idle; what the operators do; whether the trucks are following the best route; whether other factory traffic obstructs them.)

2. A supermarket manager asks you to study the possibilities of improving the design and layout of the store. Besides making observations of your own,

you can (a) question the staff, but not ask them to collect information which they wouldn't collect normally; (b) experimentally rearrange goods on display stands, but not rearrange the stands; (c) experimentally alter the checkout procedure, but not alter the equipment used, such as the cash registers. You can, of course, *suggest* these alterations or any others, when the study is completed. Plan your investigation, and draw up tentative headings for the report.

PART FIVE: *COUNSEL IN PARTING*

CHAPTER TWENTY

THE BIRTH OF A BOOK

Orientations

In Parts One and Two we studied the writer's craft in its widest bearings, and considered what it should always be, however applied. In Parts Three and Four we examined what is special in different types of writing. Publication, which for most writers is the ultimate issue, never came fully under the spotlight. We glanced at it, but moved on. Now the time has arrived to face it squarely.

Publishing, in this chapter, means the large-scale kind: book publishing. Apart from being the most important, it is stable enough to be definite about. Behind all the upheavals of the book trade there is a certain long-term permanency. With literary items smaller than books —with short stories and plays, poems and scripts for broadcasting—the media and the market are in constant flux. Even where an organization goes on uninterruptedly, as the BBC does, policies change and personalities change. The only rule never liable to become outmoded is that you should understand what the author of a book should do, and then apply that lesson to your own type of writing under your own conditions, so far as it is applicable . . . which is surprisingly far, as you will find. This chapter will help you to place the hints already offered (e.g. on pages 200–3) in the context of a broader technique of professional relations.

Book publishing itself is not an impersonal abstraction, the same in all cases. While its principles are consistent, its practice is highly variable. Giving advice on 'how to get published' is not like giving advice on 'how to fill out your income tax return'. Probably no other major business reveals such a wide range of attitudes, interests, and policies. Publishers cater to a variety of readerships, at a variety of levels. You must decide roughly who you are aiming at, and choose your publisher appropriately, with the aid of the *Writers' and Artists' Year Book* and any other available sources of guidance. And you must be prepared, as ever, for a degree of self-adaptation.

For anything worth while to happen, of course, adaptation to a publisher's needs does presuppose that you have something tangible to adapt—a distinct individuality and a command of writing-in-general. You must have a style and thoughts of your own, pointing more or less in a certain direction. Merely churning out prose which you think will suit a particular market, just in the hope of raising money or breaking into print, is a recipe for failure. Scott Fitzgerald, in *The Beautiful and*

241

Damned, portrays his financially-pressed hero dashing off a magazine story in what he imagines to be the popular idiom. His wife, asked for an opinion, is coaxed into assuring him that the story is 'better than a lot of the stuff that gets published'. Needless to say, it never does get published. He produces half a dozen such stories altogether—'wretched and pitiable efforts to "write down" by a man who had never before made a consistent effort to write at all'—and they collect thirty-one well-deserved rejection slips.

We are assuming, however, that you *do* have something to offer as an author. Where do you go with it?

Publishers: Narrowing the Field

For our present purpose the word 'publisher' means a reputable one, who accepts authors' work on its merit, and brings it out under his house's imprint, taking a commercial risk on its success or failure. There are also 'vanity publishers' who print books, with little discrimination, at the author's expense. They have very limited organizations (if any) for promoting and distributing books, and it is better to avoid them. Apart from anything else, an author who deals with such a firm may give an unfortunate impression of himself to the public—an impression which some of their clients justify. The head of one vanity firm confessed that he had taken a large sum from an author to publish a work entitled *How to Make Money Writing*.

If you have an idea of value, and the capacity to handle it, you will stand a good chance of finding a genuine publisher who will say 'yes'. Genuine publishers in Great Britain bring out a total of over 30,000 books every year. There are 2,000 of them. In practice, however, your choice is far less wide. Many are small, and confine themselves to publications of a specialized type, such as local guides or regimental histories. Some small publishers, lacking a strong speciality which is economically sound, go out of business quickly, and it is as well to check the reputation and prospects of a small, unknown firm before you enter into an agreement with it.

Your choice of major publishing houses is probably limited to about 50. Run your eye over the reviews in the *Sunday Times* and *Observer*. Most of the books noticed and advertised on those pages are published by firms in the top class. These established houses combine prestige with success. They show sustained business sense and acumen as well as literary discernment. Over the years they have built up lists of books that go on and on selling, and the profits from these enable them to take chances with others.

If you have not yet made a name for yourself, always remember this element of risk which the publisher must assume. Even the largest firms have to struggle with ever-mounting financial problems—production costs, overheads, salaries, warehousing, postage, readers' fees, the cost of keeping representatives on the road. The frequent mergers and take-overs reflect their difficulties. To stay in business at all, a publisher must *sell* books. To sell them, he must hold down the retail prices to accept-able levels. Therefore he must incur losses on some, to be made up by the profits on others. Largely, it is the best-selling authors who keep a firm afloat. You, if unknown or only slightly known, are not a best-seller, and are most unlikely to become one overnight. Almost certainly, you are a risk. So look for a publisher with the resources to gamble a little, and policies and tastes which might dispose him to gamble on you.

One publishing house is emphatically not like another. Each has its own character, stamped on it, perhaps, by a personality (e.g. Victor Gollancz), or by a family tradition (e.g. John Murray), or by following up a winning streak, or attracting authors of a particular outlook. Before submitting even an idea to a publisher, make sure that this one is promising for you. It is a waste of time and money to approach one that isn't. The rule is not refuted by the case of that supreme best-seller A. J. Cronin, who wrote his first novel in a spirit of extreme diffidence, and then, instead of making an appraisal of publishers, picked one out with a pin. The novel was outstanding, and the pin, by chance, was well aimed. It is wiser not to rely on your own unique genius, or your own pin.

There is no need to spend days determining the one exactly-right firm, and then succumb to despair if rejected by that one. On the face of things at least, several will be equally suitable. Also there will be several you can eliminate. Don't try a scholarly work on a publisher of sensational fiction; don't try a sex-novel on a university press.

As I said, you can get some guidance from the *Writers' and Artists' Year Book*. However, there is no complete substitute for actually looking at a firm's recent publications. 'Recent' should be stressed. Aspects of a publisher's policy and the character of his list often change; and the changes are sometimes radical if there is new ownership or management. Study a publisher's list by getting a copy of his latest catalogue. See the kind of books he favours, the areas in which he publishes—educational books, 'literary' fiction, sensational fiction, popular history, scholarly history, and so on.

Approaching a Publisher

At what stage of your work do you begin making overtures?

With fiction, it is best to wait till you have a completed book, and then send it to whichever firm you think the most suitable. A novel must be judged as a whole. A publisher will be wary of a chapter or two submitted alone, however brilliant. Authors, notoriously, can lack staying power. Many a novel begins with a promising first chapter, then falls to pieces or gets out of hand by the second or third.

With non-fiction it is easier for the publisher to give at least a provisional decision on the basis of an outline and specimen chapter. In that field you can make a first move before getting too deeply embroiled with the text. Such a move can be most valuable in sounding out interest.

Outline and Specimen Chapter

Your specimen should be designed to whet the publisher's appetite. Recognize the pitfalls. Because you are interested in a subject yourself, it doesn't follow that everybody else is. The sample will commend you far more forcibly if you make it stimulating than if you weigh it down with mere proofs of your knowledge. Beware, also, of slipping into another misconception that leads to the same failure—the snobbery of the expert who believes he is the sole authority, or one of a tiny group of authorities; that the public knows nothing, isn't worth the courtesy of explanation, and doesn't matter. It will be obvious to a publisher that the completed book would be a dull parade of expertise, unlikely to attract anybody without specialist knowledge.

The first mistake lies in picturing the uninitiated reader as closer to you than he is, and not realizing that you have to interest him. The second lies in picturing him as further off than he is, and not even wanting to interest him. A specimen outline and text showing a just appraisal of the public envisaged, and a power to attract and excite, will take you further towards acceptance with most publishers than any display of 'cleverness'.

Your outline of the proposed book can be one of two things, preferably both: (*a*) a piece of descriptive text explaining the form of the book, its content, and the order in which the material will be presented, or (*b*) a list of chapter headings with the main topics of the chapters summarized under each. Such a list will look rather like the detailed list of contents found in the preliminary pages of many non-fiction books, including this one. (See pages ix–xiv.)

The specimen chapter which accompanies your outline need not be the first in the book—though the first may show best how you would set the scene and lead into your subject—but it should certainly embody some of the best and most characteristic material the book will contain.

Both outline and chapter should be typed, as cleanly and professionally as possible, on quarto size paper. Typing should be double-spaced with fairly wide margins. Keep at least one carbon copy, preferably two. Don't send a publisher anything on dirty paper, or with excessive crossings-out, or rusty paper-clips. You can place the typescript in a folder, with a title on the front, if you like. This will keep it clean and hold it together, but is not essential. What *is* essential is a note of your name and address, and telephone number if you have one. These particulars should be clearly typed on page 1 of your material, as well as being included in the normal way in your covering letter.

The Covering Letter

This should be a clear, compact explanation of your reasons for proposing to write the book, and any relevant facts that can help the publisher to assess its possible market. Say who you think would buy the book; in fact, list the kinds of readers for whom you are writing. A publisher likes to know that you have taken the trouble to find out the strength of possible rivalry (see pages 183–5) and can say *why* your book would fill a gap in a particular market, or meet a foreseeable demand. Publishers today frequently co-publish with an American firm, so if you can say why you think the book would interest American readers, that too can be helpful. So can information that would aid the publisher in assessing prospective sales of serial and paperback rights.

When your outline, sample text and covering letter are complete, send the package off to the editor of whichever publishing house you have chosen. Always include a stamped addressed envelope for its return. And then, *wait*. You should receive a formal acknowledgment of receipt, after which, for a time, silence will follow. Do not demand an interview. Do not telephone. Do not pester for a decision. Be patient, if necessary, for a full month before making even the most tentative inquiry. Delay may well be a hopeful sign, and when the issue is in the balance, an author can turn a publisher against him by tactless badgering.

The Publisher's Response

To a proposition put in the form suggested, most publishers will respond rather sooner than they will to a full typescript, which takes time to consider. You will hear from a staff editor. If he says 'no', accept that verdict. Don't indulge in fantasies about prejudice or vested interests. The only ground for arguing would be an error of fact. Thus he may have expressed doubts of saleability for reasons which you can refute (politely of course) from positive knowledge. He may have said, 'A, B, and C have already written books on this topic and there surely isn't room for another,' and you may know, from your own scrutiny of their books, that yours will contain material they have not used, will be quite different in approach, and will supersede all three. But such situations are uncommon, and in any case you ought to have anticipated the editor's point in your first letter, making it unambiguously clear from the outset *why* your book would be different and better.

If rejected by the first publisher on your list, try the next. Try several if necessary. Go on till one of three things happens:

(1) A publisher does express interest.
(2) You have exhausted the list and drawn blank.
(3) You have had a number of rejections *for the same reason*, and this is a reason which you can trust publishers to be right about,

such as the prohibitive cost of producing the book you have in mind (e.g. too many pictures), or the smallness of the potential market (e.g. too few enthusiasts for your subject).

Results (2) and (3) may of course be due to a reason which is not made explicit—that your work just isn't good enough. Publishers are reluctant to say so too brutally, and a fairly non-committal rejection letter is as far as they will go. You must try to read between the lines of a letter of this type. *Don't ask for a detailed criticism.* A publisher will only offer positive criticism (*a*) if he thinks that a script is promising and could be improved, and that the author is worth encouraging; or (*b*) if he is interested in publishing it, provided the author is willing to undertake certain revisions. If neither (*a*) nor (*b*) applies, the publisher rejects without comment, and you must simply accept his verdict.

To revert, however, to the first and happiest possibility: that a publisher's editor shows interest. On the strength of a specimen only, he is still unlikely to give you an instant affirmative. He may do so (after consultations within the firm) if you have performed some startling feat with an obvious public appeal, such as capturing a flying saucer. The finished story will manifestly sell, and if it turns out that you can't write well enough to sustain it to the end, he can bring in a ghost-writer to assist. Failing such an achievement, however, he will probably send you an encouraging letter, and ask for more details or more material. Or he may ask you to come and see him.

Should he want fuller information, supply it promptly, and supply it in a forthcoming, constructive spirit. If your book is to succeed, it will succeed through an alliance between your own gifts and the commercial insight of the publisher who has recognized them.

At the Publisher's End

What goes on in a publishing house during the period while the author waits? Let us start from the moment when a full typescript, say of a novel, lands on the editor's desk. Much the same applies to a non-fiction outline and specimen chapter, in the form we have been considering, except that the provisional decision can be reached sooner. The editor can study the material in less time, and get a second opinion, if he wants one, by passing it to another editor within the house.

The editor is busy, and will only 'sample' a complete new script that arrives. He can judge quickly whether it is worth getting a full report made on it. If so, he will pass it to a qualified professional reader. In most publishing houses of repute, editors are very careful indeed in assessing manuscripts. They are not biased towards rejection. They know how often best-sellers have been lost to Publisher A through some mistake of judgment or foresight which Publisher B did not commit, and they are well on guard against letting anything good slip through their hands. Your typescript will be examined in detail unless it is plainly hopeless . . . and we are assuming that it isn't.

A favourable report from a reader will lead to closer scrutiny by the editor. He may ask for a report from another reader, or read the whole thing himself. Continuing good responses, plus the editor's own recommendation, will lead to a discussion at executive level. How many copies of the book might be sold? What shape, size, and price would the book be? Would it sell to an American publisher? Might it raise problems of censorship or libel? What about the paperback prospects? Has the author a future, or is this liable to be his one and only work? Will any re-thinking and re-planning be required, and if so, is he going to be co-operative?

The last question can be crucial. An author can clear every other fence and then fall at this one, when a query from the editor draws an uncompromising reply. *Authors who are troublesome antagonize publishers.* In this field as in others, always show a co-operative spirit, so far as you can without loss of integrity.

Even after your hopes have been raised sky-high by exchange of letters and an interview at the office, the publisher may still reject you. At such an advanced stage you will be given reasons in full. Think them over, consider how far you can deal with the objections, and decide whether to tackle another firm.

Meanwhile, watch the physical appearance of your typescript. If in due course you send it elsewhere, the much-travelled material will have lost its first freshness. That condition will tell its own tale, predisposing the next publisher against you, slightly perhaps, but significantly. Replace the folder with a new one. Re-type the script wherever it seems advisable to do so; pay special attention to the first and last pages.

The Contract

When a publisher does accept you, you will be offered a contract. This is a legal document stating the terms of his obligation to you, and of yours to him. It will specify the percentage royalty to be paid to you on each copy sold, and the advance on royalties to be paid beforehand. It will include clauses defining various rights—translation, for instance, and other subsidiary rights—and probably it will include an option clause, requiring that when you write your next book, you must offer it to this publisher before going to any competitor.

Although you are free to bargain over the terms, it is better not to, especially with a first book where the publisher is taking a gamble on you. In any case a reputable publisher will certainly make you a fair offer, normal for a book of this kind, and based on his preliminary costings.

The contract guarantees that the publisher will try hard to bring out

your book within a fixed period, but this is not an irrevocable undertaking. Fire, flood, or printers' breakdown may interfere at any time,
and delays *may* be unavoidable. If your contract is for a book which the
publisher has accepted on the basis of specimen material only, you
yourself will have agreed to a date on which you undertake to deliver
the completed work. The contract for such a commissioned book—perhaps an educational book in a series—will normally include a clause
stating that the publisher will pay part of the advance on royalties 'on
acceptance' of a satisfactory manuscript. You are not at liberty to
bungle your work and still demand publication. You must meet your
publisher's expectations, and, again, make whatever revisions he asks
for, within reason. Once you have done your part, and the complete
script is finally accepted, all relevant clauses of the contract will come
into legal operation.[1]

Planning for Completion

If you originally presented your book to your publisher in the form
of a synopsis or outline, how far will the finished book adhere to it?
Probably it will differ considerably, yet remain, in substance, the same
book that you pictured from the beginning.

At whatever stage the publisher is approached, any book, whether
fiction or non-fiction, has to be planned. The organization of the actual
writing is bound to be a personal business. But always a plan should
underlie it, laying out the subject in a sequence of headings and sub-
headings, so as to give everything a place in a coherent scheme. The
scheme should be a guide rather than a rigid framework. You must feel
free to alter it as you go along. I can best illustrate the method by citing
my own experience.

I have seldom been able to decide, in advance, what the chapters of a
book are going to be, though I can always arrive at a written approxima-
tion that will enable a publisher to form an opinion. The working plan
is a logical division rather than a List of Contents.

When preparing my biography, *Gandhi*, I saw at once that it would fall
into three phases: first Gandhi's early life, then his long residence in
South Africa, then his years in his native India as a national leader.
Next, I saw that the 'early life' phase broke up into two—his childhood
and schooling in India, and his student years in England. The 'South
African' phase had three natural divisions—his practice as a lawyer, and
pioneer civil-rights campaigns on behalf of minorities; his invention of
a new social philosophy and a non-violent technique of direct action;
and his application of these to secure the repeal of racist laws. The later
'Indian' phase seemed to have four divisions: Gandhi's local reform

---

[1] For further information on the details of publishing, the role of literary
agents, and related matters, see David St. John Thomas, *Non-Fiction: a
Guide to Writing and Publishing*, David & Charles, 1970

work after he returned from South Africa; the first stage of his national leadership against British rule; the second stage, sharply different from the first; and the final years, including the British transfer of power and Gandhi's last public activities and assassination.

It could all be laid out as a provisional plan like this:

A. *Early life*
   1. Childhood and schooldays in India
   2. Studies in England

B. *South Africa*
   1. Legal practice and pioneer civil-rights campaigns
   2. The new social philosophy and technique of action
   3. Application of these to combat racist laws

C. *India*
   1. Local activities after return from South Africa
   2. First stage of national leadership
   3. Second stage of national leadership
   4. Indian independence, final campaigns, assassination

Under each sub-heading, further divisions emerged with further study of the material on Gandhi's career. There were points of overlap. There were also gaps—thus, he did not go straight from England to South Africa, though the interim was only a small fraction of his life. Yet the scheme made it possible to marshal all the facts, and gradually determine the right proportions and perspectives.

In the upshot, division A-1 produced two chapters; A-2, one chapter; B-1, a chapter and a half; B-2 and 3 together, with overlap, a chapter and a half; C-1, three chapters; C-2, four chapters; C-3, three chapters; C-4, two chapters. Total, eighteen. I could not have defined these eighteen chapters before my main researches and writing started. But the logical division, summed up in the plan, enabled the chapters to take shape as I worked.

Clearly, this step-by-step arrangement of the life of a real person can be applied to fictitious ones. A novel can be organized very much as the biography was, whether it covers the seventy-eight years of *Gandhi*, or seventy-eight days or hours.

Editing and Production

So you finish your commissioned book (typed, of course, in the style and format advised for the specimen) and take it in. Your publisher can still reject it, but having invested time and money in you, he will publish if he possibly can. He has probably scheduled it for a publication date, and rejection or indefinitely deferred finalization can cause havoc all along the line in a number of departments. No one wants that to happen.

The editor and at least one professional reader will examine the whole script, and begin to raise the same issues that are raised when an acceptable work is brought to them already completed. They may approve of it as it stands. Or they may approve in substance, but suggest changes in detail. Or they may require extensive re-writing. As I remarked before, few people realize how different a published book often is from the typescript which the author handed in. Even a novel may be the outcome of collaboration between author and editor, to a greater extent than either would publicly acknowledge. And even where very little else is changed, the title is apt to be the publisher's rather than the author's . . . and to be different again in the American edition.

Co-operate. Demur by all means at any proposed changes, but give reasons for doing so, and agree gracefully to the change if you have none. Never mount the high horse, never make a stand out of mere pique or indignation. After all, the process of revision is not one-sided. You too can have second thoughts before letting the script go to the printer. Remember, though, that the text which goes to him should be as nearly definitive as you can make it. When the proofs come to you for correction, you can still make alterations; but in view of the cost, they must be kept to the barest minimum—a word here, a phrase there. Do not imagine that you will be allowed to re-write your book in proof.[1]

The one part of it which the editor may ask you to add at a late stage is the index, if any, which can't be attended to until the book is in page proof and the page numbering is known. This is a matter of discretion. Some authors compile their own index. Others leave the job to a professional indexer whom the publisher finds. The author may have to pay the indexer's fee.

Aids to Publicity

Besides compiling or delegating your index, you will probably be expected to do two further bits of writing. Somebody will send you a questionnaire for the firm's publicity department. On this you fill in information about yourself and your book, and any ideas you have for its promotion. Treat this form with respect and complete it with care, especially the last part. You may well know people who could be helpful —lecturers, for instance, willing to mention the book to audiences, or places where your work has a special bearing on local concerns. Booksellers in a district where you are known will often make a special display if the publisher's representative arranges it with them. You and your book may also get publicity from local press, radio, or television. Publishers always welcome an author's constructive, practical ideas on publicity.

[1] See Appendix Three for a guide to proof-correction.

The second piece of writing you will be asked for is a draft blurb to go on the jacket. It may surprise you to learn that these fulsome out-pourings are often, basically, the work of the author himself; and that while an editor may have re-written them, the fulsomeness is not always added by him. Authors are remarkably ready to describe themselves as the World's Greatest Authority on So-and-So, and apply superlatives to their own style. Avoid all this. Avoid vanity. Write a factual blurb, summing up the book's contents in an arresting form, that will catch the eye of the browser who picks it up, and guide reviewers along correct lines. Leave the praise to your editor.

Publication and After

About a year from the delivery of your final script—perhaps more, probably not much less—your book is published.

Whereupon, you may find, disconcertingly little happens. Reviews should appear, but they are not likely to come through in an instant flood. They may go on trickling in for months. Still, there is no need to worry about missing any. Your publisher will get copies from a press-cutting agency, and send you one of each, if you ask. The publicity department will have tried to get your book noticed in the press, sending it to every suitable literary editor. You may be able to suggest further, unthought-of media where you happen to know that the chances of a review are good: you may, for example, have a friend on the staff of the *Brewer's Argus*. But never go beyond suggestions. You can't exert pressure on a paper to mention your book, nor can you expect your publisher to exert it.

Welcome all reviews, even unfriendly ones. Bad publicity is usually better than no publicity. However, don't take either the pleasant or the unpleasant too seriously. Their effect on sales—the crucial issue—is rarely decisive. If you have glowing reviews, don't assume that high sales will result, and squander your royalties in anticipation. Conversely, if you have hostile ones, be calm. They need not hurt you much. Never quarrel with them. You are justified in writing to a paper to answer *if*, and only if, its reviewer has committed an outright misrepresentation of fact. Otherwise, keep quiet. He has a perfect right to dislike you, and you will only look silly if you complain. The best thing to do with adverse criticism is to learn from it, and meet valid objections by re-vising your book, if and when it reprints or goes into a second edition.

Your attitude to reviews should be the attitude of the true 'pro' in general. Maintain it always. When a journalist interviews you, and the interview is printed, don't explode over some trifling error; be glad that the paper has noticed you at all. When readers write to you, answer them appreciatively and courteously. When a society invites you to speak, don't treat it with contempt because it is small and parochial and not very well-informed. Appreciate the fact that the society is paying you the compliment of wanting to meet you. Accept invitations as often as you can, and give your best every time—to the Nether Bidding Church Women's Guild, as to the Royal Society of Literature.

Signs of the progress of your fame may be dauntingly meagre. Push ahead regardless. More is apt to be going on than you ever know about. For every reader you meet or hear from, there may well be hundreds who never contact you. Presently—if you have the gift, the application, the attitude—a feedback will come. Not perhaps after the appearance of your first book, but after the second or third. You will go among strangers and find that they have heard of you. Television producers will consult you, newspaper columnists will seek you out. Other publishers than your own will want to get you on their lists. You won't be able to tell when exactly the thing happened, or why or how. But you will reap one of the writer's supreme rewards: the discovery—the perpetually fresh, astonishing discovery—that you mean far more to your fellow-mortals than you ever thought you did.

Exercises

1. Put yourself in the position of a publisher's editor. Somebody has sent you an outline, and two specimen chapters, of a projected book on football *or* the West Indies *or* the treatment of cancer. The book has potentialities: its subject is interesting and the author seems to have new, original material. But the text submitted doesn't do full justice to the theme. It needs heavy working-over and rehandling.

Compose a letter to the author expressing interest, but saying (tactfully) that you will only be interested in publishing his book if he revises according to your directive. Then give him a specific criticism of his work that will enable him to see clearly what you want. You must leave no room for future disputes over your meaning.

When you have done this, put yourself in the author's position. You have received the letter. Compose a reply to it.

2. Some years from now, you have become a celebrity and are writing your autobiography. Make a plan for it, as on page 249, with a paragraph under each sub-heading to show what aspects of your life you would put in that section. You can halt at the present day, or go on into an imaginary future.

3. Write a short essay on what you have learnt from *The Art of Writing Made Simple*. If you have learnt little or nothing, and feel that you could do a better book on the subject yourself, explain how you would go about it.

SUGGESTED BOOKS FOR FURTHER READING AND REFERENCE

Writing, Thinking, Language, Media in General

Boulton, Marjorie. *Saying What We Mean*. Routledge & Kegan Paul, London, 1959.

Chase, Stuart. *The Tyranny of Words*. Methuen, London, 1938.

Flesch, Rudolf. *The ABC of Style*. Harper, New York, 1964.

Foerster, Norman, and Steadman, John. *Writing and Thinking*. Houghton Mifflin, Boston, 1931.

Fowler, H. W., and Fowler, F. G. *The King's English*. Oxford University Press, London, 1930.

Gondin, William R., Edward, W., and Dodding, James. *The Art of Speaking Made Simple*. W. H. Allen, London, 1970.

Gowers, Sir Ernest. *The Complete Plain Words*. (Pelican). Penguin Books, London, 1962.

Graves, Robert, and Hodge, Alan. *The Reader Over Your Shoulder*. Jonathan Cape, London, 1943.

Gunning, Robert. *The Technique of Clear Writing*. McGraw Hill, New York, 1952.

Hayakawa, S. I. *Language in Thought and Action*. George Allen & Unwin, London, 1965.

Jepson, R. W. *Clear Thinking*. Longmans, London, 1962.

McLuhan, Marshall. *Understanding Media*. Routledge & Kegan Paul, London, 1964.

Ogden, C. K. *Basic English*. Routledge & Kegan Paul, London, 1940.

Orwell, George. *Shooting an Elephant and Other Essays*. Secker & Warburg, London, 1950.

Partridge, Eric. *Usage and Abusage*. Hamish Hamilton, London, 1965.

Quiller-Couch, Arthur. *On the Art of Writing*. Cambridge University Press, London, 1950.

Stebbing, Susan. *Thinking to Some Purpose*. (Pelican). Penguin Books, London, 1959.

Thouless, Robert H. *Straight and Crooked Ihinking*. Pan Books, London, 1963.

Vallins, G. H. *Good English*. Pan Books, London, 1951.

Better English. Pan Books, London, 1953.

The Best English. Pan Books, London, 1963.

Précis, Comprehension and English Composition. Odhams, London, 1957.

254   *The Art of Writing Made Simple*

Waldhorn, Arthur, Zeiger, Arthur, and South, Ronald and Joan, *English Made Simple*. W. H. Allen, London, 1967.
Williams, Francis. *Dangerous Estate*. Arrow Books, London, 1959.

Authorship

Cowley, Malcolm, et al. (editors). *Writers at Work*. (Three series.) Secker & Warburg, London, 1958, 1963, 1967.
Maugham, W. Somerset. *The Summing Up*. Penguin Books, London, 1963.
Maurois, André. *The Art of Writing*. (Translated by Gerard Hopkins.) The Bodley Head, London, 1960.

Novels

Bergonzi, Bernard. *The Situation of the Novel*. Macmillan, London, 1970.
Church, Richard. *The Growth of the English Novel*. Methuen, London, 1951.
Forster, E. M. *Aspects of the Novel*. Edward Arnold, London, 1927. (Penguin Books, London, 1962.)
Lubbock, Percy. *The Craft of Fiction*. Jonathan Cape, London, 1926.
Neill, S. Diana. *A Short History of the English Novel*. Jarrolds, London, 1951.

Short Stories

Beachcroft, T. O. *The Modest Art: a Survey of the Short Story in English*. Oxford University Press, London, 1968.
O'Faolain, Sean. *The Short Story*. Collins, London, 1948.

Plays

Bogard, Travis, and Oliver, William I. *Modern Drama*. Galaxy Books, (Oxford University Press), New York, 1965.
Druten, John van. *Playwright at Work*. Hamish Hamilton, London, 1953.
Jeans, Ronald. *Writing for the Theatre*. Edward Arnold, London, 1949.
Wellwarth, George E. *The Theatre of Protest and Paradox*. MacGibbon & Kee, London, 1965.

Poetry

Brewer, R. F. *The Art of Versification*. John Grant, Edinburgh, 1937.
Day-Lewis, C. *The Poetic Image*. Jonathan Cape, London, 1947.
Hamer, E. *The Metres of English Poetry*. Methuen, London, 1954.
Reeves, James. *Understanding Poetry*. Heinemann, London, 1965.
Sansom, Clive (editor). *The World of Poetry*. Phoenix House, London, 1959.

Non-fiction

St. John Thomas, David. *Non-Fiction: a Guide to Writing and Publishing*. David & Charles, Newton Abbot, 1970. (This book includes much general information on author–publisher relations.)

Journalism

Wainwright, David. *Journalism Made Simple*. W. H. Allen, London, 1972.

Williams, Francis. *Dangerous Estate*. Arrow Books, London, 1959.

Radio

McWhinnie, Donald. *The Art of Radio*. Faber & Faber, London, 1959.

Milton, Ralph. *Radio Programming*. Geoffrey Bles, London, 1968.

Television

Bakewell, Joan, and Garnham, Nicholas. *The New Priesthood: British Television Today*. Allen Lane, the Penguin Press, London, 1970.

Hood, Stuart. *A Survey of Television*. Heinemann, London, 1967.

Swinson, Arthur. *Writing for Television*. Adam & Charles Black, London, 1960.

Worsley, T. C. *Television: the Ephemeral Art*. Alan Ross, London, 1970.

Reports

Gaum, C. G. *Report Writing*. Prentice-Hall, New York, 1954.

Kapp, R. O. *The Presentation of Technical Information*. Constable, London, 1948.

Mitchell, John. *A First Course in Technical Writing*. Chapman & Hall, London, 1967.

Souther, J. W. *Technical Report Writing*. Wiley, New York, 1957.

Reference and Miscellaneous

Author's and Writers Who's Who. Burke's Peerage Ltd (6th ed.) 1971.

Bartlett's Familiar Quotations. Macmillan, London, 1968 edition.

Brewer's Dictionary of Phrase and Fable. Cassell, London, 1970 edition.

Carey, G. V. *Mind the Stop*. Penguin Books (Pelican), 1971.

Chambers Biographical Dictionary. Chambers (revised ed.) 1968.

Concise Oxford Dictionary. Oxford University Press, London, 1964 edition.

Concise Oxford Dictionary of English Literature. Oxford University Press, 1971.

Dictionary of Modern English Usage. (H. W. Fowler, revised by Sir Ernest Gowers.) Oxford University Press, London, 1965.

Hadyn, J. and Vincent, B. *Dictionary of Dates and Universal Information*. Dover Publications (new impression), 1969.

Oxford Companion to English Literature. Oxford University Press, London, 1967.

Oxford Dictionary of Quotations. Oxford University Press, London, 1953.

Penguin Dictionary of Modern Quotations. Penguin Books, 1971.

Penguin Dictionary of Quotations. Penguin Books, London, 1967.

Rees, H. *Rules of Printed English.* Darton, Longman and Todd, 1970.

Roget, P. M. *Thesaurus of English Words and Phrases.* Longmans, (new ed.) 1962.

Titles and Forms of Address. Adam and Charles Black, (revised ed.) 1966.

Ward, A. C. (ed.) *Longmans Companion to Twentieth Century Liturature.* Longmans, 1970.

Whitaker's Almanack (annual). J. Whitaker and Sons Ltd.

Who's Who (annual). Adam and Charles Black.

Writers' and Artists' Year Book. Adam & Charles Black, London. Published annually.

The Writer's Guide. Issued from time to time (not annually) by the Writers' Guild of Great Britain, London.

TWO LISTS OF 'CLASSICS': LUBBOCK AND BROPHY

List One

Sir John Lubbock offered his list of the Hundred Best Books in a lecture entitled 'The Choice of Books', which was published in 1887. He based the list partly on his own judgment, but chiefly on a consensus. These were the books which he found to be recommended most often. The scope is narrowed by two limitations. He left out all books by authors living at the time. He also left out nearly all works of science, arguing, rightly, that while science was important, virtually any given book would be superseded, and therefore few should be included.

The list is not quite fair. For instance, Lubbock counts all the novels of Scott as one book. But such details can be passed over. He shows us an interesting phase in the movement of literary ideas. Most of the list still illustrates the standard Christian-classical culture of Victorian England. Yet certain awarenesses have begun to creep in. Lubbock does know that other cultures exist, and seven of his titles acknowledge the fact. Two of these, however, are western writers' presentations of eastern material. The 'orthodox' proportion remains well above 90 per cent by any reckoning.

Here are the Hundred Books. (Bear in mind Lubbock's rule against authors who were alive at the time of compilation, such as Ruskin and Tennyson, whom he would otherwise have put in.)

The Bible; the *Meditations* of Marcus Aurelius; Epictetus; Aristotle's *Ethics*; the *Analects* of Confucius; St. Hilaire's *Le Bouddha et sa Religion*; Wake's *Apostolic Fathers*; Thomas à Kempis's *Imitation of Christ*; St. Augustine's *Confessions*; the *Koran* (portions of); Spinoza's *Tractatus Theologico-Politicus*; Comte's *Catechism of Positive Philosophy*; Pascal's *Pensées*; Butler's *Analogy of Religion*; Taylor's *Holy Living and Dying*; Bunyan's *Pilgrim's Progress*; Keble's *Christian Year*.

Plato (selected); Xenophon's *Memorabilia*; Aristotle's *Politics*; Demosthenes's *De Corona*; Cicero (selected); Plutarch's *Lives*; Berkeley's *Human Knowledge*; Descartes's *Discours sur la Méthode*; Locke's *On the Conduct of the Understanding*.

Homer; Hesiod; Virgil; Talboys Wheeler's digests of the Indian epics *Mahabharata* and *Ramayana*; the Persian epic *Shah-nameh*; the *Nibelungenlied*; Malory's *Morte d'Arthur*.

The *Shi-king* (Chinese poetry); Aeschylus (*Prometheus* and the Orestes trilogy); Sophocles's *Oedipus Tyrannus*; Euripides's *Medea*; Aristophanes (*The Knights* and *The Clouds*); Horace; Lucretius.

Chaucer's *Canterbury Tales* (expurgated); Shakespeare; Milton (selected); Dante's *Divina Commedia*; Spenser's *Faerie Queene*; Dryden; Scott's poems; Wordsworth (selected); Southey (*Thalaba* and *The Curse of Kehama*); Pope (selected); Burns; Byron's *Childe Harold*; Gray.

Herodotus; Xenophon's *Anabasis*; Thucydides; Tacitus's *Germania*; Livy; Gibbon's *Decline and Fall of the Roman Empire*; Hume's *History of England*; Grote's *History of Greece*; Carlyle's *French Revolution*; Green's *Short History of England*; Lewes's *History of Philosophy*.

The Arabian Nights; Swift's *Gulliver's Travels*; Defoe's *Robinson Crusoe*; Goldsmith's *Vicar of Wakefield*; Cervantes's *Don Quixote*; Boswell's *Life of Johnson*; Molière; Sheridan (principal plays); Carlyle's *Past and Present*.

Bacon's *Novum Organum*; Smith's *Wealth of Nations* (part of); Mill's *Political Economy*; Cook's *Voyages*; Humboldt's *Travels*; White's *Natural History of Selborne*; Darwin (*Origin of Species* and *Voyage*); Mill's *Logic*.

Bacon's *Essays*; Montaigne's *Essays*; Hume's *Essays*; Macaulay's *Essays*; Addison's *Essays*; Emerson's *Essays*; Burke (selected); Smiles's *Self-Help*.

Voltaire's *Zadig*; Goethe (*Faust* and *Autobiography*); Jane Austen (*Emma* or *Pride and Prejudice*); Thackeray (*Vanity Fair* and *Pendennis*); Dickens (*Pickwick* and *David Copperfield*); Lytton's *Last Days of Pompeii*; George Eliot's *Adam Bede*; Kingsley's *Westward Ho!*; Scott's novels.

It is hard to see any logical way of counting which makes this list come out to exactly a hundred. However, Lubbock sometimes counts an author as 'two' when the two recommended books are very different (e.g. Hume's *History* and *Essays*). On this basis we might count Goethe's *Faust* and *Autobiography* as two, and if we also count Talboys Wheeler's Indian epic-digests as two, we have the round number.

List Two

Brigid Brophy's anti-list was compiled in collaboration with Michael Levey and Charles Osborne. It appears in *Fifty Works of English Literature We Could Do Without*, published in 1967. 'English' includes 'American' but excludes translations. Each item is accompanied by a short critical essay explaining why the authors regard it as overrated and expendable.

Here are the fifty.

Beowulf; the York Mystery Plays; Spenser's *Faerie Queene*; Ben Jonson's *The Alchemist*; Shakespeare's *Hamlet*; Bunyan's *Pilgrim's Progress*; Defoe's *Moll Flanders*; Fielding's *Tom Jones*; Gray's *Elegy*; Goldsmith's *She Stoops to Conquer*; Sheridan's *The School for Scandal*.

Wordsworth's *The Daffodils*; Scott's *The Bride of Lammermoor*; Lamb's *Essays of Elia*; De Quincey's *Confessions of an English Opium*

Eater; Newman's *The Dream of Gerontius*: Hawthorne's *The Scarlet Letter*; Elizabeth Barrett Browning's *Aurora Leigh*; Oliver Wendell Holmes's *The Autocrat of the Breakfast Table*; Dickens's *Pickwick Papers*; Trollope's *The Warden*; Charlotte Brontë's *Jane Eyre*; Emily Brontë's *Wuthering Heights*.

Melville's *Moby Dick*; Whitman's *Leaves of Grass*; Lewis Carroll's *Alice in Wonderland*; Thomas Hughes's *Tom Brown's Schooldays*; Palgrave's *Golden Treasury*; Blackmore's *Lorna Doone*; Mark Twain's *Huckleberry Finn*; Hardy's *Tess of the D'Urbervilles*; Gerard Manley Hopkins's poems; George Moore's *Esther Waters*.

A. E. Housman's *Collected Poems*; Francis Thompson's *The Hound of Heaven*; J. M. Barrie's *Peter Pan*; Kipling's *An Habitation Enforced*; H. G. Wells's *The History of Mr. Polly*; Galsworthy's *Forsyte Saga*; Norman Douglas's *South Wind*; Somerset Maugham's *The Moon and Sixpence*; Virginia Woolf's *To the Lighthouse*; D. H. Lawrence's *Lady Chatterley's Lover*; Rupert Brooke's *1914 Sonnets*.

Edith Sitwell's *Collected Poems*; T. S. Eliot's notes on *The Waste Land*; Aldous Huxley's *Point Counter Point*; William Faulkner's *The Sound and the Fury*; C. S. Lewis's *The Silver Chair*; Ernest Hemingway's *A Farewell to Arms*.

The reasons for rejection are too various to summarize here. The only point which must be made is that the naming of a work by an author does not always imply a general dismissal of that author. Thus, *Hamlet* is included mainly as being the wrong Shakespeare play to admire: 'Do the English deserve the poet of *Antony and Cleopatra*, *A Midsummer Night's Dream* and the Sonnets, when they pick on *Hamlet* as his cardinal work?' Sometimes, however, a work is named as simply the most glaringly over-valued specimen of an author who is over-valued generally; and there are various gradations between.

ALTERATIONS AND CORRECTIONS IN PROOFS

The first rule about altering proofs is: avoid it if possible. Get your script as nearly right as you can before it goes to the printer. Every change costs money, and no publisher can afford to let an author revise his book substantially at the proof stage.

However, small changes may occur to you which are really important, and can be made without serious rearrangement of the type. Also, you must go over the proofs to pick out and correct actual errors, so that when the book is finally produced it will be as nearly free from misprints, and mis-readings of your script, as it can possibly be. (Don't be annoyed, either with yourself or with the printer, if a few oversights get by in the published version. A few very often do.)

For these purposes there is a standard set of symbols. You can use the same symbols at an earlier stage, for amendments to your own script. To make a correction or alteration which you are sure of, use ink of a colour that will stand out from the typescript or print. To indicate a query, where you think there should be a change but are not certain, use pencil.

B.S. 1219 : 1958

NOTES ON THE USE OF SYMBOLS FOR CORRECTING PROOFS

All corrections should be distinct and made in ink in the margins; marks made in the text should be those indicating the place to which the correction refers.

Where several corrections occur in one line, they should be divided between the left and right margins, the order being from left to right in both margins, and the individual marks should be separated by a concluding mark.

When an alteration is desired in a character, word or words, the existing character, word or words should be struck through, and the character to be substituted written in the margin followed by a /.

Where it is desired to change one character only to a capital letter, the word ' cap ' should be written in the margin. Where, however, it is desired to change more than one character, or a word or words, in a particular line to capitals, then one marginal reference, ' caps ', should suffice, with the appropriate symbols made in the text as required.

Three periods or full stops (constituting an ellipsis, see No. 61) should be used to indicate an omission, except where the preceding sentence has been concluded, in which case *four* full stops should be inserted, the first of which should be close up to the preceding word.

Normally, only matter actually to be inserted or added to the existing text should be written on the proof. If, however, any comments or instructions are written on the proof, they should be encircled, and preceded by the word PRINTER (in capitals and underlined).

(Words printed in italics in the marginal marks column below are instructions and not part of the marks).

SYMBOLS FOR CORRECTING PROOFS

No.	Instruction	Textual mark	Marginal mark
1	Correction is concluded	None	/
2	Insert in text the matter indicated in margin	⋏	*New matter followed by* /
3	Delete	Strike through characters to be deleted	♂
4	Delete and close up	Strike through characters to be deleted and use mark 21	♂
5	Leave as printed	. . . . under characters to remain	*stet*
6	Change to italic	——— under characters to be altered	*ital*

No.	Instruction	Textual mark	Marginal mark
7	Change to even small capitals	≡≡≡ under characters to be altered	*s.c.*
8	Change to capital letters	≡≡≡ under characters to be altered	*caps*
9	Use capital letters for initial letters and small capitals for rest of words	≡≡≡ under initial letters and ≡≡≡ under the rest of the words	*c. & s.c.*
10	Change to bold type	∼∼∼ under characters to be altered	*bold*
11	Change to lower case	Encircle characters to be altered	*l.c.*
12	Change to roman type	Encircle characters to be altered	*rom*
13	Wrong fount. Replace by letter of correct fount	Encircle character to be altered	*w.f.*
14	Invert type	Encircle character to be altered	↺
15	Change damaged character(s)	Encircle character(s) to be altered	✗
16	Substitute or insert character(s) under which this mark is placed, in 'superior' position	/ through character or ∧ where required	*under character (e.g. ⤳)*
17	Substitute or insert character(s) over which this mark is placed, in 'inferior' position	/ through character or ∧ where required	*over character (e.g. ⤳)*
18	Underline word or words	—— under words affected	*underline*
19	Use ligature (e.g. ffi) or diphthong (e.g. œ)	⌣ enclosing letters to be altered	*⌣ enclosing ligature or diphthong required*

No.	Instruction	Textual mark	Marginal mark
20	Substitute separate letters for ligature or diphthong	/ through ligature or diphthong to be altered	*write out separate letters followed by* /
21	Close up—delete space between characters	⌒ linking characters	⌒
22	Insert space*	⅄	#
23	Insert space between lines or paragraphs*	> between lines to be spaced	#
24	Reduce space between lines*	(connecting lines to be closed up	*less* #
25	Make space appear equal between words	⎮ between words	*eq* #
26	Reduce space between words*	⎮ between words	*less* #
27	Add space between letters*	⎮⎮⎮⎮⎮⎮ between tops of letters requiring space	*letter* #
28	Transpose	⌐⌐ between characters or words, numbered when necessary	*trs*
29	Place in centre of line	Indicate position with ⌐ ⌐	*centre*
30	Indent one em	⌐	□
31	Indent two ems	⌐	□□
32	Move matter to right	⌐ at left side of group to be moved	⌐
33	Move matter to left	⌐ at right side of group to be moved	⌐

* Amount of space and/or length of re-spaced line may be indicated.

No.	Instruction	Textual mark	Marginal mark
34	Move matter to position indicated	[ ] at limits of required position	*move*
35	Take over character(s) or line to next line, column or page	⊏	*take over*
36	Take back character(s) or line to previous line, column or page	⊐	*take back*
37	Raise lines*	over lines to be moved / under lines to be moved	*raise*
38	Lower lines*	over lines to be moved / under lines to be moved	*lower*
39	Correct the vertical alignment	‖	‖
40	Straighten lines	through lines to be straightened	=
41	Push down space	Encircle space affected	⊥
42	Begin a new paragraph	before first word of new paragraph	*n.p.*
43	No fresh paragraph here	between paragraphs	*run on*
44	Spell out the abbreviation or figure in full	Encircle words or figures to be altered	*spell out*
45	Insert omitted portion of copy NOTE. The relevant section of the copy should be returned with the proof, the omitted portion being clearly indicated.	λ	*out see copy*
46	Substitute or insert comma	/ through character or λ where required	,/
47	Substitute or insert semi-colon	/ through character or λ where required	;/

*Amount of space and/or length of line may be included.

No.	Instruction	Textual mark	Marginal mark
48	Substitute or insert full stop	/ through character or ⋀ where required	⊙
49	Substitute or insert colon	/ through character or ⋀ where required	⊙
50	Substitute or insert interrogation mark	/ through character or ⋀ where required	?/
51	Substitute or insert exclamation mark	/ through character or ⋀ where required	!/
52	Insert parentheses	⋀ or ⋀ ⋀	(/)/
53	Insert (square) brackets	⋀ or ⋀ ⋀	[/]/
54	Insert hyphen	⋀	|-|
55	Insert en (half-em) rule	⋀	en
56	Insert one-em rule	⋀	em
57	Insert two-em rule	⋀	2 em
58	Insert apostrophe	⋀	⁹⁄
59	Insert single quotation marks	⋀ or ⋀ ⋀	⁹⁄ ⁹⁄
60	Insert double quotation marks	⋀ or ⋀ ⋀	⁶⁶⁄ ²⁹⁄
61	Insert ellipsis*	⋀	.../
62	Insert leader	⋀	⊙⋯
63	Insert shilling stroke	⋀	⊘
64	Refer to appropriate authority anything of doubtful accuracy	Encircle words, etc. affected	(?)

* See notes on use of symbols.

MARKS TO BE MADE ON PROOF, OR PROOFS, AFTER READING

Mark	Meaning
'Revise' (and signature)	Correct and submit another proof.
'Revise and make-up' (and signature)	Submit another proof in page form.
'Revise, make-up and impose' (and signature)	Submit another proof in page form and imposed.
'Clean proof' (and signature)	Submit clean proof to reader. If a specific number of proofs is required, this shall be stated. NOTE. This mark is intended for use only by printers' readers.
'Press' (and signature)	Print off.

Where the printer has drawn the author's attention to any particular point by means of a query (see No. 64), it is desirable that the author should settle the query or, if the text is already correct, strike through the query.

Extract from B.S. 1219 : 1958, *Recommendations for Proof Correction and Copy Preparation*. Reproduced by permission of the British Standards Institution, 2 Park Street, London W1A 2BS, from whom copies of the complete Standard may be obtained.

INDEX